LYRICAL DIARY

Christian Gerhaher
LYRICAL DIARY

*Lieder from Franz Schubert
to Wolfgang Rihm*

TRANSLATED BY
Shaun Whiteside

faber

This English translation first published in 2025
by Faber & Faber Limited
The Bindery, 51 Hatton Garden
London EC1N 8HN

First published in German as *Lyrisches Tagebuch* in 2020
by Verlag C.H. Beck oHG, München

Typeset by Agnesi Text, Hadleigh, Suffolk
Printed and bound by CPI Group (UK) Ltd, Croydon, CR0 4YY

All rights reserved
© Verlag C.H. Beck oHG, München, 2020
Translation © Shaun Whiteside, 2025

The right of Christian Gerhaher to be identified as author of this work
has been asserted in accordance with Section 77 of the Copyright,
Designs and Patents Act 1988

A CIP record for this book
is available from the British Library

ISBN 978–0–571–35770–3

Printed and bound in the UK on FSC® certified paper in line with our continuing
commitment to ethical business practices, sustainability and the environment.
For further information see faber.co.uk/environmental-policy

Our authorised representative in the EU for product safety is
Easy Access System Europe, Mustamäe tee 50, 10621 Tallinn, Estonia
gpsr.requests@easproject.com

2 4 6 8 10 9 7 5 3 1

To my dear and admired friends Sally Cavender,
John Carewe and James Cheung

CONTENTS

Prelude with Low-flying Fighter Jet   1
   Straubing, August 1984

Lyrical Dramaturgy   37
   London, September 1999

Schumann's Abstract Opera   59
   Berlin, 24 February 2010

Tradition and Role-Playing   81
   Munich, 12 October 2013

The Souls of the Crags   99
   Berlin, 7 September 2016

Farewell to the Familiar   123
   Straubing, November 2017

Drama of the Moment   147
   Frankfurt, April 2014

Intermezzo   161
   Elmau, September 2019

Holliger's Lunar Landscape   171
   Zurich, 25 March 2018

Hope – Love – Faith   203
   Munich, 3 February 2017

Rihm and Goethe: Building a Programme *Weimar, November 2018*	221
Steles in an Ice Field *London, December 2018*	255
Art Nouveau Rose *Lisbon, 5 September 2019*	285
Meaning or Being *Munich, December 2020*	303
Schubert's Lied Legacy *Helsinki, January 2021*	323
Coda with Stifter *Madrid, February 2021*	357
Notes	363
Acknowledgements	389
Index	391

PRELUDE WITH
LOW-FLYING FIGHTER JET

STRAUBING, AUGUST 1984

Liebesbotschaft
Robert Schumann: *Aus dem Liederbuch eines Malers* (6)

Wolken, die ihr nach Osten eilt,
Wo die Eine, die Meine weilt,
All meine Wünsche, mein Hoffen und Singen
Sollen auf eure Flügel sich schwingen,
Sollen euch, Flüchtige,
Zu ihr lenken,
Daß die Züchtige
Meiner in Treuen mag gedenken!

Singen noch Morgenträume sie ein,
Schwebet leise zum Garten hinein,
Senket als Tau euch in schattige Räume,
Streuet Perlen auf Blumen und Bäume,
Daß der Holdseligen,
Kommt sie gegangen,
All die fröhlichen
Blüten sich öffnen mit lichterem Prangen!

Und am Abend in stiller Ruh'
Breitet der sinkenden Sonne euch zu!
Mögt mit Purpur und Gold euch malen,
Mögt in dem Meere von Gluten und Strahlen
Leicht sich schwingende
Schifflein fahren,
Daß sie singende
Engel glaubt auf euch zu gewahren.

Ja, wohl möchten es Engel sein,
Wär' mein Herz gleich ihrem rein;
All meine Wünsche, mein Hoffen und Singen
Zieht ja dahin auf euren Schwingen,
Euch, ihr Flüchtigen,

Hinzulenken
Zu der Züchtigen,
Der ich einzig nur mag gedenken.

ROBERT REINICK

Clouds, rushing eastwards,
To where the One, my own, is waiting,
Let all of my desires, my hopes, my songs
Take flight upon your wings,
And guide you,
Fugitives, to her,
That my chaste love
May faithfully think of me.

Dreams of morning sing around her,
Float quietly into the garden,
Settle like dew in shady spots,
Strew pearls on flowers and trees,
So that at the appearance
Of the fair one
All the joyful blossoms
Open with brighter beauty.

And in the evening in quiet peace
Spread out towards the setting sun,
Paint yourself with purple and gold,
And in the sea
Of embers and beams
Sail like bobbing boats,
And make her believe she sees
Singing angels round you.

Yes, angels they would be,
If only my heart were as pure as hers;
All my desires, my hopes, my singing

Draw hither on your wings,
To guide you,
Fugitives,
To the chaste one,
The only one I may remember.

The place I come from is a little like the Wild West. Straubing lies in the great alluvial plain of the Danube, the wide horizon to the north disappearing into the Bavarian forest. It gets very hot in the summer, and my friend's farm was dusty with corn. I worked there once for a few days, cycling the ten kilometres there and back. The work was hard, but what I remember most distinctly is the sting of the grain dust, particularly during the rapeseed harvest. It was impossible to describe all the different colours in the millions of grains. My young farmer friend and I couldn't tear our eyes away; every colour was there, except perhaps blue. We stood there, smoking like cowboys and talking about motorbikes. And then I would cycle home again. In the evening there was much still to be said, and we talked on the phone.

Then something happened that I have never experienced since. We were living at the edge of the German Democratic Republic – East Germany – at the end of the Western world; Bohemia and the Iron Curtain were less than fifty kilometres away. A low-flying fighter jet – they flew all the time in those days – approached the farm. The noise could be heard over the telephone, and we stopped talking. It flew on. And we resumed our conversation. Then the same plane reached my parents' house. I was speechless; we both were. We immediately sensed what a unique experience was connecting us. We talked some more about motorbikes, about the harvest, about the workers on the farm. And yet the bond forged by what we had just experienced was much more profound and elemental than the one established by our words.

Lovers hope for similar moments when they spend an evening apart. They agree to look at the moon at a particular time, wherever they may be. They don't have the same perspective, but they have a shared illusion – that they are seeing, feeling and thinking the same thing, at the same time. Words are superfluous; they would only get in the way.

Two hundred years ago many messages of love were written and much music composed for them, relying on this same shared illusion. Some of these songs are particularly important to me. The very first song-cycle in the entire lied tradition, Beethoven's *An die ferne Geliebte* ('To the Distant Beloved'), with its six lieder, is one such: clouds, streams, birds and wind – they are all supposed to be the lover's messengers, inanimate or animate, but not real human go-betweens. As if these messengers have the gift of reason, they are to tell the beloved that he misses her because she is so far away – that is the limit of what they can say. As if the beloved didn't know in any case that her friend loves her and longs for her. The gesture is more important than the message, just as the artificial togetherness when far apart may be more important than the exchange of words, shared thought more important than speech. That gesture does not distinguish only the poems of Alois Jeitteles, set by Beethoven, but also Schubert's *Liebesbotschaft* ('Message of Love') and Schumann's, the first lied of the *Schwanengesang* and the last of *Aus dem Liederbuch eines Malers* ('From a Painter's Song Book', Op. 36). These lieder conjure natural events capable of quickly reaching far-off places, so swiftly that the message is still warm when it arrives, even if it is not especially rich in content.

Ungeduld

Franz Schubert: *Die schöne Müllerin* (7)

[...]

Ich möchte mir ziehen einen jungen Star,
Bis daß er spräch die Worte rein und klar,
Bis er sie spräch mit meines Mundes Klang,
Mit meines Herzens vollem, heißen Drang;
Dann säng er hell durch ihre Fensterscheiben:
Dein ist mein Herz und soll es ewig bleiben.

Den Morgenwinden möcht' ich's hauchen ein,
Ich möcht' es säuseln durch den regen Hain,
O, leuchtet' es aus jedem Blumenstern!
Trüg' es der Duft zu ihr von nah' und fern!
Ihr Wogen, könnt ihr nichts als Räder treiben?
Dein ist mein Herz und soll es ewig bleiben.

[...]

WILHELM MÜLLER

I wish I could train a young starling,
Until it could repeat my words purely and clearly,
Until it could speak with my mouth's sound,
With the full, hot urging of my heart;
Then it would sing clearly through her window panes:
Yours is my heart, and will be always.

I would like to breathe it into the morning winds,
I would like to whisper it through the bosky grove,
O that it might gleam from every blossom-star!
That their scent might carry it to her from near and far!
O stream, can you do no more than turn the wheel?
Yours is my heart, and will be always.

STRAUBING, AUGUST 1984

The two middle verses of *Ungeduld* ('Impatience'), the seventh lied of Schubert's song-cycle *Die schöne Müllerin*, are messages of love, although of a particular kind. Here the object of devotion is close by, in the same place, but she has yet to find out how lucky she is. For a message of love to be perfect, the couples communicating (or not quite communicating) have already declared themselves. In *Die schöne Müllerin*, on the other hand, the apprentice miller is one of many, along with his fellow workers, who worship the miller's daughter. Over the course of the cycle he obsessively imagines more and more intensely his relationship with the girl for whom he will eventually drown himself in the millstream. And it is this delusion that drives him to send messages to the miller's daughter, although he cannot entrust them to another person – he doesn't dare – any more than he could dare speak them to her himself.

This idea is put quite bluntly – and here again there is as yet no couple, only the lover's desire – in Aloys Schreiber's *Blumenbrief* ('Flower Letter'), also set by Schubert. The message is not about something that can be said. It is simply that being together with the unknown beauty is utterly inevitable. Should it fail to come about, then death must surely follow.

The living warmth of the greeting in Mendelssohn's setting of Lenau's *An die Entfernte* (op. 71 no. 3) is intended to be vivid: the distance the beloved travels should be no further than a rose can survive in bloom as a message of love, no further than sound can carry or a nightingale can bring straw to its nest. What is important is the freshness of the message; conversely it expresses that desired experience cannot be guaranteed by messages alone. The addressee in *Was bedeutet die Bewegung?* ('What is the meaning of this motion?') from Goethe's *West-östlicher Divan* expresses just this: 'Oh, the true message of the heart, / The breath of love, refreshed life, / Comes to me from its mouth alone, / Can give me his breath alone.' In this poem, also set by Schubert (as *Suleika I*), the perspective of the distant beloved herself is revealed. Whereas in the

Beethoven–Jeitteles setting the 'west' indicates the winds blowing westwards from the east, here the wind is identified as 'east', blowing from Weimar (Goethe) to Frankfurt (Marianne von Willemer).

While in all the lieder mentioned here the beloved seems to live in the open countryside, which is why the message is always able to reach her directly, the lover in the poem written by Marianne von Willemer is described as going about his business behind the high walls of his city. Particularly in *Ach, um deine feuchten Schwingen* ('Ah, Your Wings So Moist') – another *Divan*-poem written by Marianne von Willemer, set by Schubert as *Suleika II* – the heralding wind assumes a different gender. The beloved herself speaks much more empathetically to the west wind about the man's feelings – a message from her to him, then – wishing that it might hide all her pain and not grieve her distant beloved. No male sender seems capable of such altruism. In the pain of their separation, they are capable of feeling nothing but the pain and distress of their own longing, which the person to whom the message is addressed is begged to assuage.

Die Taubenpost ('Pigeon Post'), at the end of Schubert's *Schwanengesang*, finally gives the messenger, a pigeon in this instance, a name: 'It is called: Longing.' Here I feel I have reached the heart of the matter: if we consider not the real female affection articulated exclusively in the *Suleika* lieder, but the male equivalent, which focuses solely on the sender's own painful longing, and writes it in the wind and water, we might be inclined to suspect that the intention is not so much reunification with the longed-for woman, but rather that it is this expressed desire itself that is the object of passionate interest. In Joseph von Eichendorff's novel *Aus dem Leben eines Taugenichts* ('From the Life of a Good-for-nothing'), the hero, who imagines himself in a state of happy longing, is attracted for the entire book by fantasies rather than by the love of a real woman. As a reader I have no desire to know what his life would be like once it were to resume an orderly course or his love if it were to blossom in real life. It's no surprise that the wonder of this book must end where a man's everyday love life begins, unworthy as it is of description. And that is where every 'message of love' has to conclude: longing would end if the couple were allowed, or indeed compelled, to live together, if self-preoccupied infatuation were to make way at last for mutual love.

In Beethoven's *An die ferne Geliebte*, it is not only nature, both animate and inanimate, that is summoned as a messenger. In the first and sixth poems it is love songs themselves that seem to exist simply as their own message, overcoming time and distance, and ubiquitously available: 'For the sound of song escapes / Every space and every time, / And a loving heart reaches / What blessed a loving heart.' The beloved waiting in the distance may then sing the message back, as in Goethe's poem *An die Entfernte* ('To the Distant One') set by Schubert – sung messages of love appear to be the only imaginable alternative to a message conveyed by nature. At any rate the messages of Beethoven's distant beloved ('What from my full breast / Rang without false artistry, / Just aware of its own longing') should be clearly perceived as an expression of unadulterated emotion: no affects, only private feeling; no sentimentality, only something jointly felt; nothing less than uniqueness, nothing beyond compare. All of that is to sound once more from her lips, at a shared moment, at the beginning of night – a very private meditation shared over a great distance.

Here the song takes the place of nature; the poet assumes nature's 'naturalness', he wants to proceed 'without artifice'. Here – in the very first song-cycle, and even before folk songs were collected in Germany – the dialectical symmetry of the art song and the folk song is addressed. Still, a utopia – the lied – must be art, yet it does not derive its credibility from art. The lied does not emerge from past memory accorded to birds, streams, clouds and winds; it must be the present. It is then a very short distance from that utopia, that artistic illusion, to present reality, from Beethoven to Schubert, who put that idea – without a programme, of course, but in its first perfect form – into practice.

In the Beethoven, however, between the first and the sixth poem, there are four lieder that the lyrical self of the lover has clearly already sung, because at the end the poet declares, somewhat surprisingly: 'Then embrace these songs / Which I sang to you, beloved' – even though they are in fact the cause of all the fuss in the first place. These four poems are simply an expressive form of lamentation (songs 2 and 5) and the stated desire for a swiftly delivered message (songs 3 and 4). In the third poem the loved one is captured as if through a lens: it is first birds, singing as they sail high and light, who cover the distance most quickly and directly. In the next stanza the message, still in the major key, is passed to clouds, as mist, through which the birds, dropping lower, now need to pass. Then the beloved can be seen in close-up, sitting in the bushes, from here on in the minor key. Lastly, light breezes and the stream whisper to her that at least someone far away is still thinking of her.

The five stanzas of the third song show how, just at the very moment the lied genre is coming into being, Beethoven is determined to individualise the stanzas and thus make them vivid within the song. He is unable to use the technique of instrumental variation – neither text nor voice will stretch to that – but there are traces of it, in the interplay of major and minor, and in the way in which the music rhythmically articulates the poem. This is achieved not by *staccato* or slurs or accents, but by note values that, as in the major–minor modulation, focus attention on the meaning of the poem as it develops through the stanzas. Quaver pauses separating syllables certainly indicate that a difference between *legato* and *parlando* is intended to emphasise the importance of the words within the musical context (see music example 1 overleaf). First, single crotchets are integrated within the quaver context via long vowels ('*Hö*[-hen]', '*spä*[-hen]'),

1 Ludwig van Beethoven: *An die ferne Geliebte*:
'Leichte Segler in den Höhen', bars 105, 109 and 114–17

2 Ludwig van Beethoven: *An die Ferne Geliebte*:
'Leichte Segler in den Höhen', bars 118–25

then, later the syllable '*sin*[-nend]' is elongated, even though it is actually spoken with a short vowel – a sound equivalent to its meaning. Finally, whole phrases become disembodied into an entirely un-voice-like line of quavers alternating with quaver pauses – connoting ease and levity. The variety of the vocal line is reflected in the piano part through a remodelling of the original quaver-triplet movement, giving the song an agitated twelve-quaver character. It is varied by dotted-quaver rhythms, tied and untied crotchets, syncopated quavers and even two bars with little *a cappella* phrases over chords, recitative-style (see music example 2).

This suggests that Beethoven is attempting a great variety of articulation when it comes to textual interpretation, at a time when the vocabulary for such notation of the vocal part did not even exist. In fact it didn't exist in any sense, but it was soon rendered unnecessary by the new style of melodic declamation, for example in Schumann and Wagner. For present-day performers it is a curiosity to come across notation of vocal articulation of this kind. In *Wozzeck* Alban Berg, still inexperienced in the banalities of the art of singing, wrote some sixty different kinds of vocal articulation. (Someone, apparently, has counted them . . .) No one would presume to understand or determine precisely all their meanings, or even make them sound distinctive, but it should still be clear that the composer is seeking to achieve and convey a fantastical range of aural possibilities.

For that reason, particularly in performance, I have never found it a practicable solution to observe slavishly the length of the notes in the third song of Beethoven's *An die ferne Geliebte*. The various syllable lengths, with a notation in quavers or crotchets, can hardly evoke an exact idea of sound. Curiously, it isn't even really audible when one does attempt to follow the note values precisely. Particularly with note values as short as the ones in this song, the nature of different consonants or chains of consonants restricts the ability to achieve rhythmical precision, especially when set against instrumental sound. To me, that seemingly almost 'natural' artistic freedom can be understood as the expression of dramatic fidelity to the work, because the required precision can be achieved only by accepting a degree of interpretation. The greatest possible literal fidelity can, paradoxically, lead a performer beyond the sound at the heart of a work. As far as I am concerned, this is one of many indications that fidelity to the work is to be preferred to fidelity to the author as a guiding principle in the performing arts. However, it is clear that fidelity to the work does not have to involve an explicit rejection of the author's *stated* will but can in fact be the execution of the author's *implied* will. Who would feel obliged to accept, for example, Berg's instruction that some scenes in *Wozzeck* (street, inn, etc.) must have a naturalistic stage set? This is why the delightful saying that 'the work knows more than the author' is in no way an anarchic justification for artistic randomness or high-handedness on the performer's part.

My conclusion with regard to Berg's *Wozzeck* lies not in seeking a finite solution to the problem – for example, by only speaking or only singing – but in developing a sound appropriate to the dramatic situation and combining it with a plausible interpretation of the score. Then, with the means available, such as articulation, dynamics, intonation, coloration and vibrato, one might even attain far more than sixty different kinds of vocal presentation, because essentially each note to be performed, every word that a singer/actor needs to communicate, is a unique and incomparable sound event.

In the fourth song of *An die ferne Geliebte*, exuberance breaks through. The inanimate trio – the cloud, the west and the stream – which in the previous song were granted being and meaning by the birds, are now brought to life by the originator of the message. He wants to be there; he wants the clouds to carry him along; he wants to share the wind's pleasure as it touches his beloved's hair. Reminiscent of *Eifersucht und Stolz* ('Jealousy and Pride') from Schubert's *Müllerin*, in which the miller orders the stream, 'Turn round!', most beautiful of all is his desire that the stream should simply flow backwards as soon as it has absorbed the beloved's reflection. It is the desire for a response – as it were via post-chaise, telegram or television set – that will convey to the lover her every detail, not only her tears flowing into the stream, not only verbal description, but sound and picture. He longs to see, even to feel, how she is, far away in the distance. Water stands in inanimate apposition to his own physical sensuality – we shall soon experience that device once again in Schubert's *Müllerin*, in which the miller, his own life severely restricted, needs an alter ego: the brook.

In *Liebesbotschaft*, the sixth song of Robert Schumann's opus 36, quoted above, we can find its inversion. In this lied, an aural embodiment of the ethereal, virtually a sung *perpetuum mobile*, the designated messengers – the clouds – appear as perfect carrier pigeons, as they do in *Die Taubenpost* from Schubert's *Schwanengesang*. They are ideal embodiments of the sender's longing: metamorphous in colour and shape, they no longer seek to communicate anything concrete; they are mere apparitions. The beloved, if she were then to think of the sender, would be moved only subliminally to do so, as if untouched by any desire of her own, which is also why she is referred to as chaste and faithful. All of the clouds' appearances ('all of my desires, my hopes, my songs'), however they might present themselves – as dew in shady spots, as pearls on flowers on trees, as little ships, painted purple and gold in the sea of glowing rays, on which tiny angels sing – they can ensure only that she remembers him: for her he is all that exists.[1] This chauvinist, somewhat exhibitionistic enthusiasm is a game for which the writer needs an addressee. Perhaps she shouldn't even be present. No answer to or engagement with his outpourings seems to be even desirable. *In extremis* the essence of *Liebesbotschaft* appears to be that the most important thing about the 'song to the distantly abiding beloved' may be the distance itself.

This lied was an epiphany for Gerold Huber and me. Even as young students we had to confront an ignorance that failed to grasp the song's world-shifting remoteness from reality. Eric Sams wrote of the song beginning with a too excessive sweetness.² For me this is a startling expression of a reluctance to understand something that threatens to afflict us all when our sophistication is challenged too excessively by singularity. At any rate, in the first recording that the two of us were to make, at Bayerischer Rundfunk, we had to defend our interpretation against the experienced and indeed excellent sound engineer, who wanted the song to be delivered in a denser, more impasto-like tone than we would have wished. But our vision for the lied, which sounds like the immortalisation of any desire to believe, was rewarded: the recording attracted the interest of our agent, and she gave us our first really important performance, in May 1999 at the Schubertiade in Lindau.

With the main motif that begins *attacca* – a dotted scale rising from the third to the octave before falling again to the fifth – we associate an immediate expression of blissful transfiguration, completely lacking any sense of affirmation but at the same time avoiding indeterminacy. We always perform the lied as slowly as is humanly possible – as long as I don't end up out of breath and neither does the phrase, and it doesn't simply fall apart.

But this air is not the illustrative breath and whisper that in many respects appears in Beethoven's 'Liebesbotschaft'. Rather it is a breath marked by a curious heaviness, which makes singing itself the subject in addition to distance – as in the two framing songs of Beethoven's *An die ferne Geliebte*. This is not done explicitly, however, as in the Beethoven, but through the singing itself, in sensuality: singing may be experienced as singing. Then I use as little vibrato as possible, keeping the amplitude to a minimum. The colour is supposed to be bright and light. And all the parentheses – 'Wo *die Eine, die Meine* weilt' ('To where *the one, my own,* is waiting') and 'Daß *der* Holdseligen, / *Kommt sie gegangen* / All die fröhlichen / Blüten . . .' ('So that *at the appearance of the fair one* / All the joyful blossoms . . .') simply need enough air and enough duration to be recognised as such, to be able to make themselves understood. And yet they also need enough power not only to signify that sensuality, but to embody it in concrete terms, as sung and played phrases. It is not sensuality that the lonely and separated couple described above is missing, but something present in abundance for the complacently longing lover: it is lied as self-celebration.

The last example taught me the extent to which a sentence that is interrupted as a musical phrase ('So that at the appearance of the fair one [piano interlude], / All the joyful blossoms open with brighter beauty') must receive all the greater attention from the singer. Because the important thing here is to preserve the impression of the infinite – embodied throughout by the poem's whole *perpetuum-mobile* character, and epitomised by the enjambement and the sudden pentameter in the last line of the stanza. Even when sung, the sentence as a whole may be kept alive by virtue of the fact that the dynamic at which the voice pauses at the beginning of the piano interlude is precisely resumed at its re-entry.

At the melodic climax Schumann has written an *ossia*, an alternative up to a sixth lower, in which the vocal line reaching an A flat, or even a B flat in the original, can be bypassed. From the very beginning, the high original struck Gerold Huber and me as counter to the essence of the lied, because it is too aria-like, and I was glad not to be able to sing it beautifully in a vocally technical sense, as with the ending of Dr Marianus's aria in Schumann's *Szenen aus Goethes Faust* ('. . . needing mercy'). Sung lower, this passage expresses a greater indeterminacy, and corresponds more to the transfigured femininity than the convinced upward swing to the definitively conclusive high G.[3] Perhaps these upward *ossias* are grapes that were too sour for me (like the fox in the fable finding the grapes were hanging just too high to be reached), or at least those fruits, when I did manage to get hold of them, were not sweet enough. However, this lied also ends in glorious indeterminacy when Reinick writes and Schumann sings: 'guide you, fugitives, / To the chaste one, the only one I may remember'. May he remember only her and no one else, or may he only remember her but not lead his life with her?

Today the problem of the message of love no longer exists. We can go wherever we like, or we can phone people up or chat via our computer. Only the deeper, sensual experience of the other is absent both then and now – the vaguely recognised timbre of the voice (i.e. over the telephone) cannot deceive us about that. Even seeing the moving face when FaceTiming is only a pale reflection of the situation in which two people touch each another, breathe the same air, are affected by the same rain, the same light and the same wind, burning the same air as they smoke two cigarettes. So I still find it all the more extraordinary how shocked my friend and I were by that brief interconnection of sensual and cognitive experiences. I hear the fighter jet over the telephone and imagine how loud it must be, the physical power of it, the noise that isn't perceived solely by the eardrum, but that prompts a profound and terrible shudder in the hair and skin. And then the sound in the right ear, against the receiver communicating the distant situation, lessens and the sound in the unfiltered left ear becomes louder, because the jet is now reaching my house – and vice versa for my friend. Never since have I had such a shared, simultaneous, sensual and virtual experience over a long distance.

But the grief of the past at the inability to communicate even to the most rudimentary degree over long distances has perhaps become the most important literary motif of the history of the lied. And even today the lied remains its most bewitching realisation.

Some Messages of Love

An die ferne Geliebte
Ludwig van Beethoven; op. 98

I

Auf dem Hügel sitz ich spähend
In das blaue Nebelland,
Nach den fernen Triften sehend,
Wo ich dich, Geliebte, fand.

Weit bin ich von dir geschieden,
Trennend liegen Busch und Tal
Zwischen uns und unserm Frieden,
Unserm Glück und unsrer Qual.

Ach, den Blick kannst du nicht sehen,
Der zu dir so glühend eilt,
Und die Seufzer, sie verwehen
In dem Raume, der uns teilt.

Will denn nichts mehr zu dir dringen,
Nichts der Liebe Bote sein?
Singen will ich, Lieder singen,
Die dir klagen meine Pein!

Denn vor Liedesklang entweichet
Jeder Raum und jede Zeit,
Und ein liebend Herz erreichet,
Was ein liebend Herz geweiht!

―――

On the hill I sit gazing
Into the blue misty land,

Looking for the far-off tracks
Where I found you, beloved.

Far away am I from you
Bush and valley separate us,
Lying between us and our peace
Our joy and our torment.

Oh – you cannot see the gaze
Hastening so ardently towards you,
And the sighs disperse
In the space dividing us.

Will nothing reach you,
Nothing be love's messenger?
I want to sing, I want to sing songs
That tell you my pain.

For the sound of song escapes
Every space and every time
And a loving heart reaches
What blessed a loving heart.

2

Wo die Berge so blau
Aus dem nebligen Grau
Schauen herein,
Wo die Sonne verglüht,
Wo die Wolke umzieht,
Möchte ich sein!

Dort im ruhigen Tal
Schweigen Schmerzen und Qual.
Wo im Gestein
Still die Primel dort sinnt,

Weht so leise der Wind,
Möchte ich sein!

Hin zum sinnigen Wald
Drängt mich Liebesgewalt,
Innere Pein.
Ach, mich zög's nicht von hier,
Könnt' ich, Traute, bei dir
Ewiglich sein!

———

Where the mountains so blue
Appear out of
The misty grey,
Where the sun casts its last light
Where the cloud drifts,
That is where I would like to be.

There in the peaceful valley
Pain and torment fall silent
Where among the crags
The primrose dreams in silence
And the wind breathes softly,
That is where I would like to be.

For the pensive wood
Yearns the force of my love,
My inner pain.
Ah, were I not drawn away from here
Could I, true one,
Be with you forever.

3

Leichte Segler in den Höhen,
Und du Bächlein, klein und schmal,
Könnt mein Liebchen ihr erspähen,
Grüßt sie mir viel tausendmal.

Seht ihr Wolken sie dann gehen
Sinnend in dem stillen Tal,
Laßt mein Bild vor ihr entstehen
In dem luft'gen Himmelssaal.

Wird sie an den Büschen stehen,
Die nun herbstlich falb und kahl,
Klagt ihr, wie mir ist geschehen,
Klagt ihr, Vöglein, meine Qual.

Stille Weste, bringt im Wehen
Hin zu meiner Herzenswahl
Meine Seufzer, die vergehen
Wie der Sonne letzter Strahl.

Flüstr' ihr zu mein Liebesflehen,
Laß sie, Bächlein klein und schmal,
Treu in deinen Wogen sehen
Meine Tränen ohne Zahl!

———

Light birds sailing on high
And you, narrow little brook,
If you see my sweetheart
Send her many thousands of greetings.

If, clouds, you should see her walking
Pensively in the silent valley,
Let my picture appear before her
In the airy space of heaven.

Should she be standing by the bushes
Autumnally pale and bare
Let her know what has befallen me,
Birds, tell her of my pain.

Silent westerly winds, bring
Waving to my heart's choice
My sighs, that fade
Like the sun's last ray.

Whisper to her my pleas of love,
Little brooklet, let her see
Faithfully in your ripples
My numberless tears.

4

Diese Wolken in den Höhen,
Dieser Vöglein muntrer Zug
Werden dich, o Huldin, sehen,
Nehmt mich mit im leichten Flug!

Diese Weste werden spielen
Scherzend dir um Wang' und Brust,
In den seidnen Locken wühlen,
Teilt ich mit euch diese Lust!

Hin zu dir von jenen Hügeln
Emsig dieses Bächlein eilt.
Wird ihr Bild sich in dir spiegeln,
Fließ zurück dann unverweilt!

These clouds in the heights,
These birds' cheerful skein,
Will see you, graceful one,
Take me along on your breezy flight!

These west winds will play
Jokingly around your cheek and breast,
Will burrow in your silken locks,
If only I could share your delight!

Towards you from those hills
Busily dashes this brook.
If her image is reflected in you
Flow back then straight away!

5

Es kehret der Maien, es blühet die Au.
Die Lüfte, sie wehen so milde, so lau,
Geschwätzig die Bäche nun rinnen.
Die Schwalbe, die kehret zum wirtlichen Dach,
Sie baut sich so emsig ihr bräutlich Gemach,
Die Liebe soll wohnen da drinnen.

Sie bringt sich geschäftig von kreuz und von quer
Manch weicheres Stück zu dem Brautbett hierher,
Manch wärmendes Stück für die Kleinen.
Nun wohnen die Gatten beisammen so treu,
Was Winter geschieden, verband nun der Mai,
Was liebet, das weiß er zu einen.

Es kehret der Maien, es blühet die Au.
Die Lüfte, sie wehen so milde, so lau.
Nur ich kann nicht ziehen von hinnen.
Wenn alles, was liebet, der Frühling vereint,
Nur unserer Liebe kein Frühling erscheint,
Und Tränen sind all ihr Gewinnen.

———

May returns, the meadow is in bloom.
The breezes blow so soft, so mild.
The brooks babble along.
The swallow returns to the welcoming roof
So busily building its bridal chamber
Where love shall dwell.

Eagerly, from all around
It brings soft things to the bridal bed,
Some warming things for the little ones.
Now the spouses live so faithfully together.
What winter has parted May has brought together,
It knows the way to reunite the lovers.

May returns, the meadow is in bloom.
The breezes blow so soft, so mild,
Except that I cannot move from here.
Springtime reunites all that loves –
Yet no springtime appears for our love
And tears are its only reward.

6

Nimm sie hin denn, diese Lieder,
Die ich dir, Geliebte, sang.
Singe sie dann abends wieder
Zu der Laute süßem Klang.

Wenn das Dämmrungsrot dann ziehet
Nach dem stillen blauen See,
Und sein letzter Strahl verglühet
Hinter jener Bergeshöh;

Und du singst, was ich gesungen,
Was mir aus der vollen Brust
Ohne Kunstgepräng erklungen,
Nur der Sehnsucht sich bewußt:

STRAUBING, AUGUST 1984

Dann vor diesen Liedern weichet,
Was geschieden uns so weit,
Und ein liebend Herz erreichet,
Was ein liebend Herz geweiht!

ALOIS JEITTELES

Then embrace these songs,
Which I sang for you, beloved.
And in the evening sing them yourself
To the lute's sweet sound.

When the setting sun then moves
Towards the still blue lake,
And its last ray dies away
Behind this mountain peak;

And you sing what I had sung,
Which from my full breast
Rang without false artistry,
Just aware of its own longing:

Then give way to these songs,
Which had separated us so far,
And a loving heart achieves
What a loving heart had vowed.

Liebesbotschaft
Franz Schubert: *Schwanengesang* (D. 957) (1)

Rauschendes Bächlein, so silbern und hell,
Eilst zur Geliebten so munter und schnell?
Ach, trautes Bächlein, mein Bote sei du;
Bringe die Grüße des Fernen ihr zu.

All' ihre Blumen, im Garten gepflegt,
Die sie so lieblich am Busen trägt,
Und ihre Rosen in purpurner Glut,
Bächlein, erquicke mit kühlender Flut.

Wenn sie am Ufer, in Träume versenkt,
Meiner gedenkend das Köpfchen hängt,
Tröste die Süße mit freundlichem Blick,
Denn der Geliebte kehrt bald zurück.

Neigt sich die Sonne mit rötlichem Schein,
Wiege das Liebchen in Schlummer ein.
Rausche sie murmelnd in süße Ruh',
Flüst're ihr Träume der Liebe zu.

LUDWIG RELLSTAB

Rushing brook, silvery and bright,
Do you hurry so lively, so quickly, to the beloved?
Oh, trusty brook, be my messenger;
Bring the greetings of the distant one to her.

All of the flowers that she has tended in the garden,
Which she wears so sweetly in her bosom,
And her roses with their purple glow,
Refresh them, little brook, with your cooling waters.

If, lost in dreams by the riverbank,
She hangs her head as she remembers me,
Comfort the sweet one with a friendly glance,
For the beloved will soon return.

When the sun sets with its reddish glow,
Rock my darling into slumber.
Lull her with your murmurs into sweet peace,
Whisper to her dreams of love.

Der Blumenbrief
Franz Schubert; D. 622

Euch Blümlein will ich senden
Zur schönen Jungfrau dort,
Fleht sie mein Leid zu enden
Mit einem guten Wort.

Du Rose kannst ihr sagen,
Wie ich in Lieb' erglüh',
Wie ich um sie muß klagen
Und weinen spät und früh.

Du, Myrte, flüstre leise
Ihr meine Hoffnung zu,
Sag': auf des Lebens Reise
Glänzt ihm kein Stern als du.

Du Ringelblume deute
Ihr der Verzweiflung Schmerz;
Sag' ihr: des Grabes Beute
Wird ohne dich sein Herz.

ALOYS SCHREIBER

Little flowers, I want to send you
To the fair maiden there,
Beg her to end my suffering
With a kind word.

You, rose, can tell her
How I burn with love,
How I must lament for her
And weep night and day.

You, myrtle, whisper softly
My hopes to her,

Say: on life's journey
No star shines for him like you.

You, marigold, show
Her the pain of despair,
Tell her: the grave's prey
Will be his heart without you.

An die Entfernte
Felix Mendelssohn: *Six Songs*, op. 71 (3)

Diese Rose pflück' ich hier
In der weiten Ferne,
Liebes Mädchen, dir, ach dir,
Brächt' ich sie so gerne!

Doch bis ich zu dir mag ziehen
Viele weite Meilen,
Ist die Rose längst dahin;
Denn die Rosen eilen.

Nie soll weiter sich in's Land
Lieb' von Liebe wagen,
Als sich blühend in der Hand
Läßt die Rose tragen;

Oder als die Nachtigall
Halme bringt zum Neste,
Oder als ihr süßer Schall
Wandert mit dem Weste.

NIKOLAUS LENAU

This rose I pluck here
In the foreign land,

To you only, darling girl,
I would love to bring it!

Before I can return to you
Travelling many miles,
The rose will be long gone;
So swiftly roses fade.

Never further into the land
Love from love should venture,
Than blossoming in the hand
A rose can be carried;

Or than the nightingale
Brings straws to the nest,
Or than her sweet sound
Wanders with the wind from the west.

Suleika I
Franz Schubert; D. 720

Was bedeutet die Bewegung?
Bringt der Ost mir frohe Kunde?
Seiner Schwingen frische Regung
Kühlt des Herzens tiefe Wunde.

Kosend spielt er mit dem Staube,
Jagt ihn auf in leichten Wölkchen,
Treibt zur sichern Rebenlaube
Der Insekten frohes Völkchen.

Lindert sanft der Sonne Glühen,
Kühlt auch mir die heißen Wangen,
Küßt die Reben noch im Fliehen,
Die auf Feld und Hügel prangen.

Und mir bringt sein leises Flüstern
Von dem Freunde tausend Grüße;
Eh' noch diese Hügel düstern,
Grüßen mich wohl tausend Küsse.

Und so kannst du weiter ziehen!
Diene Freunden und Betrübten.
Dort, wo hohe Mauern glühen,
Find' ich bald den Vielgeliebten.

Ach, die wahre Herzenskunde,
Liebeshauch, erfrischtes Leben
Wird mir nur aus seinem Munde,
Kann mir nur sein Atem geben.

    JOHANN WOLFGANG VON GOETHE,
    MARIANNE VON WILLEMER

What is the meaning of this motion?
Does the east wind bring me happy news?
Its wings' fresh stirring
Cools the heart's deep wounds.

Caressingly it plays with the dust,
Sends it flying up in light little clouds
Drives to the safety of the grapevine
The cheerful swarm of insects.

Eases gently the sun's glow,
Cools my hot cheeks too,
Kissing the grapes while fleeing
That adorn the field and hill.

And its quiet whisper brings me
From my friend a thousand greetings;
Even before these hills darken,
I am greeted by a thousand kisses.

STRAUBING, AUGUST 1984

And so you can now move on!
Serve the friends and the afflicted.
And where high stone walls glow,
I will soon find my much beloved.

Oh, the true message of the heart,
The breath of love, refreshed life,
Comes to me from its mouth alone,
Can give me his breath alone.

Suleika II
Franz Schubert; D. 717

Ach, um deine feuchten Schwingen,
West, wie sehr ich dich beneide:
Denn du kannst ihm Kunde bringen,
Was ich in der Trennung leide!

Die Bewegung deiner Flügel
Weckt im Busen stilles Sehnen;
Blumen, Auen, Wald und Hügel
Stehn bei deinem Hauch in Tränen.

Doch dein mildes sanftes Wehen
Kühlt die wunden Augenlider;
Ach, für Leid müßt' ich vergehen,
Hofft' ich nicht zu sehn ihn wieder.

Eile denn zu meinem Lieben,
Spreche sanft zu seinem Herzen;
Doch vermeid' ihn zu betrüben
Und verbirg ihm meine Schmerzen.

Sag' ihm, aber sag's bescheiden:
Seine Liebe sei mein Leben,

Freudiges Gefühl von beiden
Wird mir seine Nähe geben.

        JOHANN WOLFGANG VON GOETHE,
                MARIANNE VON WILLEMER

Oh, how your damp wings,
West wind, I envy you:
For you can bring him message
Of how I am suffering in separation.

The movement of your wings
Wakes in the breast still longing;
Flowers, meadows, wood and hills,
Stand at your breath in tears.

But your mild, soft draft
Cools the weary eyelids;
Oh, of suffering I could die
If I did not hope to see him again.

Hurry, then, to my beloved,
Speak softly to his heart;
But avoid saddening him
And hide from him my pain.

Tell him, but say it modestly:
His love is my life,
A sense of joy in them both
Being near to him will give me.

Die Taubenpost
Franz Schubert: *Schwanengesang* (D. 957) (14)

Ich hab' eine Brieftaub' in meinem Sold,
Die ist gar ergeben und treu,

Sie nimmt mir nie das Ziel zu kurz,
Und fliegt auch nie vorbei.

Ich sende sie viel tausendmal
Auf Kundschaft täglich hinaus,
Vorbei an manchem lieben Ort,
Bis zu der Liebsten Haus.

Dort schaut sie zum Fenster heimlich hinein,
Belauscht ihren Blick und Schritt,
Gibt meine Grüße scherzend ab
Und nimmt die ihren mit.

Kein Briefchen brauch' ich zu schreiben mehr,
Die Träne selbst geb' ich ihr:
Oh, sie verträgt sie sicher nicht,
Gar eifrig dient sie mir.

Bei Tag, bei Nacht, im Wachen, im Traum,
Ihr gilt das alles gleich,
Wenn sie nur wandern, wandern kann,
Dann ist sie überreich.

Sie wird nicht müd', sie wird nicht matt,
Der Weg ist stets ihr neu;
Sie braucht nicht Lockung, braucht nicht Lohn,
Die Taub' ist so mir treu!

Drum heg' ich sie auch so treu an der Brust,
Versichert des schönsten Gewinns;
Sie heißt: die Sehnsucht – kennt ihr sie? –
Die Botin treuen Sinns.

JOHANN GABRIEL SEIDL

I have a carrier pigeon in my employ
Which is all devoted and loyal.
It never falls short of its goal,
And never flies past it.

I send it out many thousands of times
To ply its trade every day,
Past many a kind place
On to the beloved's house.

There it looks through the window secretly,
Spies on her gaze, her step,
Passes on my greetings playfully
And picks up hers in return.

No letter I need to write any more,
My tear even give I to it;
Oh, it certainly never will lose it,
As the pigeon eagerly serves me.

By day, by night, waking or dreaming,
It's all the same to this bird;
As long as it can wander, wander,
It is amply rewarded.

It does not become tired or weary,
The route is always fresh and new;
It needs no enticement nor prize,
So loyal is the pigeon to me.

And that is why I hold it in faith to my breast,
Ensuring the finest reward;
It is called: Longing – do you know it? –
The messenger of a faithful heart.

An die Entfernte
Franz Schubert; D. 765

So hab' ich wirklich dich verloren?
Bist du, o Schöne, mir entflohn?
Noch klingt in den gewohnten Ohren
Ein jedes Wort, ein jeder Ton.

So wie des Wandrers Blick am Morgen
Vergebens in die Lüfte dringt,
Wenn, in dem blauen Raum verborgen,
Hoch über ihm die Lerche singt:

So dringet ängstlich hin und wieder
Durch Feld und Busch und Wald mein Blick;
Dich rufen alle meine Lieder:
O komm, Geliebte, mir zurück!

JOHANN WOLFGANG VON GOETHE

So have I really lost you?
Have you, fair one, fled from me?
Still echoes in familiar ears
Every word, every sound.

Just as the wanderer's gaze at morning
Vainly pierces the air,
When, hidden in the blue expanse
High above him, the lark sings:

So fearfully back and forth wanders
Through field and bush and wood my gaze;
To you all of my songs are calling:
O come, beloved, back to me!

LYRICAL DRAMATURGY

LONDON, SEPTEMBER 1999

> Here one may certainly admire man as a mighty genius of construction who manages to assemble an infinitely complicated conceptual cathedral on moving foundations and as if on flowing water; of course, to stand on such foundations it must be a building as if made of spiders' webs, delicate enough to be carried along by the waves, solid enough not to be blown apart by the wind.
>
> FRIEDRICH NIETZSCHE (sadly not about Schumann)[1]

Robert Schumann's output in terms of lieder may be only about half as extensive as that of Franz Schubert, the 'inventor' of the genre, but it is marked by an idiosyncratic consistency. From the outset this is expressed in what can be perceived as a unique drive towards a structured conception. It can be discerned in many respects in relatively familiar dramaturgical ideas in the compositions dating from Schumann's first year as a lieder composer – in the three most important cycles, but also in smaller forms. Glimpses of the conceptual freedom and diversity of his later years make their appearance early, for example in the *Andersen-Lieder*, op. 40, which, with their downright malicious emotional descent, prepare the way for the more abstract *Lenau-Lieder*, op. 90, ten years later.

The conceptual diversity is astonishing from the start. *Aus dem Liederbuch eines Malers*, op. 36, from 1840 might be a painter's portfolio imagined in sound, a kind of vocal sonata. The first lied is a cheerful movement; the second, third and fourth lieder form a scherzo with three romance sections; this is followed by a dramatic lied close to Goethe's *Erlkönig* and Heine's *Die Lorelei*, the whole concluding in the sixth song with an endless melody. The 'small' *Liederkreis*, op. 24, settings of poems by Heinrich Heine, is in my view (apart from the three *Romanzen und Balladen*, op. 49) Schumann's most ironic cycle, above all because of the contrast provided by the highly romantic, longing-filled lieder that interpose themselves into the sequence: 3 *Ich wandelte unter den*

Bäumen ('I Wandered Beneath the Trees'); 5 *Schöne Wiege meiner Leiden* ('Lovely Cradle of My Sorrows'); and 7 *Berg' und Burgen schau'n herunter* ('Mountains and Castles Gaze Down').

Frauenliebe und Leben ('A Woman's Love and Life'), op. 42, could in fact be a 'Life of Mary' – a daring and exciting attempt to explain Schumann's textual reduction of Adelbert von Chamisso's cycle of poems.[2] If we wish to stop short of that and still pay homage to the phenomenon of this 'untimely' cycle, we can do so in a less spectacular way: with respect not only for the formal structure, but also for the psychologically gripping understanding of the poetry of the Biedermeier period.[3] There is no need to damn and incriminate this musically compelling and sensitive cycle with banal references to textual anachronisms; among intellectuals the rejection of the cycle seems to be something one can almost take as read. If the agreement of every work of art with the ethical conviction of the recipient or interpreter were required for its survival, our spiritual world would suddenly be very empty.

The other 'lied opuses' from Schuman's first 'lieder year' often reveal an autobiographically based character. As examples we might cite *Myrthen* ('Myrtles'), op. 25, and the three settings of opus 30 – both of which will be discussed below.[4] They all have a cyclical form that places them beyond mere collections and that can be perceived with varying degrees of clarity.

In the ageing man's view of invigorating and adored youth there is only a very faint connecting thought in the lyrics of the relatively unknown *Lieder und Gesänge*, op. 27. On the other hand, this opus has a sequence that connects the individual lieder quite unambiguously in a musical sense: introduction – continuation – resignation – resumption – conclusion. Equally we might mention two ballade triptychs: *Drei Gedichte von Emanuel Geibel*, op. 30, brings together three views of a man, from the free artist – *Der Knabe mit dem Wunderhorn* ('The Boy with the Magic Horn') – through the humble – *Der Page* ('The Page') – to the victorious – *Der Hidalgo*

('The Hidalgo'). In the background is the trial, which was reaching its conclusion, surrounding Schumann's marriage to Clara, whose legal permission to marry in the closing song, *Der Hidalgo*, leads to exuberant joy and unconcealed triumph: 'The zither was for the ladies / The blade for the rival. / So let's have an adventure. / The sun's fire is already spent / Beyond the mountains. / Moonlit night's hours of dusk / They bring news of love, / And with either flowers or wounds / I will return tomorrow.' *Drei Gesänge*, op. 31, as if by way of balance, reveals the characters of three women evoked in poems by Chamisso, the first and third of which are engagingly unique and authentic. The ritornello-like chorale of the third song, *Die rote Hanne* ('Red-haired Hannah'), effectively yields into Hanne's fate, which she had hoped might be rather better, and the listener has to follow her. The first song, *Löwenbraut* ('Lion's Bride'), is ecstatically, sensually, almost manically wistful. But in between the two, there is the massive contrast of the *Die Kartenlegerin* ('The Fortune Teller') – a portrait of loquacious immaturity and unnerving superstition, which, with its inflection of a superficially humorous operetta couplet, can only be trying to provoke revulsion in the listener.

Later the structures incline slightly more towards symmetry. *Lieder und Gesänge III*, op. 77, for example, begins and ends lightly, with difficult transitions to and from *Geisternähe* ('Nearby Spirits'), a backward-looking 'message of love' that stands at its centre. Or the cycles' structures incline to the conceptual, for example the theme of 'loss and farewell' in *Sechs Gesänge*, op. 89, settings of Wilfried von der Neun, concluding with *Röselein* ('Little Rose'), often delivered with the flirtatiousness of a soubrette, but which for me embodies an exquisite unworldly acceptance of destiny – the only song known to me that parallels Mahler's *Urlicht*. Or they approach abstraction and a sensual heightening of poetic language (as in *Lieder und Gesänge IV*, op. 96, and *Sechs Gesänge*, op. 107), or to involve the interpretation of figures from literary history

(Wilhelm Meister in opus 98a, for example; Elisabeth Kulmann in opus 104; Mary Stuart in opus 135).

Later, another caesura in Schumann's life was to be significant. The death of the two Mendelssohn siblings in quick succession might explain the two heroic cornerstones of the *Byron-Lieder*, op. 95: a song for Fanny, *Die Tochter Jephtas* ('Jephtha's Daughter') – an anonymous, unknown figure, as Fanny was virtually unknown as a composer – and, indisputably, one for Felix, *Dem Helden* ('To the Hero)'. These two monumental songs are linked to each other by *An den Mond* ('To the Moon'), a lament for them both.[5]

I find two absurd late works – the carnivalesque and bloodthirsty *Husarenlieder*, op. 117, with texts by Nikolaus Lenau, and a curious assemblage of three settings of Gustav Pfarrius, op. 119, gripping, brutal and comical. In the Pfarrius songs we are first presented with a fairy-tale idyll that could not be lovelier; it's hard to imagine a life becoming any more marvellous. Then comes a warning: things will not stay this way, because the owl is threatening the little bird. Finally the owl turns into a creature who greedily sucks a birch tree dry and leaves it to bleed to death. Once again, as in the *Kerner-Lieder*, op. 35, poems are forced into an association that is entirely unintended by the poet, and are thus made to express a peculiarly free and visionary affiliation. Even in the other little cycles (opp. 45, 51, 53 and 64), in performance I always find the enthralling sense of an entirely deliberate connection.[6]

I would ask you to forgive this simplistic and subjective vision of Schumann's songs. The only important thing for me is to make clear my conviction that every Schumann lieder opus is fundamentally characterised by ideas of cohesion both formally and in terms of content, and that each has its own new and different form and dramaturgy.[7] This cannot be expressed more effectively, explained more comprehensively, than by Richard Strauss's comment on instrumental music, that 'the poetic idea also embodies the form-giving element'.[8] The cyclical musical form thus develops in a unique way, following the poetic idea that corresponds to the respective poems on which the songs are based, not in terms of congruence, but by following their inspiration.

In both musical and linguistic terms Schumann's concept of the lied challenges 'meaning': it assumes no clear semantic attitude towards either the poem or the music but rather towards the combination of the two or – on a still higher plane – towards the combination of lieder into cycles. Like Friedrich Nietzsche's linguistically sceptical essay of 1873, 'About Truth and Lies in the Extra-moral Sense', Schumann's programmatic vocal chamber music anticipates conceptual artistic designs, crucial trends in the twentieth century. I wish that in the following quotation Nietzsche had also spoken of the 'intuitive' in Schumann, while in reality he had nothing good to say about him.[9]

> There are eras in which the rational man and the intuitive man stand side by side, one fearful of intuition, the other scornful of abstraction; the latter as irrational as the former is inartistic. [. . .] While the man led by concepts and abstractions only fends off unhappiness without deriving happiness for himself from the abstractions, while seeking the greatest possible freedom from pain, the intuitive man, standing in the middle of a culture, already harvests from his intuitions, apart from fending off evil, a continuously flowing enlightenment, encouragement, salvation. Admittedly he suffers more violently *when* he suffers; indeed he also suffers more often because he does not try to learn from experience and keeps falling into the same ditch that he has fallen into before.[10]

In Schumann's work the programmatic and cyclical principle can act within the meaning of a narrative (*Kerner-Lieder*, op. 35) or even of a drama (*Dichterliebe*, op. 48); it can create symmetrical geometrical forms (*Lieder und Gesänge III*, op. 77) or floral patterns; it can follow philosophical convictions (*Lieder und Gesänge IV*, op. 96;

Romanzen und Balladen III, op. 53) and tend towards the abstract[11] (e.g. *Zwölf Gedichte aus 'Liebesfrühling'*, op. 37, and *Drei Gesänge*, op. 83). But this cyclical work can also be – and frequently is – the expression of Schumann's notoriously gloomy sense of life, when, as in the particularly significant *Kerner-*, *Andersen-* and *Lenau-Lieder* (opp. 35, 40 and 90), innocent poems are brought together in such a way that they demonstrate the badness of the world.

In September 1999 I made my first appearance at London's Wigmore Hall, which, thanks to William Lyne and John Gilhooly (its two most highly laudable artistic directors), has become the most important venue for my collaboration with Gerold Huber. On this occasion I covered for Gerald Finley, singing alongside the magnificent, legendary Edith Mathis and accompanied by the wonderful pianist Julius Drake in a performance of Schumann's *Myrthen*. She was rightly uneasy, because I had never sung these songs before. In spite of that, everything went well, and the cycle, which I had quite honestly not known before, immediately became very important to me. It is quite close to three somewhat remote Schumann song-cycles, because in all three of these works two singers, a man and a woman, sing alternately. These are the *Wilhelm-Meister-Lieder*, op. 98a; the *Liebesfrühling*, op. 37; and the *Liederalbum für die Jugend*, op. 79. The last two differ from *Myrthen* and the *Wilhelm-Meister-Lieder* in that they contain duets alongside conventional solo songs.

For a long time I thought the *Liederalbum für die Jugend* was a collection of songs assembled solely with pedagogical intent, to bring young people to the art of words and their sounds, and of sounds and their words. In my adolescence that wouldn't have dragged me away from my personal archetype as 'Strong Vanya Oven', the young man who reclines by the hearth throughout his youth, passively gathering his strength in order to take his place in the world all the more actively later on. I much preferred

Schumann's programmatic piano music (although only as a listener). And yet, and here again – given the sensual experience of performance – I became fully aware of Schumann's systematic and programmatic will: apart from the interpolation of duets and even ad lib. tercets, the cycle includes a kind of aesthetic in a nutshell: the conviction that the art song came into being not only because of the new possibilities of contemporary lyric poetry[12] but rather that it could be seen as a consolidation and refinement, indeed as a further development and inherent goal of children's songs and folk songs. It is here that we see a great, indeed diametrical, difference from Brahms, who uses his experiences in the field of the art song nostalgically, to gild his 'folk songs' as if they were cherubs.

The sequence of the 29 lieder of the *Liederalbum für die Jugend* does not take the form of a steady escalation; rather its constituent parts develop gradually, moving both forwards and backwards, towards what the cycle finally arrives at: large-format art songs, inclining towards a symphonic sound, such as song 28, *Lied Lynkeus des Türmers* ('Song of Lynceus the Watchman'), and song 29, *Mignon*. The latter was also published as the first song of the *Lieder, Gesänge und Requiem aus Goethes 'Wilhelm Meister'*, op. 98a/b.

In *Mignon*, however, another aspect of the programmatic conception of the *Liederalbum für die Jugend* becomes apparent. In this final song, the 'youthful' appearance of spring, universally present throughout the cycle, undergoes, with 'Italy', an intensification of the idea of 'spring and youth'. In the *Liederalbum für die Jugend* two statements about the meaning of the art song are brought together through an association with folksong: one, structural, on the possible framework of its development, and the other demonstrating in exemplary fashion the potential for the interpretative setting of a poem.

Each of Schumann's great song-cycles brings together texts by a single poet: *Zwölf Gedichte*, op. 35 – Justinus Kerner; *Liederkreis*, op. 39 –Joseph von Eichendorff; *Dichterliebe*, op. 48 – Heinrich

Heine. This is very different from Schumann's wedding present to his wife Clara: the 26-part cycle *Myrthen*, op. 25, is a collection of poems by eight different authors. For that reason – and also because the two singers alternate – it is often viewed merely as a kind of anthology. But the fact that each of its four books closes with two songs on texts evoking a couple standing faithfully together reveals a mind that is organising material architecturally. It seems as if here too – for the first time, incidentally – Schumann has developed a unique formal principle not repeated and unrepeatable in other song sequences, marked by a purpose and expressing itself in the content of the poems as well as in their arrangement and relationship to one another.

Schumann explicitly chose as his title the word 'Myrthen' with an 'h'. In German the name of the myrtle plant is actually written without an 'h', but there is also evidence of this orthography in the writings of Goethe and Jean Paul, for example. Myrtle twigs have been strewn at festive occasions since ancient times, and bridal crowns woven from them. This cycle, then, is a metaphorical bridal decoration, but it is unmistakably also a collection of the thoughts, sounds and desires that Robert Schumann associates with the marriage for which he has fought so hard. In *Myrthen* Schumann applies to an excessive degree a method that occurs frequently in his work, letters of the alphabet translated into musical notes in melody and harmony, to emphasise the word *Ehe* (marriage). (In German the note B is indicated by the letter H.) For example, the accompanying melody in the right hand of song 3, *Der Nussbaum* ('The Walnut Tree'), begins with the fifth leap E–H, which the singing voice immediately completes with H–E. The following song, *Jemand* ('Someone'), begins in E minor, bitterly symbolising the original refusal of consent from Clara's father Friedrich Wieck (the introduction ends with E, followed by a repeated fall of a fifth in the voice from H to E), before ending in E major (fourth leap from H to E). Song 16, *Räthsel* ('Riddle'), in turn circles around the letter 'H' and the note H. So the spelling of the song-cycle's title and the name of the eponymous plant with an 'h' may also be essential.

Myrthen, op. 25

Book I
1. *Widmung* ('Dedication') – Friedrich Rückert
2. *Freisinn* ('The Free Spirit') – Johann Wolfgang von Goethe
3. *Der Nussbaum* ('The Walnut Tree') – Julius Mosen
4. *Jemand* ('Somebody') – Robert Burns / *Lieder aus dem Schenkenbuch im Divan* ('Songs from the Book of the Cupbearer in the *West-östlicher Divan*' – Johann Wolfgang von Goethe
5. *Sitz'ich allein* ('If I Sit Alone')
6. *Setze mir nicht, du Grobian* ('Don't Set Down for Me, You Oaf')

Book II
7. *Die Lotosblume* ('The Lotus Flower') – Heinrich Heine
8. *Talismane* ('Talismans') – Johann Wolfgang von Goethe
9. *Lied der Suleika* ('Song of Suleika') – Marianne von Willemer, Johann Wolfgang von Goethe
10. *Die Hochländer-Witwe* ('The Highland Widow') – Robert Burns / *Lieder der Braut* ('Songs of the Bride') – Friedrich Rückert
11. *Mutter, Mutter* ('Mother, Mother')
12. *Lass mich ihm am Busen hangen* ('Let Me Rest upon His Chest')

Book III
13. *Hochländers Abschied* ('Highlander's Farewell') – Robert Burns
14. *Hochländisches Wiegenlied* ('Highland Lullaby') – Robert Burns
15. *Aus den hebräischen Gesängen* ('From the Hebrew Melodies') – Lord Byron
16. *Räthsel* ('Riddle') – Catherine Maria Fanshawe / *Zwei Venetianische Lieder* ('Two Venetian Songs') – Thomas Moore

17 *Leis' rudern hier* ('Row Gently Here')
18 *Wenn durch die Piazzetta* ('When through the Piazzetta')

Book IV
19 *Hauptmanns Weib* ('The Captain's Woman') – Robert Burns
20 *Weit, weit!* ('Far, far!') – Robert Burns
21 *Was will die einsame Thräne?* ('What Does the Lonely Teardrop Want?') – Heinrich Heine
22 *Niemand* ('Nobody') – Robert Burns
23 *Im Westen* ('In the West') – Robert Burns
24 *Du bist wie eine Blume* ('You Are like a Flower') – Heinrich Heine
25 *Aus den östlichen Rosen* ('From Eastern Roses') – Friedrich Rückert
26 *Zum Schluss* ('Farewell') – Friedrich Rückert

Schumann later organised the somewhat randomly composed songs, which at first colourfully reflected one another as in an amorous kaleidoscope, into four groups, which were published as four books. This arrangement also seems to go beyond the pure practicalities of publishing and commercial viability, and to correspond to an order governed by content. In the 'exposition', up to and including song 6, the person and gender of the two lovers are crucial. A Madonna-like worship is expressed in *Widmung*, metaphorically transposed male heroism and journeying in *Freisinn*, extravagant longing but also erotic identification in *Der Nussbaum*. *Jemand* alludes to the eventually coerced permission for the wedding – or at least to a positive turn of events. (Clara and Schumann had to take Friedrich Wieck to court to secure permission for their marriage.) In the two *Schenkenbuch-Lieder* (songs from the 'Book of the Cupbearer' in Goethe's *West-östlicher Divan*) we find the characterisation of the fictional stag night's bachelor, offended in court by his future father-in-law (perhaps with some justification) accusing him of excessive alcohol consumption.

The second book, songs 7–12, is devoted to the idea of a shared life. In *Die Lotosblume*, attention turns to the erotic – mutual now, but characterised by its current unattainability. In *Talismane* there is the vision of God's guidance ('lead me along your path') in marriage ('when I act') and jointly created art ('when I write') albeit in a border-crossing pantheistic sense ('God's is the East / God's is the West'). In *Suleika* it is the wife's submission to his commands expected by the future husband. Here a certain identification with the 'couple' consisting of Willemer and Goethe, writing on unequal terms, should not be too quickly dismissed. Finally, in the subsequent three songs, there are the associated implications for the wife: the danger of loss in *Die Hochländer-Witwe* as well as a farewell to her own youth and her mother (or her father: 'Leave me alone . . .') in the two *Lieder der Braut*.

The third book (songs 13–18) might be seen as a kind of 'development', with a view of the shared life and the bridal pair's return to personal goals as they turn their minds back to themselves as subject: *Hochländers Abschied* is about the move, or rather the return, to everyday life; *Hochländisches Wiegenlied* about inherited family characteristics. This is followed by *Aus den hebräischen Gesängen*, a work that in my view is central not only to this cycle but to Schumann's song-writing and indeed the German-language art song as a whole. It is like a weirdly prophetic evocation of Orphic shadows. Only two weeks after Schumann had begun to compose vocal chamber music, he made this ineffable declaration of the inescapability of creative melancholy, whose spell and profundity I find it difficult to escape. I would, however, sing it even more often if I did not have the greatest respect for the F sharp initiating 'Auf, von der Wand die Laute', which needs not only to be fully voiced, but also to convey the melancholic impulse that runs through the song, as it does through the whole of Schumann's work (see music example 3). In fact this song reveals an ideal balance between vocal elasticity and declamation – the dramatic and musical essence that I feel as inherent in the work requires it to be sung not too quietly and intimately, nor with too much attack, preserving a middle way between urgency and argument. However, as Eric Sams stresses,[13] Julius Körner's translation of Byron's poem, courtesy of the family-owned publishing house of the Schumann Brothers, does not contain much of the compelling poetry of the original about the healing of Saul by David's harp-playing. It is a song that clearly illustrates the dominance of the idea of the composer of the lied over the will of the poet (in this case the translator). This volume,

3 Robert Schumann: *Myrthen*, op. 25 no.15, 'Aus den hebräischen Gesängen', bars 7–16

devoted to imagined life together, then ends with three more or less comical but still tender and cheerful after-echoes: *Räthsel* and *Zwei Venetianische Lieder.*

Finally, the fourth book (songs 19–26), unites the many wide-ranging interests, obligations and tribulations of the couple, as they reach the middle of their lives, with mutual affection underlying everything: shared struggle and self-determination (*Hauptmanns Weib* and *Niemand*) – parting and renunciation (*Weit, weit!* and *Im Westen*) – as well as remembering and forgetting (*Was will die einsame Träne?*) And the longing for everlasting love (*Du bist wie eine Blume*) – and assurance of it (*Aus den östlichen Rosen*) – and its transcendental guarantee (*Zum Schluss*) – step into the foreground as they close the cycle.

Myrthen, perhaps one of the loveliest presents ever given to a loving and beloved person, is not just an illustrated statement, but to some degree also a description of the anticipated shared journey, so long awaited and the subject of such longing, a comprehensive vision of the hoped-for eternal bond between two lovers and hence also a cheering promise. But the familiar end of the Schumanns' story as a couple cannot be entirely ignored. After Schumann's admission to the psychiatric institution in Endenich on 4 March 1854 Clara saw him only once, two days before his death, on 27 July 1856. In my view there is already a hint of the *Geistervariationen* ('Ghost Variations'), WoO 24 – the work with which Robert bade farewell to their life together as pictured in *Myrthen* – not only in the *Hebräischen Gesängen* or in *Zum Schluss* but also in the songs, which would prove so prospectively empathetic and true of the loss that Clara Schumann, the young mother of the seven children they shared, would suffer after fewer than sixteen years of marriage.

Schumann's chamber music for multiple voices can no longer be avoided, even though it is unusual and didn't meet with the wide acceptance that the composer hoped for. We are not talking here about lieder opuses with several singers, as with *Myrthen*, which contains only solo lieder and no duets. These multi-voice works are unusual because in its classical form (with one singer and pianist) the lied is devoted entirely to the personal: it combines a fundamentally individual vocal colour, the singer's timbre, in contrasting combination with the 'objective' colour of the piano, one of very few instruments with a single sound quality throughout its range, with only one register. This juxtaposition is a guarantee that the fundamental illusion of the lied performance is maintained – the illusion that an individual, the singer of the lied, expressing himself subjectively in the 'lyric first person', is addressing one entirely personally – while the sound of the piano in principle tends to embody the impersonal, the objective. This may help to explain how and why, at the start of the nineteenth century, the ideal of the Second Berlin Lieder School, the concept of a lied that was simple in every respect – a lied that effectively accompanied itself, sang itself and above all explained itself – collapsed. That concept had been lost not only since Schubert, a shift that with and through him had become impossible to ignore, but also marks one of the beginnings of the 'Romantic' in music.

In the chapter about *Wasserflut* ('Flood') in his book about Schubert's *Winterreise*, the tenor Ian Bostridge writes about the phenomenon that 'good' singers of lieder should create in the audience precisely this impression of being personally addressed.[14] I would even claim that a seemingly personal address to each member of the audience as a clause in the contract within the recital room is practically in the nature of lied singing. And the chief means used to accomplish this is the personal, unmistakable sound of the singer's voice. The less this sound inclines to the general, the universal, and the more highly developed the colouristic skill at bringing to life the idea being represented, the more likely that this kind of understanding and communication can be maintained – because of course it is an illusion; everyone is aware of that. Even if an audience member thinks that the performer has 'lived' the lieder being performed, it is clear that even this is only part of the performance. The more concrete the performance becomes, the more naturalistic the imaginative suggestion of the singer, the more remote the performer's attitude is from the largely abstract lyrical conception of the lied and the closer to the more concrete play of musical drama. The tendency towards abstraction that I would generally ask of the lied has nothing to do with the fact that the illusion of the singer's individuality is a requirement for its performance.

In Schumann, however, we encounter a curious group of songs partially scored for several voices. The fact that a cyclical fundamental idea once again predominates is no surprise, given Schumann's work with lieder and his understanding of literature, but this underlying idea is a peculiarly narrative one. These lieder are stories, more or less comprehensible plots, small constellations of love.

This is perhaps seen in the most well-balanced and most immediately comprehensible way in the two Spanish-inspired compilations from Emanuel Geibel's translations, and particularly in the later of these works, the *Spanische Liebeslieder* ('Spanish Love Songs'), op. 138, with four-hand piano accompaniment. Here we have two ideal pairs of a kind that often appear in operas. On the one hand we have a soprano and a tenor, with the tenor's predictable infidelity and the soprano's corresponding lovesickness representing one of the most common lied subjects, found particularly frequently in German-language folksong and in its art-song adaptation, and the 'serenade' – *Ständchen* – the seduction of the object of desire, who is subsequently left literally holding the baby. Here the situation is only temporary, as in all the works that we shall now consider – remarkably in the context of Schumann – things turn out well. The cycle begins with the lament of the heartbroken girl, followed by the duet of the two unhappy women who want to die: the soprano out of disappointment, the alto only because she has been separated by fate from her beloved, the baritone. In their two solo songs (5 and 8), the other major theme of the *Spanische Liebeslieder* appears: the communication between the lovers, separated but awaiting one another, via animate and inanimate nature, the 'message of love'.[15] The 'surging Ebro' (Spain's second-longest river, along with morning dew, poplars, paths and birds) is to assure the baritone's beloved on his behalf that he still loves her, while the alto remains unable to recover from their sad farewell – she speaks of the well water that is seeping into the weeds and is therefore unable to pass on a message. In the end, however, all melancholy and sadness are resolved, and the cycle ends with an idyll.

While in these op. 138 songs we find solidly distributed and sternly maintained role models, in the *Spanische Liederspiel* ('Spanish Love Play'), op. 74, the amorous main characters are limited to soprano and tenor, characterised in their two solo songs, 6 and 7. There we also hear (as in the *Spanische Liebeslieder*) of the longing for death in response to unfulfilled love, which in song 4 they are able to admit to themselves but not to each another. Only the late declaration of love by the tenor in song 7 is the prelude to their happy union. In this cycle alto and bass play only an impersonal role; they are mere augmentations of the feelings of the actual protagonists, elaborating on their chief concerns in the lower voices (songs 1–3, 8), and thus completing the song in quartets into a choric whole – like the comments of the chorus in Greek tragedy, and also in song 10 of the *Spanische Liebeslieder*.

Things become a bit more abstract in the two cycles based on Friedrich Rückert's poetry collection *Liebesfrühling*. So, for example, in the *Minnespiel* ('Play of Devotion'), op. 101, also scored for soprano, alto, tenor and bass, the soprano and the tenor address each another even more directly than in their *Spanische Liederspiel* duet (song 4) and the two central themes of serenade and messages of love also make their appearance in songs 1 and 7. But here and in the cycle as a whole the various aspects of love are related to one another less sequentially than associatively. Consequently, they create the impression of a symbolic combination of themes (rose, tree, gardener, wreath, glass, shelter, jewellery, shield, east wind) and a transcendental reflection, which is made particularly clear in the central, almost impersonal *Mein schöner Stern* ('My Beautiful Star'), song 4. In addition, we cannot easily identify a shared concluding idea (along the lines of the 'Spanish' quartets) that will give purpose to all four 'protagonists', as the oath of love between two people at the end is sung by all four singers. Yet even in the *Minnespiel* we cannot simply sideline the idea of a love story, since this four-part declaration does have a causal relationship with what preceded it.

Last of all a quite unusual work, even though, like the *Minnespiel*, it inclines to abstraction: the *Zwölf Gedichte aus Rückerts Liebesfrühling* ('Twelve Poems from Rückert's *Springtime of Love*'), op. 37, another work for two singers and piano. Here Robert and Clara Schumann complemented each other not only as lovers or musicians, but also as composers: she wrote songs 2, 4 and 11 and he the remaining nine songs. The fact that they selected texts from Rückert's collection *Liebesfrühling* of 1821, the year of the poet's greatest happiness in love and marriage, is an ideal match for the collaboration of the recently married Schumanns.

Like *Myrthen*, the *Liebesfrühling* sequence starts with the beginning of their love story from his perspective (song 1) – and from hers (song 2). But it is striking that at the end of hers, the subject of separation is addressed – probably in line with the duet, song 7, in which the feast of springtime, the initial infatuation, lasts only three days. This is followed by a kind of round-dance reflection by both about the possibility of loving one another in a real and stable way, and about the conditions under which this can happen, for example in the well-known poem *Liebst du um Schönheit* ('If You Love for Beauty'), song 4, in which the only cause of love is identified as love itself. Love is reflected metaphorically in springtime (5), and the songs detail which external (6) and internal (7) obstacles it overcomes. In song 8 the motif of the message of love is spectacularly overcome in a dream, when the distant lover is given wings that render the messages unnecessary. In song 9 doubt is cast on the meaning of the message of love itself, since love is not expressed through communications, but ideally physically, directly – yes, it is the merging of all finite, worldly details (song 10). And so, after overcoming their separation, which can also make erecting boundaries against other people necessary (song 11), in the last duet (song 12) the two lovers are finally able to sing of the absolute mutuality of their love, equalled only by comparably indivisible, immediately effective entities such as the sun, the clouds, flame and springtime itself.

While language can also be more artificial, more abstract in the two Rückert cycles than in the two 'Spanish' works, their content is highly concrete. Hence the collaborative work of *Liebesfrühling* has become, not only ideally but also physically, a work between two people, even though it describes a sequence of thoughts rather than of actions.

These ensemble works, mostly scored for several voices, even though different weight may be given to their narrative character, are at root less concerned with spirituality conveyed through sound than is typical of Schumann's solo art songs. Instead I see works with very song-like traits, but also with the character of adventure; works that do not so much concentrate on introspection (thoughts, situations or the person in the role), but declare themselves primarily in interpersonal sequences of actions and situations. Because of the many possible combinations of voice types involved, this also makes the colouristic sophistication of the sung text less important.

The illusionistic effect of the timbre of the lied singer's voice is immediately lost when more than one voice sings during a song (and also within a cyclical work). The imagination of a personal expression based on the individual sound of the performer's voice is irrevocably lost. The uniquely intimate character of the lied has gone, and solo songs interspersed among them can no longer compensate. Instead to some degree they assume the character of an aria – *Mein schöner Stern* (op. 74 no. 4) perhaps less than the others.

These cycles, particularly the two 'Spanish' genre pieces, seem to me more closely related to Schumann's large-scale vocal works. Lacking a choir, they are perhaps transitional pieces between the 'pure' song-cycles and the oratorios (*Paradise and the Peri, Requiem for Mignon, The Pilgrimage of the Rose*), the opera *Genoveva* and even the *Scenes from Goethe's 'Faust'*. As in those works, in the ensemble song-cycles one senses a vision of the world inclined towards the meaningful and the peaceful, or at least a willingness to embrace human destiny in all its God-given orderliness and legitimacy – rather than being defeated by its inexplicability, which is in my view the world presented by Schumann's pure lieder. For that reason I see them as being the more powerful expression of his personal feelings, an account of his own life, which in the course of the thirteen years of his lieder-writing career was increasingly overshadowed by despair.

Those larger-scale vocal works, in which people rather than ideas engage with each other, appear to me to be the embodiment of the ideal that Schumann had of the world and an orderly life in it. The sound-world of these works sometimes strikes me as a bit kitsch. As an example of this I might cite the opening movement of *The Pilgrimage of the Rose*, the oratorio that is able to dispense with the orchestra in favour of a piano accompaniment and is thus, in the manner of a singspiel, even closer to the song-cycles considered here. In my opinion this sound-world is by no means a depiction of Schumann's lived reality. It is perhaps the expression – possible only in and through music – of his desperate yearning for a less flawed world.

SCHUMANN'S ABSTRACT OPERA

BERLIN, 24 FEBRUARY 2010

Am farb'gen Abglanz haben wir das Leben.
ROBERT SCHUMANN, *Scenes from Goethe's 'Faust'*, no. 4

We have our life in colourful refraction.

A close friend, a true scholar of music, literature and philosophy, told me late in 2009 that he had recently watched James Cameron's incredibly successful Hollywood blockbuster *Avatar*. Perhaps a certain sense of superiority towards cinematic entertainment, particularly of American origin, had influenced his judgement in advance, but at any rate he said the film had been a great – if predictable – disappointment.

A few months later I travelled to Berlin to take part in a performance of Schumann's greatest work as part of his 200th anniversary celebrations. I don't know why every conceivable events organiser jumps on the bandwagon when there are birth and death anniversaries to be celebrated. But then, Schumann himself did the same for Goethe's centenary – by setting the last scene of *Faust, Part II*, 'Mountain Gorges', to which he then added extra parts and an overture to form the *Szenen aus Goethes Faust* (*Scenes from Goethe's 'Faust'*).

The day before the general rehearsal I went to the cinema. *Avatar* was showing in the same building as my hotel, and in 3D, which I had never experienced before. My curiosity got the better of me – and the almost pietistic spirit of the culture vulture that was still rampant in me at the time fell silent. (Since then I have shamelessly devoted myself to watching bad films as a form of escapism.) And what an experience it was!

The film, its plot and its aesthetic are to some degree predictable for large parts, but I'm not sure whether that on its own is sufficient to justify a negative review. How many works of art, including those that we consider very significant, are similarly consistent in their outward appearance, comprehensible and designed to achieve maximum effect! The plot was entirely *Faust*[1] – or at least a lot of it was. A paraplegic young man, whose twin brother has just died, arrives on the moon of Pandora,[2] on which an element indispensable to humanity, with the beautiful name of unobtanium, is mined. His brother was a member of a group of scientists, somewhat unrealistically devoted to philanthropy, who were exploring the nature of Pandora, and also its indigenous, 'primitive' population, the Na'vi. Special devices are capable of transferring the life spirits (sensory perception, action and will, everything, in fact) of selected researchers on or in so-called avatars. The name comes from the Sanskrit (*Avatara* means 'descent'), where it refers to the manifestation of a divine principle in humans or animals. The actual bodies of the Na'vi, restored to real life and onto which the respective 'entelechy' of the researchers is projected by means of these same devices, act as avatars,[3] so that the scientists can live unnoticed among the target civilisation. However, the machines work only with a DNA identity connected to an individual Na'vi body. So the paralysed, intellectually hopelessly underqualified (all right, so not everything in the film is *Faust*) but DNA-identical twin brother of the deceased is the only one who can save the scientific project (avatars are valuable and an extremely rare commodity).

The motivations of the protagonists are very different: while the scientists want to pursue their experiments, the people running the moon base (its director is a real devil, a colonel, the Mephisto of our plot) are interested in limitless unobtanium mining. For that reason the young hero, Jake Sully, an ex-soldier, is recruited by the mining company operating on Pandora to engage in industrial espionage. In his case the lure is finance for restorative spinal treatment. But soon Jake Sully is taking greater delight in the fact of being an avatar, which puts all human sensuality in the shade; what's more, he falls in love with a Na'vi, and really wants to do his own thing. Of course, the Faustian idea gets a bit lost here. Soon there isn't much talk about unconditional striving for knowledge; the scientists seem increasingly to lose the thirst for knowledge, too, and their concern with third-party funding becomes their main focus. Even Faust's rigorous quest for experience makes way for Sully's do-goodery (first as a human, then as a Na'vi). In the end he goes over to the other side, and after a rather cack-handed John-Wayne-style showdown he incapacitates his 'earthly residue' (*Faust Part II*, V:11,954), but without ever leaving his academic study or suffering from an excess of redundant learning. The important thing, however, is that the viewer himself has all kinds of experiences through which his own earthbound nature is seemingly transcended. Personally, I found it breathtaking.

The most moving things that I remember from this film are the 'mountain gorges' (the title of the last scene in *Faust Part II*), where the lovers rise up into a colony of dragons living on small flying mountains on round, moonlike clumps of rock linked only, if at all, by flowing water and lianas. These mountains remind me of Goethe's mystic and enigmatic stage directions for three 'holy anchorites distributed along the slopes, living among rocky clefts' in the last scene of *Faust*, particularly the direction for the Pater Ecstaticus: 'floating up and down', even though this is supposed to symbolise the levitation of an enlightened man. The image of these floating clumps of mountain, obviously inspired by the Huangshan range in terms of both form and vegetation, may be hard to grasp as an idea, but it is quite overwhelming in its impact. It is only a visual event, but I can hardly think of an image that held me so immediately spellbound – the closest might be Leonardo's *Madonna of the Rocks*. This overwhelming impact was very similar to what I felt when I first heard Schumann's *Scenes from Goethe's 'Faust'* – in a live broadcast on television, and with a conductor who looked like Schumann himself . . .

Then, on the other hand, on something like the peak of those mini-moons, another idea appears, so vivid that it looks like the fulfilment of more than *Part II* of Goethe's drama. The Na'vi climb onto the topmost crag and force the dragons living there to fly, before controlling them by riding them. The union of the two autonomous living creatures is physically accomplished by bringing together the tips of their tails, which act as cables connecting their bodies. This allows the rider's will to be transferred directly to the dragon as a spatial extension of the Na'vi's own lived experience. This is the apogee of what these primates can and want to achieve. The union with the fire-coloured dragons is, however, dangerous; it can be fatal if the two tails, with their heritage exposed, aren't compatible. Consequently, it embodies the one and only possible transcendence of the simple life of the indigenous people on Pandora, precisely because it is associated with the greatest possible risk – the loss of existence and identity.[4]

The historical Johann or Georg Faust is supposed to have attempted to fly in Venice, or at least so Philipp Melanchthon records. Many of Goethe's writings address the fascination with flight. In *Faust Part I* it is still a modest fantasy: 'Oh – if only on the mountain peaks / I could go in your dear light, / Float around mountain caves with spirits, / Weave on meadows in your twilight' (V:392–5); 'O that no wing lifts me from the ground, / [. . .] In the rays of evening I would see / The silent world at my feet, / All heights on fire, every valley calm / The silver brook flowing into golden streams. / Nor would be stemmed the godlike run / By the wild mountain with all its gorges' (V:1,074–81). In the poem *Prooemion* the idea is already given a more sensually concrete form: 'And your spirit's highest fiery flight / Is sated by the simile, the image; / It draws you, pulls you serenely onwards, / And where you wander, path and place are beautified; / You no longer count, or calculate the time, / And every step is immensity.' In *Faust Part II* it is given shape in an actual character, Euphorion – the son of Faust and Helen, Greek mythology's ultimate beauty – who, Icarus-like, is destroyed by his fantasy in the enthusiastic dissolution of boundaries: 'To soar / into the air / is my wish [. . .] I no longer want / To remain stuck on the ground; [. . .] Leave my hands / Leave my curly hair / Yet! – a pair of wings / Unfolds! / I must go there! I must! / Grant me flight' (V:9,713–900).

In *Avatar*, the 3D film, the whole spectrum of 'fiery flight' lacks the sensation of location and acceleration, and even the feeling of moist air and contact with the dragon's back – but still, I enjoyed it more than a masquerade or an Oktoberfest. And so for me as a viewer that eruptive extension of life through flight on a dragon was a momentary highlight that it seemed to me worth clinging to – just as Faust says in his closing monologue. His vision of a shared activity and a constant, unhindered expansion of the human will, in which it attempts to attain meaning and significance forever is, however, both an actual and a grammatical irrealis:

> Im Innern hier ein paradiesisch Land,
> Da rase draußen Flut bis auf zum Rand,
> Und wie sie nascht, gewaltsam einzuschießen,
> Gemeindrang eilt, die Lücke zu verschließen.
> Ja! diesem Sinne bin ich ganz ergeben,
> Das ist der Weisheit letzter Schluß:
> Nur der verdient sich Freiheit wie das Leben,
> Der täglich sie erobern muß.
> Und so verbringt, umrungen von Gefahr,
> Hier Kindheit, Mann und Greis sein tüchtig Jahr.
> Solch ein Gewimmel möcht' ich sehn,
> Auf freiem Grund mit freiem Volke stehn.
> Zum Augenblicke dürft' ich sagen:
> Verweile doch, du bist so schön!
> Es kann die Spur von meinen Erdentagen
> Nicht in Äonen untergehn. –
> Im Vorgefühl von solchem hohen Glück
> Genieß' ich jetzt den höchsten Augenblick.

FAUST'S DEATH,
from GOETHE'S *Faust Part II*, V:11,569–86

> Within, a land like paradise; without
> A flood that surges to the edge.
> And as it gnaws and makes to break the walls
> A common force hurries to fill the gaps.
> Yes, I cling to that idea,
> Wisdom's final end:
> He alone deserves both liberty and life
> Who must daily conquer them.
> So, girded around by danger,
> Childhood, manhood, age shall live their days.
> I should like to see such a crowd
> Standing on free ground with a free people.
> Then I might say to the moment:
> Linger a while, you are so fair!
> The trace of my earthly days
> Must outlive the eons –
> In presentiment of such high happiness
> I now enjoy this supreme moment.

The possibility of unbroken striving is the real object of Faust's bet with Mephisto. (It's not so much a deal in the sense that all experience will be available to him until his death, but with his passing he must pay Satan the price with the loss of his soul.) This striving is something that cannot end in life because it is inseparable from being human. Faust's parting words make this very clear to everyone but Mephisto: 'The poor man wants to cling / to the last bad empty moment' (V:11,589f.). It is this visionary moment at the point of death – Faust has just had an inkling of it ('To gaze into infinity', V:11,345) – that Schumann set to music in his *Scenes from 'Faust'* with an earth-shaking quality that Goethe should have experienced at least once. Unbroken striving, at any rate, is the one helpless but unimprovable aspect of the limited human vision of the heavenly abundance of eternal perfection. The other aspect of this transcendental human desire is that human beings have the concept of eternity in the first place, and that it doesn't mean only one thing – death. So the 'supreme' moment consists, among other aspects, in this one earthly possibility of having a notion of unboundedness – albeit at the cost of a lack of continuity, because for every mortal there is only this singular moment of death in which the experience of self-abandonment can replace earthly striving.

The arts, and also religion, have always been able to speak vividly of hell, and in a reflective and illustrative way. Because it is both simple and impressive to accumulate earthly limitation, torment and pain to one's heart's content – Mephisto seems to be at work, 'the spirit that always says no' (V:1,338),[5] when the mounting suffering caused by lack of ability and lack of understanding ends up as the image of eternal sorrow. As for the opposite, however, the description of eternal unboundedness, all attempts fail. Perhaps the Captain explains it best to Wozzeck – without burdening himself with priestly euphemisms, in the magnificent words: '"Eternal", this is eternal!' (Wozzeck has to agree.) 'But then again it isn't eternal, but a moment, yes, a moment!'[6]

So when Faust says immediately before his death: 'In presentiment of such high happiness / My supreme moment I now enjoy', this does not mean that he is bringing his striving to an end within a deep sense of pleasure – in fact he ends it only in death. Rather he is enjoying the still unreal idea of human eternity, just as the glorification of all things earthly on the basis of their very earthliness is ultimately the only option open to a human being in search of transcendence.

Schumann closes this part (section 2, no. 6, 'Faust's Death') with perhaps the most beautiful and uplifting funeral march ever written. This is not necessarily intended for Faust himself but is in very general terms the expression of mourning for the insight into earthly limitation and transience, just as music may be only consolation for the dismay that it has itself caused.

In Schumann's work, Mephisto's preceding blasphemous provocation, 'He falls, it is accomplished' (line 11,594), quoting Christ's last words from St John's Gospel, is not, as in Goethe, angrily contradicted ('It is over!'; 11,595). Instead Schumann leaves it with Jesus' last word. It is expressly a sign of the extent to which the Romantic Schumann wanted to glorify the incessant earthly striving in the Faust figure, even elevating him to godlike status, while the classicist Goethe rejected Faust's immoderation. For me, though, it is also a sign of the extent to which Schumann, even more than Goethe, deliberately advocates earthliness. After all, with this textual amendment, he must knowingly have exposed himself to the accusation of atheism. Simply leaving a blasphemy to stand and comparing the antihero Faust with Jesus can hardly be described as Christian.[7]

Sadly, it is probably only a rumour that Goethe suggested that if his incommensurable drama should ever be performed, the actor playing Faust in *Part I* should play Mephisto in *Part II* and vice versa. Still, the actors Gustaf Gründgens and Will Quadflieg used it to justify their role swap in the two parts.[8] At any rate, it is all about how the guilt cannot be placed entirely on Faust's shoulders because it is Mephisto who precipitates the death and damnation – from Valentin, Gretchen and her mother, to Philemon and Baucis. But how much of that guilt belongs to Faust? Hence the fateful consequences of his hubris are not only an oversight. And does Schumann lift such an indissoluble entanglement with the earthly onto a pedestal? I think he does, because for him entanglement with guilt is part of the indissoluble principle of male aggrandisement – *Verselbstung* ('selfing') – as in Goethe's poem *Prometheus*, contrasted as a redemptive principle with feminine *Entselbstigung* ('de-selfing'), as in the poem *Ganymed*. That is also more or less the message of the closing words of Goethe's drama ('The eternal feminine / Draws us up', V:12,110f.). And Schumann structures his *Scenes from 'Faust'* by placing this opposition at its very centre.[9]

*

This work, for solo voices, choir and orchestra, is framed on the one hand by 'Faust's Transfiguration',[10] the last scene although the first to be composed, which, as the third section, closes the work as a whole and in which Faust's essence is rescued by the modest essence of Gretchen (who returns as Una poenitentium), and on the other by the overture, the last to be composed but placed at the beginning. In my view this overture represents the academic study often identified with Goethe's *Faust* as the centre of the scholar's tragedy. It is here, in Goethe's drama, that the plot begins not only with the problematisation of man's epistemological limitation, but also with the rebellion against the 'ink-stained age' (as Schiller calls it). In Schumann we hear a grey D minor battling the will's futile attempt to achieve a scientific understanding of the world.[11] After many gentle interruptions – fantasies of an existence that delights man's sense and sensuality – D minor finally makes way for a no less grey but still dazzling D major. It is here that the new life begins with Mephisto's and Faust's handshake, which also confronts us all of a sudden with the 'Superman', the term by which the Earth Spirit ironically addressed Faust at the beginning (V:490). There is no longer any need to lament the human condition – at last life can be grasped and understood in action.

Lying between the overture and third part the two main related parts now develop in parallel – although they are forced by the nature of the musical plot to run sequentially (in the narration of an oratorio this might have been handled differently).[12] The first section presents texts from *Part I* of Goethe's drama and deals with Gretchen becoming passively guilty (love (no. 1) – despair (no. 2) – damnation (no. 3)), while the second section with texts only from *Part II* of the drama addresses Faust's becoming actively guilty[13] (awakening (no. 4) – blinding (no. 5) – death (no. 6)). Both parts share the pattern: life – crisis – death, which may be observed both in the despairing Gretchen and in Faust triumphant until the end. At the same time, given the evident parallels in the shape of their content, the two parts represent the polarity between masculinity, which, despite all efforts, remains bounded, and unfettered, boundary-breaking femininity.

In his assembly of the text, which not only leaves most of *Faust Part I* untouched, but leaves out the three middle acts of *Part II* entirely, Schumann attempts a consistent interpretation of the subject matter, quite at odds with the abundance found in Goethe. The fundamental thematic problems – the limitation of knowledge and the sensual breaking of boundaries – are seen as having their origins in the opposition of female and male, and are resolved. And yet the symbolic and thematic mirroring, abundant in Goethe's drama (Romantic/Classical Walpurgisnacht; Auerbach's Cellar/Imperial Court; scholar's tragedy in *Faust Part I*/scholar's farce in the second act of *Faust Part II*, and much else besides),[14] runs parallel to the examination of the triad of life – crisis – death in the cases of both Gretchen and Faust, and is thus represented in Schumann's compilation of the text. This clearly proves once again his outstanding grasp of literature. Some colleagues of Schumann's, however, after a superficial study of the *Scenes from 'Faust'*, spoke of the boredom emanating from the work. They explained this among other things by commenting on the weak and random selection of textual passages – an explanation that didn't exactly say much for their own powers of judgement.

Beyond this, I think that Schumann's textual compilation not only enabled the only possible musical access to Goethe's most important work so far, but also created a singular concept of music theatre. Attempts have been made to classify the *Scenes from 'Faust'* as an oratorio, but not with any great success. Defining the term 'oratorio' is very difficult compared with defining 'song' or 'opera'. To me, however, the only thing that *Scenes from 'Faust'* has in common with an oratorio is that it is generally given a concert performance, with choirs behind the orchestra and soloists in front of it.[15]

I would describe Schumann's *Scenes from Goethe's 'Faust'* as an 'abstract opera'.[16] Abstract because there is no organised plot, just one with unusually large time leaps, and also because the repetition of the pattern life – crisis – death adds a reflective level to the structure. We could say that the phrase is a contradiction in terms, because an opera is a very concrete work of art, which – unlike the poem and the lied, which do incline to abstraction – should be comprehensible to the very end. To this I would reply that in the case of Schumann's *Faust* only the form is abstract and not the content, as is so often the case with poems and lieder. Goethe's work, even its *Part II*, must ultimately be labelled a drama, even if some parts of *Faust Part II* seem almost like an epic in verse (not unlike Dante's *Divine Comedy*); episode seems to follow episode, and there is little in the way of discernible dramatic plot. Schumann's work can thus doubtless also be called an opera. I do not believe that an alternative term such as 'vocal symphony' is helpful – its variations are too diverse and consequently too difficult to grasp (for example, Beethoven's Ninth Symphony, Mahler's *Das Lied von der Erde* and Eighth Symphony, Mendelssohn's *Walpurgisnacht*, Shostakovich's Thirteenth Symphony ('*Babi Yar*') and Eisler's *Deutsche Sinfonie*).

So using the term 'opera' for Schumann's *Scenes from Goethe's 'Faust'* would have practical consequences for its presentation. A staged performance would no longer be seen simply as an experiment, like a staged *B minor Mass* or a danced Requiem, but rather as an obvious way of grasping this highly sensual piece in visual terms as well. And how well that coincides with Goethe's intentions! Then the possible failure (as is possible with every opera production) would not be proof that oratorios are unstageable in principle, but rather a reason to attempt another staging.

Schumann's *Faust* also has something in common with his only opera, *Genoveva* – the particularly vivid declamation expressed in constantly changing dynamics and agogics (the former being variations in volume, the latter the shaping of the tempo in musical performance). In essence every bar, or every half-bar, needs to be checked for its agogic–dynamic significance.[17] In *Faust* this applies not only to recitative passages such as large stretches of Faust's central argument with Care (*Part II* no. 5 'The Blinding of Faust'); in Goethe's *Faust Part II* this plays a vitally important role in the theatrical plot.[18] Even truly abstract content, such as Faust's grand aria after awakening (*Part II* no. 4), thrives on this declamatory swell. How else could one bring a plot point that is closer to Plato's cave metaphor than any traditional operatic situation[19] – an intrigue, an awakening to love, or a plan to overthrow or murder someone – so vividly to life?

It is perhaps still comprehensible in traditional terms when, at the start of this part, the sun can rise as the embodiment of truth, with a great discharge of dynamic and colourful power that then continues to grow – bright, ear-splitting fanfares lead to the first irruption of the merely human. But then the sudden awareness that the excessively bright white light is unbearable to human beings requires an explanatory aria that extends and evaluates the range of human knowledge.

> So ist es also, wenn ein sehnend Hoffen
> Dem höchsten Wunsch sich traulich zugerungen,
> Erfüllungspforten findet flügeloffen;
> Nun aber bricht aus jenen ewigen Gründen
> Ein Flammenübermaß, wir stehn betroffen;
> Des Lebens Fackel wollten wir entzünden,
> Ein Feuermeer umschlingt uns, welch ein Feuer!
> Ist's Lieb? ist's Haß? die glühend uns umwinden,
> Mit Schmerz und Freuden wechselnd ungeheuer,
> So daß wir wieder nach der Erde blicken,
> Zu bergen uns in jugendlichstem Schleier.
>
> So bleibe denn die Sonne mir im Rücken!
> Der Wassersturz, das Felsenriff durchbrausend,

Ihn schau' ich an mit wachsendem Entzücken.
Von Sturz zu Sturzen wälzt er jetzt in tausend,
Dann abertausend Strömen sich ergießend,
Hoch in die Lüfte Schaum an Schäume sausend.
Allein wie herrlich, diesem Sturm ersprießend,
Wölbt sich des bunten Bogens Wechseldauer,
Bald rein gezeichnet, bald in Luft zerfließend,
Umher verbreitend duftig kühle Schauer.
Der spiegelt ab das menschliche Bestreben.
Ihm sinne nach, und du begreifst genauer:
Am farbigen Abglanz haben wir das Leben.

'FAUST'S AWAKENING',
from GOETHE'S *Faust Part II*, V:4,704–27

Thus it is, when a yearning hope,
To its supreme desire trustingly has risen,
And finds the portals of fulfilment open wide;
But now bursts from those eternal depths
An overwhelming blast of flame; we stand appalled:
We wanted to light life's torch.
A sea of fire engulfs us, what a fire!
Is it love? Or hate? that blazing sweeps around us.
With pain and joy in colossal change,
So that we glance earthwards again,
To shelter in our most youthful veil.

So shall stay the sun at my back!
The waterfall that crashes through the rocks
I gaze upon with burgeoning delight.
From fall to fall it surges in a thousand
Upon thousand streamlets pouring out,
High in the air spray dashing against spray;
Alone how gloriously sprouting from this storm
Arches the coloured rainbow's lasting change.

BERLIN, 24 FEBRUARY 2010

> Soon cleanly drawn, soon blurring with the air,
> Spreading around airily cool showers.
> This reflects all human endeavour.
> Think on it and you will grasp more clearly:
> We have our life in colourful refraction.

This aria includes a number of violent outbursts alternating with *dolce* and *legato* passages. On the one hand it is the expression of Faust's overwhelming will reawakening after the sleep of oblivion. It does also testify, however, to a certain enthusiasm that applauds the recognition of the relativity of human perception, half angrily but also euphorically. This almost peaceful agreement to the placing of man between light and dark, in the colourful refraction of light, leads to the thought that Faust might already have given himself up to the human condition and no longer wishes to transcend it by striving. The suspicion arises at this point almost even more than it does at the moment of Faust's death. Schumann's aria is in fact a breathlessly enthusiastic sequence of astonishment and stupefaction in the face of such near-superhuman greatness. And so already here we can see the appearance of the final tragically earthbound nature of Faust, and of mankind in general, in that the absolute requirement to be understood can be grasped only through anthropomorphic concepts ('Is it love? Is it hate?', V:4,711), and hence only as a reflection of the infinity surrounding us.

At the heart of the aria is the central phrase, the sound of which could not have been better understood: 'Am farb'gen Abglanz haben wir das Leben' ('We have our life in colourful refraction', V:4,727). Schumann leads up to this phrase over five bars with a quiet and curiously enigmatic modulation, which, to me, bows fervently to Goethe's Colour Theory when the word in question develops from it. After the vain attempt to go beyond the terrestrial, the sentence is a declaration of love to this world, and Goethe's pantheism – the

Spinozism of the 'Deus sive Natura' ('God or Nature') – may here find its best imaginable, that is sensual, expression.

The 'elastic' balance that might emerge in a performance of this scene, and which would ideally correspond to a balance between lyricism and both vocal and orchestral power, never really manifests itself concretely, of course, but appears at best as an idea. Many passages in Schumann's *Faust* seem like this to me. In my idea – developed through much listening and many performances – of how this work should sound, there also lies a sadness that I will never really be able to experience it in that way. And the hope of hearing the work one day in 'eternal life', entirely as we have imagined it or even better, is defeated by the insight that while the whole of both Schumann's and Goethe's *Faust* may be a parable of the Absolute, the concept of the Absolute is also man-made and a parable cannot become actuality. So, if there is an eternity, one will not be able to linger there by listening to a perfect performance of the *Faust-Szenen*; that's over then.

And so we are left with the hope that, for example, in no. 1, in which Gretchen and Faust meet for the first time in the garden, the 12/8 rhythm will not run away with itself, and that the duplets, rather as they do in 'Die Sennin' ('The Shepherdess'), Schumann's op. 90 no. 4),[20] embodying the entry of the demonic into the loving world of the triplets, will be given the necessary weight, and that the syllable ratio of 2:1 on a crotchet is comprehensible, not making necessary a broadening to 3:1, which swallows up elegance and concision. Or that in the concluding violent march after Faust's blinding (no. 5), I shall be able to reach the end with the necessary breadth and weight and not sing the high G sharp with inappropriate thinness. Or that shortly before Faust's death I shall be able to sing the words 'Verweile doch, du bist so schön' ('Linger here, you are so fair') lyrically and yet expansively. Or that perhaps the most beautiful of all choral movements, 'Waldung, sie schwankt heran' ('Woodland wavers into view'), the beginning of the third section, does not end too quickly. The list could go on. But much else will remain imperfect and cannot be even a metaphor for the Absolute.

But still – one difficulty may not in fact be one: I am often uncomprehendingly asked to conclude Dr Marianus's incomparable aria with the alternative version with the high G on the words 'Gnade bedürfend' ('In need of mercy', 12,019). To be perfectly honest, I can't sing that. I've never managed to do so convincingly; it's too high for me. Whenever I've tried, it has always sounded squeezed or distorted. But in fact I don't find the resolution of the high version to the fifth of the concluding G minor or to the third of the B major of the following no. 6 at all satisfactory. Perhaps because a high note sounds too triumphal here, but specifically because it clearly implies a conclusion, which is not at all helpful because Marianus' text continues into the following number. For this reason the low version, which is able to transition via the leading note A in a very long sustained *attacca* into the B major of no. 6, is much better and more sensible. Heinz Holliger says this too, by the way, so it must be right.

> Alles Vergängliche
> Ist nur ein Gleichnis;
> Das Unzulängliche,
> Hier wird's Ereignis;
> Das Unbeschreibliche,
> Hier ist's getan;
> Das Ewig-Weibliche
> Zieht uns hinan.
>
> CHORUS MYSTICUS,
> from GOETHE'S *Faust Part II*, V:12,104–11

> Everything ephemeral
> Is only parable;
> The unattainable
> Becomes event,
> The indescribable
> Here it is done;
> The eternal feminine
> Draws us up.

Already during Faust's death it is clear that both Faust the character and *Faust* the work of art must remain entirely earthbound. This brought it painfully home to me for the first time that sadly nothing can come of the idea that the arts can get us on the trail of eternity. All hope of hearing this piece, my favourite work (apart from many lieder), perfectly one day in Paradise – should such a thing exist – in order to eradicate all the inadequacy of contemporary performances and plumb maximum sensuality, is doomed, and it's not alone. Just as all religion remains an earthly effort to achieve a celestial goal, in spite of all its transcendental claims, so does all art.

For me, one example that can clearly demonstrate this hostile line to us is Schumann's reworking of the 'Chorus mysticus' that concludes his and Goethe's work. The first version is, as we know and appreciate, something like a 'spherical' stride into the superhuman; that's what it actually sounds like towards the end of the first part (up to bar 27) – Schumann's 'realisation in sound' of Goethe's 'harmony of the spheres'. And yet here there is another tumble into the deeply human: the fugal, loud, affirmative deployment of the choral groups, although they flee towards the conclusion into a kind of illustration of an event in the universe, as if a spaceship were flying slowly from the thrilling image of a glorious nebula (coloured only for human eyes) into the bleak expanses of the universe. It's all meant to be super-terrestrial and trans-human, but, even so, it's not a way for us to find ourselves moving towards eternity.

There is, however, a second version of the 'Chorus mysticus' in which, at the point where these choral entries begin (I often find these loudly affirmative fugues difficult to bear), with an under-developed, very long (11-minute) choral passage, the few lines of text are treated almost paratactically, with the same melodic phrase transposed in sequence in several voices. This version – about five minutes longer, even though it is several bars shorter – is hardly ever performed. In the many performances in which I have taken part, I have never experienced it. I have, however, been able to hear a recording. My impression is this: it's a bit long-winded. I can almost hear the denigrators of Schumann's late work saying, 'It's weak, it's boring, it's yet another typical outpouring of a weakened, sick mind.' In this version there is in fact less opportunity for lurid agitation. Not much happens, and the same words and motifs are repeated again and again with dynamic steadiness. Everything seems to be slowly relinquishing the many sensual and spiritual stimuli that the 12,000 lines of Goethe's *Faust* and the however-many bars of Schumann's have left behind, to replace earthly meaningfulness with repetition and something approaching babbling. Yet perhaps this is the clearest demonstration of the mundane fact that all sensual or spiritual attempts to capture the fullness of eternity – or even only guess at it – are doomed to fail. Because of the seemingly endless repetitions, the effect cannot avoid a certain melancholy – an expression of grief at the unsatisfactory nature of man, with his limited destiny, and hence an almost contrasting conclusion to the popular and uplifting first version of the 'Chorus mysticus'.

In *Wilhelm Meisters Wanderjahre* Goethe writes: 'The composer sets bar division and bar movement against poetic rhythm. But here the mastery of music over poetry soon becomes apparent; for if poetry, as if appropriate and necessary, always had its quantities in mind as purely as possible, for the musician a few syllables are resolutely long or short; at will the musician destroys the most conscientious process of the maker of rhythm, and even transforms prose into song, where the most wonderful possibilities emerge.'[21] And yet the differences in what the arts are capable of are only gradual; they are not of transcendental significance. The closing words and the closing music of *Faust* might appear diverse and esoteric, but what they are setting out to achieve is an appropriate expression of the complicatedness of the terrestrial; out of that terrestrial complicatedness, in a desire for the transcendental and the dissolution of boundaries, they create a gripping beauty that evokes the beyond in a way that we can imagine it in the here and now. This conclusion is not a manifestation of transcendental equivalence, it is not a transgression against terrestrial experience; it remains earthbound and is ultimately an affirmation of the human condition. The 'parable' remains earthly, and 'The unattainable / becomes event' means not only *now*, but also *here*, only here – in our earthly world.

I hope that eventually a director unafraid of using all means at their disposal will realise this sequence of ideas of extreme sensuality – ideally, however, without *Avatar*-style 3D-film, which will inevitably quickly become dated. But also the traditional theatre, given the limits on illusion imposed by the proscenium arch, would probably not be the right place for Schumann's *Faust-Szenen*.

Ideally we might need a theatre like the one imagined by Richard Wagner for the performance of Goethe's *Faust*,[22] in which not a distant stage but the space around the audience becomes the location for a total experience of the dissolution of human boundaries, without an orchestra in between. But to do that one would have to abandon what I have long imagined as a successful staging of the *Faust-Szenen*: painted borders and vistas, with images of paintings selected by Goethe (by Adam Elsheimer and others), lighting moods and sky colours such as rose, blue, yellow, orange and grey, like the ones that the Asam family painted on church ceilings.

Whether we could replace that with holograms or whatnot, I couldn't say. With the old techniques, however, we would know that everything is and should be illusion. And then one would be able to devote oneself entirely to the meaning conveyed with the sensory impression of colour.

TRADITION AND ROLE-PLAYING

MUNICH, 12 OCTOBER 2013

Ich liebe der Frost.

I love them frost.

IGOR STRAVINSKY's reply
to Othmar Schoeck, when he called
his music *etwas kühl* ('somewhat reserved')[1]

Apart from Schumann's *Dichterliebe* it was Mahler's *Lieder eines fahrenden Gesellen* ('Songs of a Wayfarer') that made me want to be a singer. Even now the recording with Hermann Prey and the Amsterdam Concertgebouw Orchestra under Bernard Haitink is sacred to me; there is nothing more beautiful. The printed score, which my parents gave me for Christmas (with the score of the *Kindertotenlieder* ('Songs on the Death of Children'), which was on the other side of the LP), is still sacred to me. These cycles immediately became icons for me, and they still are, not least because of the technical vocal difficulties that they pose, particularly the 'Wayfarer' songs. I looked at the score in disbelief, because I couldn't imagine how I would ever be able to sing these songs. At my first performances I went on stage with a metaphorical white flag, plagued by anxiety.

Currently the *Gesellen-Lieder* form the core of my repertoire, and they remain a crucial touchstone of my professional singing. I don't think I've sung, practised or rehearsed even *Dichterliebe* as often. It may be that no other cycle is as clear to me as this one: for all its brevity, in terms of its content it is utterly complete, and sums up in exemplary fashion the whole of the lied tradition up to that point. I would entrust nearly anything to an amateur singer – except this work. It lays bare the challenges of Mahler's lieder writing as a whole, and in my view there is no way an actor or amateur would be able to sing it without creating serious difficulties for himself or his audience, just as it is almost impossible for a layman to sing a demanding operatic score.

From a technical point of view the comparison with opera singing is far from irrelevant. The outbursts in the third song require a supremely confident handling of vocal power, similar to that demanded by opera singing in many dramatic situations. Yet in the last song there are intimate lyrical passages so exposed that a precisely calculated economy of power is required in order, for example, to sing 'vom allerliebsten Platz' ('from the loveliest place of all') *pianissimo*, without any scratchiness or needing to retreat into falsetto.[2] However, I would not wish to conclude from this that Mahler, opera conductor as he was, was attempting to import an operatic approach to singing into the art song. Otherwise he would not have provided such careful annotations, particularly in the lower dynamic range, and supplied such a strikingly large number of instructions for the opera singers who gave the first performances of his concert works. Conversely, I think that the techniques of the art song – particularly in terms of vocal colour and variety of vibrato – could also achieve interesting effects if transferred to the operatic stage.

The aesthetic tradition from which the *Gesellen-Lieder* are drawn is in my view above all the one created by Schubert.[3] The folksong-like simplicity, the uncomplicated content, the long cantilenas whose dynamic difficulty reminds me of the *messa di voce* of Italian operas (held notes with rising and falling volume), the setting of the lyrics inclining towards homophony (I am referring here to the often rhythmically regular chordal accompaniment to the melodic vocal line), and particularly the ubiquitous changes in mode between major and minor – formally, all of this amounts to a kind of continuation of Schubert's legacy. In terms of content, it is the nature poetry that establishes a particular kinship with Schubert's two principal cycles. It undermines the only rudimentarily declared tragedy of love in the *Gesellen-Lieder*, as seen particularly in Schubert's *Die schöne Müllerin* (although here the emotional rejections are made extensively explicit),[4] in terms of a healing and integrative effect, an external reference designed to ease suffering.[5] But nature, on the other hand, may also appear as the reflection or even the confirmation of the protagonist's vulnerability and despair.[6]

Wenn mein Schatz Hochzeit macht
Gustav Mahler: *Lieder eines fahrenden Gesellen* (1)

Wenn mein Schatz Hochzeit macht,
Fröhliche Hochzeit macht,
Hab' ich meinen traurigen Tag!
Geh' ich in mein Kämmerlein,
Dunkles Kämmerlein!
Weine! wein'! Um meinen Schatz!
Um meinen lieben Schatz!

Blümlein blau! Blümlein blau!
Verdorre nicht, verdorre nicht!
Vöglein süß! Vöglein süß!
Du singst auf grüner Heide!
Ach, wie ist die Welt so schön!
Ziküth! Ziküth!

Singet nicht! Blühet nicht!
Lenz ist ja vorbei!
Alles Singen ist nun aus!
Des Abends, wenn ich schlafen geh',
Denk ich an mein Leide!
An mein Leide!

from *DES KNABEN WUNDERHORN*

When my darling has her wedding,
Her joyful wedding day,
That is a sad day for me!
I go into my room,

> Dark room,
> I weep, weep for my darling!
> For my beloved darling!
>
> Little blue flower, little blue flower!
> Fade not, fade not!
> Oh, sweet little bird, sweet bird!
> You sing on the green heath!
> Oh, how is the world so fair!
> Chirrup! Chirrup!
>
> Sing not! Bloom not!
> Springtime is over!
> All singing is done!
> In the evening, when I go to sleep,
> I think of my suffering!
> Of my suffering!

With their turns in the piano's treble line, the opening bars of the first of the *Gesellen-Lieder* sound a bit like a continuation of the right-hand piano garlands of *Der Leiermann* ('The Hurdy-Gurdy Man'), the last song of *Winterreise*.[7] The structure of the song can be rendered in the form A–B–A', in that the third verse musically resembles the first. The whole A part, like the A' part that returns after the nature-related middle section, is stuck in a purely subjective perspective. This could not be better demonstrated than in music, because in Mahler, as in Schubert, the music is not a commentary on the textual content of the lied (the hurdy-gurdy man on the one hand, the wedding music on the other), but is in each case simply the music of the lied itself.

The references to nature in the B part, as well as the whole of the second *Gesellen* lied, are intended as exuberantly and entirely positive, until the gaze of the lyrical self turns with disappointment inward: 'Nun fängt auch mein Glück wohl an?! / Nein! Nein! Das ich mein', / Mir nimmer, nimmer blühen kann!' ('Is my happiness beginning now? / No! No! I believe / That it can never ever blossom!'). This paves the way for the dramatic, violent and self-destructive third song of the cycle. Here, and in the second part of the concluding fourth song, nature, if it appears at all, assumes the threatening and doom-laden expression of the later *Müllerin* lieder and the whole of *Winterreise*. 'Wenn ich in den Himmel seh', / Seh' ich zwei blaue Augen steh'n, / Wenn ich im gelben Felde geh', / Seh' ich von fern das blonde Haar' ('When I look into the sky, / I see two blue eyes there, / When I walk in the yellow field, / I see blond hair from afar') the lyrics begin[8] – but immediately these idyllic references are perceived as illusions. In the last song the sentence 'Ich bin ausgegangen in stiller Nacht, / Wohl über die dunkle Heide' ('I went out in the still of the night, / across the dark heath') recalls the wintry walks of *Winterreise*, just as the linden tree in this song specifically recalls *Der Lindenbaum* ('The Linden Tree'), the fifth song of Schubert's cycle, which promises the peace and calm of a possible but not inevitable death. Just as death is toyed with as a possibility in Schubert's cycle, in the *Gesellen-Lieder* the linden tree is not really ominous, but points the way to a final emotional stillness, an almost purifying calming of the previous emotional extremes.[9]

The peace at the end of the *Gesellen-Lieder* is typical of Mahler's song-cycles,[10] and I take it as characteristic of Mahler's lied aesthetic: the end promises redemption in the form of a predictable eternity. In this sense the *Lieder eines fahrenden Gesellen* returns in the end to *Die schöne Müllerin*, albeit in a somewhat dispassionate way, and also to the world of the last song of *Winterreise*, *Der Leiermann*,[11] in which the protagonist brings his crisis to a conclusion, because this is one way in which the last words of the *Gesellen-Lieder* can be understood: 'War alles, alles wieder gut! / [. . .] Lieb und Leid, und Welt und Traum!' ('Everything, everything was good again! / Love and pain, and world and dream!'). So this little cycle combines both of Schubert's Wilhelm Müller cycles and takes them further.

There is one very striking discrepancy between the Schubert cycles and Mahler's *Gesellen-Lieder*: duration. The Mahler, at about 15 minutes, takes only a quarter or even a fifth of the time to serve as a dramatically self-contained work. Of course, in the *Gesellen-Lieder* we do not find the detailed psychological account of deluded passion that we do in *Die schöne Müllerin*, or a multi-faceted exploration of an existential crisis as in *Winterreise*. But in these four songs Mahler manages to achieve a fully valid illumination of a cycle of events, and more of a narrative development than *Winterreise*: catastrophe – hope – relapse – new hope – disillusion – despair – illusion – desire for death – retrospection – continuation – arrival – consolation. These staging posts, with their changing characteristics, are surprisingly reminiscent of the two great Schubert cycles, particularly *Winterreise*'s milestones – each of its songs, especially since they are united by the concept of a journey.

In the *Gesellen-Lieder*, composed at the start of Mahler's song-writing career – before he takes what may be an unconscious step into modern music with the *Wunderhorn-Lieder*[12] – the prototype of the Romantic figure recurs: 'fahrender Geselle' essentially means simply 'wanderer'.[13] That this work is able to develop such strong continuity and consistency in terms of narrative, in spite of its brevity and the small number of songs, lies partly in the identity of its protagonist and his love story, which is kept very general. But it can also be traced through the melodic relationships that extend thematically across the four lieder.[14] From song to song they create, with increasing retrospection, a systematic cohesion and solidity.

Here I would like to return once more to the matter of technical vocal difficulties. As I have already suggested, these lie essentially in the fulfilment of norms in sound that are also required by opera singing. The reason for this may be found in the fact that this short 'love story' of a wayfarer is kept universal, and that it must remain so in the musical representation, so that the framework of temporal extension is not broken by too much individuality.

This has nothing to do with the identification of the singer with his role – which to my mind is to be avoided. Allowing one's own life and sensibility to flow into the performance of a role or a song has no compelling effect on the listener, and only a contingent effect on the sound produced. In my view that sound should be more the result of an attitude of intended arrangement, which requires a distancing,[15] achieved through sound, of the creative idea. Thus, an insistent brightness or a muted darkness of the voice, for example, are not the direct expression of the emotional state of the performer, but a planned means of communication, which the performer has developed in response to the work and its emotional content.

This goal of universal validity in sound may perhaps be accomplished by a compatibility of technical skill and vocal tone (in the sense of a de-individualisation of timbre). By this I mean a 'technical' singing that does not constantly attempt to take its bearings from the context of meaning to be communicated at that moment, but from a universally valid technique applied to the piece. For the *Lieder eines fahrenden Gesellen* this means that one would have to match the vocal extremes in the low registers and particularly in the many high passages with a practically exemplary placement of the voice, more in sound terms of 'narration' than of 'living out' the emotion (although the latter should be grasped only as a mood that the performer has to communicate and not live through himself). The underlying text – a substratum of texts from the collection *Des Knaben Wunderhorn*, which Mahler assembled and enriched on the basis of his own response – is already theatrical enough and rich enough in pathos.

In some passages, however, it is my intention to allow a hint of vocal individuality – a personalisation of tone – into the performance. In spite of my previous argument, I believe this is essential if the chosen basic 'universalised' sound is not to become stereotypical and monochrome; sometimes it needs enlivening with contrasts. In this way I attempt to do justice to the fact that the 'plot' of the work contains passages of concentration, needs moments of tension, and can occasionally bear the illusion of the protagonist's individuality.

This is not necessary in the first song, in which the strictly separate middle section with its nature idyll, even without 'intervention' on the part of the performer, delivers the task of imposing a formal structure. In the second song, on the other hand, the relatively brief moment in which the protagonist refers to the experience of bliss in nature to himself and his history (from 'Nun fängt auch mein Glück wohl an' – 'Now my happiness begins as well'), calls, I feel, for an intensification of the sung experience. For that reason I try to lighten the voice towards the end of this lied with a degree of *parlando*, and to restrict the breadth of the vibrato in dynamic and intonation.[16] I see comparable passages in the dream vision in the third song from 'Wenn ich in den Himmel seh' ('When I look into the sky') to the onset of reality with 'Wenn ich aus dem Traum auffahr' ('When I waken from my dream'), as well as the section about hiking in the last lied. Here, in the middle part, from 'Ich bin ausgegangen in stiller Nacht' ('I went out in the still of the night'), I try to combine a *parlando* colour with a faster tempo, and in the final section, from 'Auf der Straße steht ein Lindenbaum' ('By the road stands a linden tree'), by combining a rounder, hence somewhat darker, colour with a move into an extremely calm closing tempo as a way of stressing yet again, and once and for all, the idea of vocal universality as the quintessence of this song-cycle's performance style.

> Weihnachten frisch und gesund,
> Im frohen Geschwisterrund,
> Am Neujahr mit blassem Mund,
> An den drei Kön'gen im Grund.

So thaten die Feste sich kund
Mit Tod und Grab im Bund.
Mein Herz bleibt bis Ostern wund
Und wird nicht bis Pfingsten gesund.

FRIEDRICH RÜCKERT,
from *Kindertotenlieder*

Christmas – fresh and well,
Surrounded by cheerful siblings,
At New Year, pale-mouthed
At Epiphany under the earth.
That's how the feasts announced themselves
In alliance with death and the grave.
My heart stays sore till Easter
And will not heal until Whitsun.

In comparison with the *Lieder eines fahrenden Gesellen*, shaped into a cycle with great artificiality, Mahler's *Kindertotenlieder* ('Songs on the Death of Children') can be more easily described as a collection. The five lieder, each thematically self-contained, have no sequential plot, no structure to relate them to each other. But neither are they an open collection, perhaps like Mahler's *Rückert-Lieder*, with the only loosely connected song *Liebst du um Schönheit* ('If You Love for Beauty'), or particularly his *Wunderhorn-Lieder*. These consist of an early group of lieder composed only with piano accompaniment and a large group of later lieder in orchestral and piano versions, some of which appear in Mahler's Second, Third and Fourth Symphonies, and some of which even have an independent instrumentation as an orchestral lied (*Urlicht*). It's hard to classify them, and there's no reasonable way of performing them as a whole. Yet even the *Wunderhorn-Lieder* are more than mere individual lieder, since they represent a cohesive complex not only in a literary but also in an aesthetic sense.

In spite of their status as a collection, in comparison with the *Gesellen-Lieder* the *Kindertotenlieder* form a thematically advanced, even daring, kind of lied composition. There is no narrative, because the event has already happened, and the theme of grief is static. Ambitious attempts at interpretation – which tend to reach a peak of hopelessness in the third lied, framed by the first and the last, while the lieder in between weave in stronger forward and backward references – do not illuminate anything for me. And how tasteless would it be to impose a dramatic structure on this particular theme in order to produce a presumptive effect? The loss of children was still part of everyday life around 1900, but as is demonstrated by Friedrich Rückert's 400-plus poems about the deaths of his two children, Luise and Ernst, as a result of scarlet fever, and his helpless grief for them, even in those days one could not simply dismiss this horror as something to be expected.[17] (There are also similar poems by Joseph von Eichendorff, Karl Barth and Hoffman von Fallersleben.) Losing a child has always been terrible.

The inconsolable state that must have gripped Friedrich Rückert and his wife, and which he recorded so vividly in his poems, has nothing artistically ambivalent about it for the reader, nothing that could be understood in different ways. There can be no catharsis here, and of course there is nothing entertaining about the subject – as there might be about even the most grisly operatic murder.

So what is it that makes these lieder bearable and even popular? Alongside all their musical and linguistic attraction it may be the consolation that speaks in them, which immediately grips the reader. But consolation for what?

> Unglaublich, wie erträgt ein Herz,
> Was schon zu denken unerträglich!
> Hinhalten Hoffnungen den Schmerz,
> Ihn brechend, den sie steigern täglich.

> Man hofft und hofft, bis hoffnungslos
> Geworden das geliebte Leben,
> Dann giebt man auf die Hoffnung bloß,
> Das Leben war schon aufgegeben.
>
> FRIEDRICH RÜCKERT,
from *Kindertotenlieder*

> Incredible – how endures a heart
> Something unbearable even to think!
> Hope holds at bay the pain,
> While breaking it, and heightening it daily.
>
> One hopes and hopes until hopeless itself
> Became the beloved life.
> Only then one gives up hope,
> Life had been given up already.

Experiencing the death of one's own children must be the worst thing that can happen to a parent. I struggle to imagine that, having suffered such an experience, one might deliberately expose oneself to these lieder (but I also struggle to imagine that pain). So there is an audience the overwhelming majority of which at least will not experience the horror first hand. And because we probably don't want to try to imagine such tragedies happening to us, the distance of objectivity remains. This also applies to other aesthetic horrors, such as in *Lear* and *Wozzeck*, *The Raft of the Medusa*, *Don't Look Now* or *All Quiet on the Western Front*. None the less, I feel, as do many others, helplessly exposed when I hear the *Kindertotenlieder* – something confirmed by family, friends and others. The fact that the horror of immediacy grips us particularly hard in this instance may have to do with the aura of these poems, which were not (at least at first) destined for publication, and were intended for very private consumption, as opposed to something initially conceived as a work of art, which will always need to seek out a public.

Still, the lieder do provide consolation. It arises from the proximity to the abyss and the knowledge that we have hitherto been spared. It's as if we were being consoled for something that doesn't affect us directly. (Of course, if you are directly affected, you can also be comforted by the sense of shared suffering.) I think that the *Kindertotenlieder* can be seen and understood as a prototype of musical consolation per se. The remarkable thing in my view – and I think that this may be true of all the arts – is that the positive aspect of consolation through art, so often striven for, may indeed exist, but is by no means a requirement; art can console us only for the violence that it has itself inflicted on our vulnerability. At funerals, on the other hand, it often happens that the art performed is either self-regarding, or dulled in an effort to provide consolation. Instead we often find the consolation we seek only when the music falls silent again. (This may be a good example of the futility of artistic endeavour and ambition. In the end all human activity and yearning is pointless, even though Cicero, for example, might have imagined – and this always prompts an incredulous, disdainful smile from me – that he would survive through his literary and philosophical ambitions and works. Nothing of us will survive.)

The representational arts, which include musical performance, are about role play, about roles and playing. Authors, directors, performers always feel challenged to push these boundaries in a new way, or even to question and attack their foundations. At the 2014 Wiener Festwochen, Romeo Castellucci had a patient in a vegetative state present her own personal experience on stage in the role of Euridice. However, as she had apparently given her consent, her contribution itself became a role. And the sarcophagi on which the corpses of Elisabeth and Tannhäuser rot away in Castellucci's 2017 Munich staging, and that bear the first names of the two performers, do not represent a fundamental intrusion into their privacy. Instead this idea is shaped by the essence of play inherent in the arts: a mask still hides the identity of the two singers. Even Thomas Bernhard's theatre works, whose titles bear the names of the actors who first performed them – *Ritter, Dene, Voss, Minetti*, or indeed the play dedicated to Bernhard Minetti, which was also about him, *Einfach kompliziert* ('Simply Complicated') – do not cross this boundary. The collaborators are part of these artworks only by virtue of being actors; their privacy is hardly even touched.

> Niemand soll mich weinen sehn
> Als in Feld und Aue
> Blumen, deren Augen stehn,
> Meinen gleich, im Taue.
>
> Sollt' ich vor den Leuten weinen,
> Die, ich weiß nicht, wie sie's meinen,
> Wenn sie mir zu trauern scheinen?
> Zu den Blumen will ich gehn,
> Denen ich vertraue:
> Niemand soll mich weinen sehn,
> Als in Feld und Aue.
>
> Soll mein Leid ich ihnen klagen?
> Eignes haben sie zu tragen,
> Würden mir ihr eignes sagen,
> Und ich will nur meines sehn,
> Das in euch ich schaue,
> Blumen, deren Augen stehn.
> Meinen gleich, im Taue.
>
> Blumen schweigen still bescheiden,
> Wollen trösten nicht mein Leiden,
> Noch an meinem Weh sich weiden.
> Niemand soll mich weinen sehn

Als in Feld und Aue
Blumen, deren Augen stehn.
Meinen gleich, im Taue.

FRIEDRICH RÜCKERT,
from *Kindertotenlieder*

None should see me weep
But in field and meadow
Flowers, whose eyes
Are like mine, in dew.

Should I weep in front of people
Who mean I know not what
When they seem to me to grieve?
It's to the flowers that I want to go,
The ones I trust:
None should see me weep
But in field and meadow.

Should I lament my suffering to them?
Their own they have to bear,
They would say their own things to me,
And I want to see only mine,
That I see in you,
Flowers, whose eyes are,
Like mine, in dew.

Flowers are silent, still and modest,
They don't wish to console my suffering
Or to graze on my woe.
None shall see me weep
But in field and meadow
Flowers whose eyes
Are, like mine, in dew.

I must admit that Gerold Huber and I think that an ethical–aesthetic boundary is in danger of being crossed with the last lied in Mahler's *Kindertotenlieder* – *In diesem Wetter, in diesem Braus* ('In this weather, in this storm'). In a dramatic *espressivo* that is not really appropriate as far as we are concerned, the pain is virtually screamed. And here the piano version actually seems more suitable and perhaps more tasteful because one can simply skip the dynamic outbursts with *mp*s not indicated by the composer. The heightened emotion is also contrasted with a closing lullaby, which, with its ultimately calming style, can seem rather presumptuous.

So in Mahler's *Kindertotenlieder* the privacy of Friedrich Rückert and his family tragedy lie directly and vulnerably, wounded and open, before us. Here I can see no proscenium and no stage set, no page, much less a piece of writing – particularly not in concert when the texts are effectively delivered over to musical notes, and confront us with their annihilating content as directly as if Rückert himself were speaking to us, and not a lyrical self, not the wearer of a mask. So perhaps the performance with orchestra, with its dense, weighty and seemingly difficult instrumentation, is the correct alternative because it makes the particular intimacy of piano versions – in all the Mahler lieder my favourite style of performance – to some degree impossible. Avoiding intimacy in performance is perhaps a position on which we might be able to agree.

So the fact that texts of the *Kindertotenlieder*, in Rückert's intimate language, were written as poems does not raise them above the level of autobiographical coping mechanisms, and in spite of their artistry they are a kind of diary entry, not, as so often, written with only superficial considerations about privacy and with thoughts of later publication. But why Mahler set them to music is a mystery to me. Making public something so intimate could be seen as crossing a line. (Mahler later faced similar exposure himself – under the gaze of interpretation – when details of his private life were revealed.) Because Mahler had nothing to deal with on this topic. Here it may become unpleasantly obvious why the authors of poems seldom give their permission to have them set to music. Perhaps – probably, in fact – it was empathy rather than a tired aesthetic interest that led Mahler to compose this work.

And why are the *Kintertotenlieder* performed? Not because of their overwhelming intensity, which, while often sought after, seems almost too violent. Because they are an outstanding work of art? This is only half true; Rückert's poems might be highly artistic but they are not a work of art. Still, this might be reason enough. Equally – although perhaps not – these lieder are capable of adding further injury to those who are already too deeply wounded.

THE SOULS OF THE CRAGS

BERLIN, 7 SEPTEMBER 2016

Denn: liebend zeugen, hassend morden,
Ist Menschenherzens Süd und Norden.
NIKOLAUS LENAU, *Faust*, V:295

For: begetting in love, in hatred killing
Is the human heart's south and north.

More often than not, after performances of the *Sechs Gedichte und Requiem* ('Six Poems and Requiem'), op. 90, the audience sits there very quietly, unable to show its appreciation, rather unsettled and perhaps simply baffled. That may be down to the last martial words and notes of the *Requiem*, which Schumann clearly intended in memory of Lenau. (He thought the poet had already died, when in fact Lenau didn't die until 22 August, shortly before the first rehearsal or first private performance of opus 90 in the Schumanns' house on 24 August.) Even now, from my own perspective, I can't quite understand that reaction, because these seven songs by Schumann are probably my favourite song-cycle and the one that is most important to me; over the past few years, alongside Schubert's *Müllerin*, it has unfailingly astonished, touched and inspired me. Sometimes Gerold Huber and I would be standing backstage, with the feeling that a fairly satisfactory performance had just taken place, both of us shaking our heads in amazement that something so powerful, something that moves our world as intensely as this work does, should even exist – and that we had been allowed to comprehend it for those few minutes.

Requiem
Robert Schumann: *Sechs Gedichte und Requiem*

Ruh' von schmerzensreichen Mühen
Aus und heissem Liebesglühen;
Der nach seligem Verein

Trug Verlangen, ist gegangen
Zu des Heilands Wohnung ein.

Dem Gerechten leuchten helle
Sterne in des Grabes Zelle,
Ihm, der selbst als Stern der Nacht
Wird erscheinen, wenn er seinen
Herrn erschaut in Himmelspracht.

Seid Fürsprecher, heilge Seelen,
Heilger Geist, lass Trost nicht fehlen;
Hörst du? Jubelsang erklingt,
Feiertöne, darein die schöne
Engelsharfe singt:

Ruh' von schmerzensreichen Mühen
Aus und heissem Liebesglühen;
Der nach seligem Verein
Trug Verlangen, ist gegangen
Zu des Heilands Wohnung ein.

LEBRECHT DREVES

Rest from painful efforts
And love's hot ardour;
He who blissful union
Desired in Heaven has entered
The Saviour's realm.

For him who is just shall brightly shine
Stars in the tomb's cell,
For him, who as a star in the night
Will turn up, when he beholds
His Lord in heavenly splendour.

> Intercede, holy souls,
> Holy Spirit, let comfort not be lacking.
> Do you hear? Cheerful song sings out,
> Festive sounds, to which the angel's
> Harp is singing:
>
> Rest from painful efforts
> And love's hot ardour;
> He who blissful union
> Desired in Heaven has entered
> The Saviour's realm.

These lieder, with their frightening descent into a collective death wish on the part of a lover in the sixth song, *Der schwere Abend* ('The Oppressive Evening'), cease in fact to be terrible by the end, because in *Requiem*, beginning with the dynamic *Wie Harfenton* ('Sounding like a harp'), a positive shift is accomplished: the holy souls and the Holy Spirit are appealed to, with the most shattering violence of conviction and euphoria. First of all, as if to intensify the urgency of the appeal, piano triplets accompany the lyrics, which are sung in duplets. The triplets are then followed by quadruplets and even quintuplets, which create a distressing and – more important – a very unusual sense of turmoil; quintuplets were still very rare at this period. Then there's an incredible dynamic: *Himmelspracht* ('Heavenly glory'), *Feiertöne* ('Solemn tones'), very high notes, sung *fortissimo* and with extreme intensity, not forced or 'pushed out' with breath high in the chest, but with the greatest possible expansion of the lungs, a technique that perhaps only older singers have acquired, resulting in a broad sound, but still necessarily capable of returning to a more refined tone (see music example 4).

4 Robert Schumann, *Sechs Gedichte und Requiem*, op. 90, 'Requiem', bars 31–46

Finally there is the repetition of the first verse, although it sounds very different from the first time it is heard, and with the words 'ist gegangen / zu des Heilands Wohnung ein' ('has entered / The Saviour's realm') it symbolises the imagined peace of the tormented human creature in this world. I would like to sing the final five words, if not the whole sentence, in a single breath, and not have to interrupt the flow of the lyrics out of physical necessity – but this is impossible for me in performance. The last word, 'ein' ('in') – not an especially meaningful word – must be sung for an astonishing ten beats (two and a half bars) on a single note, to depict the peace desired eternally for the soul. I have no option but to take a breath before 'Wohnung' ('realm'). Once I accepted this, once I stopped trying to conceal the fact that Schumann may well have intended such a long phrase but that I'm incapable of singing it, I have found I have enough breath and strength to attempt a small colour metamorphosis, as if accompanying the simultaneous cadence in the piano, which is intended to underline the imagined ascension into heaven in the spirit of the song as a whole, as an illustration of this change of shape and form of being (see music example 5).

5 Robert Schumann, *Sechs Gedichte und Requiem*, op. 90, 'Requiem', bars 56–62

I heard these songs for the first time in March 2002, when Ruth Ziesak sang them in Strasbourg, where I was involved in a production of *The Magic Flute*. I was delighted to be hearing chamber music again at long last. I sat in the front row of the Opéra du Rhin in the middle box, seeing and hearing everything from the perfect seat. And I thought as I always do as a member of the audience at a lieder recital: 'My God, that's difficult! How can anyone dare to give a whole recital on their own like that? How can they stand there so calmly? How can their knees not wobble and stop them projecting an even tone . . .?' But when the Lenau songs rang out, I was no longer relating the event to my own experience. The songs were sung incomparably and compellingly. Their simplicity and urgency awoke in me an overwhelming presentiment. I couldn't understand them, but I was overwhelmed. I immediately called Gerold Huber: we definitely had to learn this work.

The particular drama of opus 90, which might at first alienate many people, is not necessarily new in Schumann's work: one can hear an unsparing anti-climax of horror and despair in the opus 40 lieder, for example – four settings of poems by Hans Christian Andersen 'rounded off' with a Greek folk song, all five translated into German by Adelbert von Chamisso. They date from Schumann's first song-writing year, 1840. At first there seems to be nothing disturbing here, and yet the first song, *Märzveilchen* ('March Violets') ends with the words, 'Und Gott sei gnädig dem jungen Mann' ('And may God have mercy on the young man'). Why would such a person need mercy, when there seems to be nothing whatsoever the matter with his life? A slightly veiled uncertainty, but one that to me smacks entirely of intention: first this strange half-sentence is repeated as if it had a special meaning, and then comes that strangely stumbling conclusion, which, with an agogically unexpected upbeat to the final appoggiatura, prevents an organically

6 Robert Schumann: *Fünf Lieder*, op. 40, no. 1,
'Märzveilchen', bars 26–32

ritardando ending and might thus suggest a piece of sarcasm that is certainly present in the poem (see music example 6).

Second, *Muttertraum* ('A Mother's Dream'), more violent, because the raven at the window tells the young mother, 'Your angel will be ours / The little thief will be our food.' After that comes *Der Soldat* ('The Soldier'), the only member of the firing squad to hit his condemned friend in the heart. Finally, in the fourth song, *Der Spielmann* ('The Minstrel'), a musician has to play at the wedding of his own beloved, and in his madness he fatally stabs himself in the heart with his shattered violin. However, at this point in the cycle, after the remorseless descent into the vale of tears, the contrasting image of the concluding near-folk song *Verratene Liebe* ('Love Betrayed'), with its airy ease, cannot reach anyone, let alone cheer them up. And how could Schumann in all seriousness use the dynamic *Leicht* ('lightly') here? This song is about two lovers in a boat out at sea, observed by a star, which then falls into the water, is fished out and makes everyone at the fish market laugh with its story. This twist gives the work a quality no less intense, no less shattering, but different from that of the six *Lenau-Lieder* written ten years later (in Schumann's second song-writing year, 1850), which conclude with *Requiem*, often referred to as 'old Catholic'.[1] This is in fact simply the translation of a Latin 'spiritual poem' by Lebrecht Dreves. The publisher, Joseph von Eichendorff, reports[2] that it depicts Héloïse's lament for Abelard, although this is disputed by Kilian Sprau's commentary.[3] The more ballad-like tone of the *Andersen-Lieder* breathes a certain narrative perspective into the individual opus 40 songs, although not into the cycle as a whole, thus giving the work something concrete: it makes it seem a little like Grand Guignol, even though of course it isn't. In fact, through its conceptual organisation, it develops a deliberately artificial, basically allegorical character. Ten years later, in the opus 90 Lenau songs, this ballad-like, solid aspect makes way for something that is not figurative at all.

On this subject we might quote a literary anecdote identifying 'artistic freedom' in a new and practically irrefutable way, and which, to me, once more confirms Schumann's singular artistry. Joseph von Eichendorff published the poems by the lawyer Lebrecht Dreves in 1849. This edition also includes the translations of nineteen 'old Latin "songs" of the church',[4] the last of which forms the conclusion of the book as a whole, which Schumann used as a retrospective epitaph on Lenau's life and work, and which itself became the conclusion of the opus 90 cycle (the title *Requiem* was added by Schumann). But what Eichendorff writes in his preface to the volume that he compiled and edited is remarkable in this context, since it clearly reveals huge annoyance with the latest developments in Romantic poetry:

> Poetry too has experienced its revolution in Germany. A shallow liberalism had, beneath the magnificent mantle of cosmopolitan humanity, sobered up faith and life in this field as well, and prompted a reaction from Romanticism. But both were afraid

of their consequences, liberalism of revolution, Romanticism of the Church. But any half-measures are completely unpoetic. The younger poetry thus became radical by summarily declaring any hesitant liberalism to be mature and self-governing and led beyond faded Romanticism to its inevitable goal. Hence the poetry of the negation of everything positive began with Lenau, Anastasius Grün, and many others . . .[5]

Lenau's poetry is not analysed here by the poet himself, but at least it is evaluated by a writer as eminent as Eichendorff. Is it possible to imagine a greater affront to the artistic will on the part of this important writer, however vicariously intended, than by portraying this new poetry as deliberate and calculating? Schumann's decision to round off Lenau's conglomeration of songs, with their radical doubts concerning the purpose and meaning of human life and desire, with this religious hymn – which Eichendorff had singled out as an antidote to the poetry of his time (explicitly referring to Lenau) on the grounds that it was subversive and weak – can only be seen as disparaging. For me, if I may put it like this, there is a certain satisfaction in the way religious and artistic traditionalism is dealt a bracing lesson in liberalism, even though I personally have a great liking for Eichendorff's poetry. But how he may have intended his work, or even how he may have wanted it to be understood, is not of very great interest to me.[6]

Lied eines Schmiedes
Robert Schumann: *Sechs Gedichte und Requiem* (1)

Fein Rösslein, ich
Beschlage dich,
Sei frisch und fromm,
Und wieder komm!

Trag' deinen Herrn
Stets treu dem Stern,
Der seiner Bahn
Hell glänzt voran.

Trag' auf dem Ritt
Mit jedem Tritt
Den Reiter du
Dem Himmel zu!

Nun Rösslein, ich
Beschlagen dich,
Sei frisch und fromm,
Und wieder komm!

NIKOLAUS LENAU

Nice little horse, I
Am shoeing you;
Be fresh and obedient,
And come back one day.

Carry your master
Always devoted to the star
That to his road
Shines brightly forward.

Carry on your back
With every step
Your rider
Towards heaven.

Nice little horse, I
Was shoeing you;
Be fresh and obedient,
And come back one day.

In *Märzveilchen*, the first song of opus 40, it is the text, with its unexpected twist at the end, that makes the listener prick up their ears for a moment, or even leaves them suddenly unnerved by the last line. Accordingly, I have always thought that, as in the Peters edition of Schumann's songs that Gerold Huber and I used, the fourth and final sung verse of the *Lied eines Schmiedes* ('A Blacksmith's Song') seemed to be a repetition of the first verse of the poem, only with a simple 'Nun' ('Now') replacing 'Fein' ('Fine'). That seemed to me to be a conclusion based on the first three verses of the song, but without drawing any further meaning from them – indeed the absence of any new meaning is like a parallel to the uncertainty in the words to *Märzveilchen*, in this instance produced by Schumann himself, through the omission (alongside the third verse of Lenau's original in his *Faust* poem) of a single letter in the fifth and final verse, which I also misinterpreted as a repetition of the first verse. In fact, Lenau's verse is formulated thus: 'Nun Rösslein, ich / Beschlagen dich: / Sey Frisch und fromm, / Und wieder komm.' Plainly the error lies with Peters, with me and probably with most performances based on the 1887 collected edition of Robert Schumann's works by Clara Schumann, in which the 'n' in 'Beschlagen' was omitted, because it is still present in the first edition published by Kistner in 1850. (Schumann had added it in pencil to the printer's score, from which it was also plainly absent.) The dramaturge Andreas Meier kindly pointed out this publishing history, and hence also my not entirely minor error that resulted from it in the German edition of this book. For this reason I should, above all, remorsefully retract my misguided reproach towards Richard Stokes's English translation of *Lied eines Schmiedes*: 'And now / You're shod, / So off you go; / And be sure to come back again one day.' So in fact this verse is more or less saying, 'Now everything will turn out well – and even you, little horse, will help to see that it does!'

Richard Stokes, the great English connoisseur and translator of an unimaginably large number of texts of German-language art songs, has already pointed me in the right direction once in the past – for instance, with his translation of Goethe's *Schäfers Klagelied* (Schubert; D. 121), in which he renders the line 'Ich bin herunter gekommen' as 'I've come down into the valley'. Dieter Borchmeyer unfortunately confirmed to me that 'Ich bin herunter gekommen' actually means that the shepherd has just come down from the mountain and not that, as I had always imagined, he is a 'heruntergekommener' – a tramp, one who has come down in the world – although, when sung, it can be so beautifully coloured in that way. (I now simply think both.) And yet the last two lines remain the same, and Faust only just shies away[7] from punishing the naive repetition – expressed by the blacksmith's naively smug-sounding bliss with God and the world – by seducing his wife, deterred only by, to Faust, the horrific reappearance of a former female victim who has now sunk to being a beggar.

But Schumann does not simply leave these beautifully concluding words of the blacksmith's to stand. As with the uncertainty in *Märzveilchen*, he writes the instruction 'Der letzte Vers piano' ('The last line *piano*'), with what I see as a comparable effect. Schumann undermines the sunny attitude of the blacksmith, as if uttering that terrible and stupid phrase, 'Alles wird gut!' ('It will all be fine!'), with this dynamic. To my mind, Schumann's 'Der letzte Vers piano', hard on its heels, conveys an uncertainty regarding the purpose of life on earth, even of meaninglessness, perhaps felt by Faust and probably by Lenau (the *horror vacui* is one of the main themes in his work). It is as if one had suddenly and unexpectedly been robbed of substance – unexpectedly for the listener, at any rate.

This dynamic change – as if without motivation – has the effect on me almost of a panicky sense of hypaesthesia, a sudden and inexplicable decline in sensory perception. But the trigger for this hypaesthesia should be the way in which this line is performed: expression through reduced expressiveness, quietness or suggestiveness – which inevitably means a certain sacrifice on the part of the performer.[8]

While it's difficult to prove, this is what I feel: in these songs from opp. 40 and 90 we can see what Schumann was, among other things – an artist who thinks conceptually and who introduces perturbation, quite abruptly and hence as something of a shock, in order to develop a specific dramaturgy. But here this development is not inherent within the text or the music; this dramaturgy is not intended to follow a formal law, but instead emerges from a reflection on the meaning of music in a non-musical context, and may even add a third factor to the duality of words and music in song: a series of unconnected poems per se is brought together in a cycle and – certainly running somewhat against the grain of the individual poems – is connected through a *new* meaning, not least because of the meaning of this sequence. The idea of their connection and the meaning arising from it, which performs a meta-function, is something that I find unique in Schumann's songs. (Not that this does not occur in the work of other composers, but then it strikes me as more a matter of chance.) So here too there is a beginning that disturbs – or that disturbs me at least.

Gerold Huber sometimes speaks of a specifically Schumann-like sound, that turns the paradoxical direction inwards, and hence back on itself, and that does not seek to be, and cannot be, communicative, let alone expressive. It is in this sense that I would choose to understand the twist in the tail of this song, and here I would actually give preference to my idea of the loss of substance – even if the composition of opus 90, symmetrically organised as set out below in groups of poems, may hint at the idea that this is a stylistic cycle, which, ludically arranged in numbers and reflections, does not seek to depict any kind of existential abyss. In fact, I think that this expressive (or just non-expressive, or even anti-expressive) uniqueness, as one may also often observe in conceptual art, may be explained with reference to the following phenomenon. The concept of a work of art is no longer inserted into an existing form – in this instance, the tradition of a progressive strophic development. Rather, out of the necessity not only to avoid doing violence to the individuality of a work, but to bring it to light, a relatively specific method or technique capable of corresponding more precisely to the possibly intended message than a given template is developed – but nonetheless a method or technique that applies only to this single piece.

At any rate, from the second song onwards there is an exposition of disaster, not unlike that in opus 40, except that in opus 90 it is more sophisticated. The poems of Lenau – who seemed almost obsessed not only by a number of women, but also by the weight of the transient – do not invite as colourful a spectacle as those of Andersen. The development is also apparent over seven rather than five titles, and is therefore also less unambiguous. I would suggest that the first song, the *Lied eines Schmiedes*, which serves as a negative introduction, is followed by a group of five songs divided into two pairs – songs 2 and 3, and songs 5 and 6 – with another song in the middle (song 4). Here again the pairs are also paired to produce a depressive effect (as they are in the cycle as a whole – denying easy, let alone uplifting, accessibility), as a shorter song is not followed by a weightier one providing something approaching an outcome, a conclusion or even a catharsis; instead precisely the opposite occurs. The essentially positive message of the rather optimistic, albeit muddled; larger or at least weightier, albeit disjointed, poems and songs – songs 2 *Meine Rose* ('My Rose') and 5 *Einsamkeit* ('Loneliness') – is counteracted by the shorter but destructive songs – songs 3 *Kommen und Scheiden* ('Coming and Parting') and 6 *Der schwere Abend* ('The Oppressive Evening') – before the whole thing is rounded off by the *Requiem*.

I see this final song as in a close and almost antithetical relationship to the first: *Lied eines Schmiedes*, not least because of the ground practically opening up in the final verse, has to me the quality of antimatter, while on the contrary *Requiem*, thanks to its terrific weight and sheer overflowing length – unfamiliar in the work of Schumann and in the lied literature generally – effectively embodies matter. In the middle, not only between the two pairs but also halfway between songs 1 and 7, there is a favourite song of mine, *Die Sennin* ('The Shepherdess'), song 4. It really does fall in the middle: between two pairs, parallel but not symmetrical, and between the two framing songs that are complementary and hence even mutually referential. That central position, however, can be perceived only as part of a conceptual structure, and can hardly be experienced as such by the listener – perhaps that is why the cycle so often leaves the audience baffled. This focus on the middle connects opus 90 with the third section of Schumann's *Szenen aus Goethes Faust*, in which the central metamorphosis of Faust's earthly remains (no. 3) is framed on the one hand by the Anchorites (nos 2 and 3) and on the other by the appearance of Dr Marianus and Una Poentientium (nos 5 and 6), and these in turn by the Forest Chorus (no. 1) and the Chorus mysticus (no. 7). Not dissimilar to this arrangement the central position of *Die Sennin* in opus 90 breaks down the divisions into positive versus negative or matter versus antimatter: everything important is brought together in this single song; opposites are transcended.

Die Sennin
Robert Schumann: *Sechs Gedichte und Requiem* (4)

Schöne Sennin, noch einmal
Singe deinen Ruf ins Tal,
Dass die frohe Felsensprache
Deinem hellen Ruf erwache!

Horch, o Sennin, wie dein Sang
In die Brust den Bergen drang,

Wie dein Wort die Felsenseelen
Freudig fort und fort erzählen!

Aber einst, wie Alles flieht,
Scheidest du mit deinem Lied,
Wenn dich Liebe fortbewogen,
Oder dich der Tod entzogen.

Und verlassen werden stehn,
Traurig stumm herüber sehn
Dort die grauen Felsenzinnen,
Und auf deine Lieder sinnen.

NIKOLAUS LENAU

Bonny alpine shepherdess, once more
Sing your song into the valley,
That the happy tongue of rocks
To your vivid call awakes.

Hark, O alpine shepherdess, how your song
Entered the mountains' heart,
How your word the souls of the crags
Joyfully retells on and on!

But some day, as everything passes,
You depart together with your song,
When love has lured you away
Or when death has taken you.

Abandoned, remaining upright,
Sad and mute, will hither peer
There the ashen pinnacles,
And try to hear your songs again.

Ideally this song would be in 9/8 time. It is particularly restless. The triple-time sprightliness of the waltz rhythm isn't enough, which is why it is divided again into three per beat. Very lively, sometimes even manically vivacious pieces may sometimes be the consequence of this notation. For precisely this reason one could easily imagine *Die Sennin* in this rhythm. Strangely, however, the song is written in 3/8, even though it is largely structured in triplets. So, for example, if we look at bar 23 it initially appears unimportant whether it is written in 3/8 or 9/8; but a consideration of 9/8 helps to develop and confirm my opinion: one semiquaver is easier to halve (into two demisemiquavers) than three semiquavers (into semiquaver duplets). The difference between the two kinds of bar here, however, is that the division of the semiquaver in a 3/8 bar leads to a duplet division of a beat of the basic triple-time rhythm, while the halving of a beat of the 9/8 rhythm (also triple time), particularly in Schumann's day, would mean a considerable difficulty for notation: unusually, it would have to be written as two dotted triplet semiquavers.[9]

The first beat in bar 23 shows the right hand playing two voices on the piano – the lower voice with three semiquaver triplets, but the upper voice with only two semiquavers. I should now like to suggest that the leap of a downward seventh from B to C sharp (transposed) be seen as a duplet. The argument against this might be that the C sharp is included unison within the chain of triplets, and in this case the preceding B must have the duration of two semiquaver triplets. My interpretation is backed up, on the other hand, by the fact that the original fundamental 3/8 rhythm, which we may assume to consist of semiquaver duplets, asserts itself here for the first time. We can feel the breakthrough that the human listener, who is not a 'soul of the crags', catches a glimpse of what the song is actually based on: death, which I see represented in the song by the duplets, and the consternation at its inevitability. I also have a hunch that this seventh leap looks a bit like a duplet in the manuscript.

The first two verses of the poem are already strange in the respect that human life is depicted here only in communication with

7 Robert Schumann, *Sechs Gedichte und Requiem, Die Sennin*, bar 23

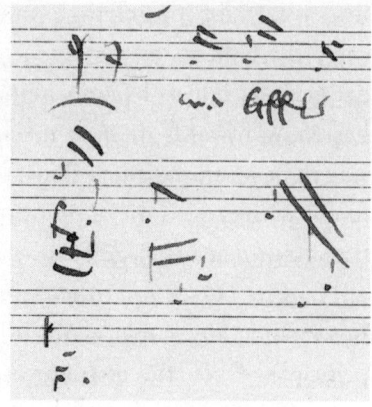

8 Robert Schumann, *Sechs Gedichte und Requiem, Die Sennin*, bar 23 (autograph manuscript)

inanimate nature: 'Felsensprache' ('speech of the crags'), 'Felsenseelen' ('souls of the crags'). In another verse that has not been set to music, mention is even made of 'Felsenchören' ('choirs of the crags'),[10] and in Lenau's *Faust* Mephistopheles speaks of Echo, as 'die alte Felsenhure' ('the old whore of the crags').[11] The shepherdess, living at her lonely altitude, can communicate only with the inanimate, with stone.

Lenau's mania consisted, among other things, in seeking, experiencing and thus explaining the incomprehensible transience of everything human, which is, certainly, always fruitless. The sheer horror of the inevitability of death finds, again and again, expression in incredulous interrogations of nature – very intensely, for example, in his poem *Ein Herbstabend*, which was set to music by Othmar Schoeck in the third movement of his work *Notturno*, op. 47, for baritone and string quartet.[12] It is in fact – and in my view spectacularly so – an anti-love message, a death message: falling leaves are now the only possible messengers, but they are messengers only of death; rather than flying they fall, lie on the ground and decay, if they are not first swept by the sluggish stream into a stagnant, putrefying pond. The winds flee, lest they should carry the laments as messages; the last birds flee from the leaves' decay so as not to have to render an account of it, and yet only hastening towards their own death. Similarly, the towering crags stay right where they are. They are not messengers of love but indifferent witnesses to the absence of the shepherdess – in the distant background at marriage or death.

Here in *Die Sennin*, the first two verses of the piano part do not include any duplets. Accordingly, the triplet functions as the principle of life, the embodiment of earthly serenity that characterises this song – almost disconcertingly – up to its conclusion. From bar 23 small duplet 'scratches' are added, and five bars later it becomes apparent why the shepherdess is able to leave her rocky world: 'When love has lured you away / Or when death has taken you.'

For that reason I find it almost crucial to the song's meaning that this first duplet should be explicitly played in this way, even though the notation could perhaps be differently interpreted. The opposite of life enters the song at this point, and from bar 23 it becomes clearly discernible in the vocal part: the first two verses do contain some duplets in the vocal part, but the basic rhythm is still in triplets. After the incursion of death and loss in bar 23, the last two verses are set exclusively in 'fatal' duplets, and in the rest of the melodic line only one single triplet appears, tellingly on the word 'Liebe' ('love'). For syllabic reasons this triplet was by no means necessary in the setting of this particular word, quite the contrary: 'Liebe' is a two-syllable word, predestined to be set as a duplet. I am all the more convinced that this interpretation, giving decisive importance to the duplets and triplets, may be attributed to this composition without overinterpreting it.

The way triplets dominate in the piano part right up to the conclusion, in spite of small duplet incursions, indicates to me that the fundamental ethos of all things earthly is represented here: serene apathy (just as the sunlight is serene) or apathetic indifference. In reality the rocks really won't mind whether the shepherdess is still there, whether she sings and whether her song still echoes off their surface, even if Lenau's last verse seems to deny this. The triplets representing life thus adapt in the end to the duplets embodying the passing of life: apathetic indifference is the true background to the initial serenity of life.

So Schumann's song ends with emotional indeterminacy. In fact the alleged sadness of the towering crags is so aberrant, within the context of the poem as well, it can be intended only as a depiction of the human perspective, a postulation of something that definitely could not be attributed to the world of rocky crags, should it have any identity at all – namely the postulation of an emotional world.

At any rate the apathy I alluded to becomes very clearly apparent in the vocal part (and whose voice is it that addresses the shepherdess – perhaps part of animate nature, to which the crags do not of course belong?) when the alternative is elicited: is the shepherdess gone because she followed her love into the valley, or because she has died? The rocks don't care; the fate of anything earthly has no value of any kind for them. The simple explanation of the disappearance of the shepherdess – love or death – seems relatively sober even in Lenau's text. In the Schumann setting, the depiction is left still less encumbered, almost eerily unperturbed, when death is laconically named as an alternative to change as the result of a marriage: death is not, as one might expect, illustrated as harmonically open, but is named when the music peacefully returns to the E major tonic (F sharp major in the original) of the middle section. Moreover, it is also noted in the *subito piano*, which reminds me of the irruption of instability in the fourth verse in the first song, because here too the power of expression is suddenly and unexpectedly renounced.

As so often in the lieder literature, I feel that here, even if the piano part itself is written *pianissimo*, guaranteeing the audibility of quieter singing, a switch to a brighter vocal colour might be appropriate as a way of effecting this instruction, because it does not diminish the intensity and comprehensibility of the performance too much, but can strengthen the sense of quietude. It's an example of a psychological phenomenon repeatedly confirmed in performance practice: you don't need to sing more softly, which is to say that you don't need to reduce the sound pressure that is helpful and necessary for the projection of the voice to a possibly detrimental degree in order to create the impression of quiet, because the same thing can be done – within limits – by brightening the timbre. By this I don't mean vowel colour, which must remain unchanged by any means – otherwise the meaning of the lyrics would be jeopardised.

However, if the terribly peaceful phrase 'or death has claimed you' sounds bright and innocent, it might create an impression of cynicism. Yet in the overall context of the song it should be clear what is meant. Apathy would be much too human; it's the colour of 'don't care'. Whether the shepherdess has got married or died is of no interest whatsoever.[13] So grief over the irrelevance of human feeling and suffering, indeed of all human existence, constitutes the core of this opus, perhaps adding a small human impulse in bar 23 when the expected three suddenly stumbles and becomes two. But that impulse is submerged again in the rest of the song when three regains the upper hand and the serenity associated with it finally turns out to be nothing more than an anthropomorphic interpretation of all earthly sameness and monotony.

FAREWELL TO THE FAMILIAR

STRAUBING, NOVEMBER 2017

Nothing is lasting but change, nothing consistent but death. Every heartbeat deals us a wound, and life would be endless bleeding to death without the poet's art. It grants us what nature refuses us: a golden age that does not rust, a springtime that does not fade, cloudless joy and eternal youth.

LUDWIG BÖRNE[1]

Here I wish chiefly to discuss Gustav Mahler's *Abschied* ('Farewell'), by lied standards the monstrously long conclusion of *Das Lied von der Erde* ('The Song of the Earth') – composed in 1907–8 and probably the composer's last song. For me there is a thread that runs ever more distinctly through the course of Mahler's lied compositions, particularly in his various *Wunderhorn-Lieder*, and most obviously in this symphonic song-cycle, particularly in its final song, and that is what I would like to address here.

When performing Mahler's songs, one can adopt a relatively uncomplicated approach to interpretation. For example, one can assume that they consist of real conversations, between girls and young men, because in many of the lieder the text takes the form of a kind of dialogue. Essentially, therefore, one could see them as small, more or less self-contained dramatic scenes. But in many of Mahler's lieder there are small ambiguities, gaps in interpretation or even contradictions, that place a crucial question mark over the seemingly uncomplicated. Here I am thinking in particular of songs based – unusually – on the combination of two poems.

Wer hat dies Liedlein erdacht?
Gustav Mahler: *Des Knaben Wunderhorn*

Dort oben am Berg in dem hohen Haus,
Da gucket ein fein's lieb's Mädel heraus,
Es ist nicht dort daheime,

Es ist des Wirts sein Töchterlein,
Es wohnet auf grüner Heide.

'Mein Herzle ist wund,
Komm Schätzel mach's gesund!
Dein schwarzbraune Äuglein,
Die haben mich verwundt!

Dein rosiger Mund
Macht Herzen gesund.
Macht Jugend verständig,
Macht Tote lebendig,
Macht Kranke gesund.'

Wer hat denn das schön Liedlein erdacht?
Es haben's drei Gäns übers Wasser gebracht,
Zwei graue und eine weiße;
Und wer das Liedlein nicht singen kann,
Dem wollen sie es pfeifen.

———

Up on the mountain, in the high house,
A fair dear girl is looking out.
She doesn't live there,
She is the innkeeper's little daughter,
She lives on the green heath.

'My little heart is sore,
Come, darling, make it well!
Your black-brown eyes
They have wounded me!

Your rosy mouth
Makes hearts well,
Makes youth understanding,
Makes dead alive,
And heals the sick.'

> Who thought up the pretty little song?
> Three geese brought it across the water
> Two grey and one white;
> And whoever cannot sing the little song,
> To them they will whistle it.

In *Wer hat dies Liedlein erdacht?* ('Who Thought up this Little Song?'), for example, two almost contradictory models are made one.[2] First of all, in the first part of the lied, there is a girl who attracts the attention of a young man visiting a mountainous region. He asks to be allowed into the 'high house' (i.e. high on the mountain) and hopes to be healed. But the end of this encounter is interpreted quite curiously by Mahler's addition of another poem: a family has been established, two children (the grey geese) and a mother (the white goose), except – the father/progenitor is absent. The young family accuses him, and brings the song and its sad truth to light.

I do not see this change only as an example of Mahler's empathy, ubiquitously present, with those who are suffering. What is special and unusual about it is the fact that the accusation not only gives the lied its title, but is also identified as the cause for the poem and thus of the lied itself ('And whoever cannot sing the little song, / To them they will whistle it.') Such self-reflexive changes to the text appear from time to time in Mahler's lied compositions – a small body of work, but one central to the genre. *Blicke mir nicht in die Lieder* ('Don't Look into My Songs'), is about the creative process as such, and *Ich bin der Welt abhanden gekommen* ('I am Lost to the World') ends with the words 'Ich leb' allein [. . .] in meinem Lied' ('I live only [. . .] in my song'). But to be presented as startlingly as we are here with the meaning of the act of composition per se – I cannot see that as contingent, as being rooted solely in the text that has been set to music by chance.

Even if the fast waltz rhythm and the very cheerful and unproblematic major key at first give us no cause for concern, on closer inspection the song appears as something fundamentally aggressive, full of wrath. There are comparable instances elsewhere in Mahler's oeuvre. In the *Rheinlegendchen* ('Little Rhine Legend'), for example, there is also a great deal of rage at the idea of living under a ruler's tyranny. But that rage about subjects not being able to determine where and how they live is not shared by the fundamental character of the setting. Perhaps here music and text are deliberately at odds, a characteristic that is commonly labelled 'grotesque' in Mahler's work.

I think that a very uncomplicated, cheerful, relaxed and entirely sentimental performance and reception of such lieder is possible, indeed widely established as one way of interpretation, and therefore even intense shifts and contradictions do not need to become problematic. It is possible simply to ignore these important details and instead follow a 'great whole'. But one can equally use these ambiguities to develop a different image of Mahler's lieder, one often contrary to expectations. Personally, I tend to go in that direction, not in order to distance myself from the status quo but simply out of the conviction that these lieder are not conventional, consistent structures and certainly not operas in miniature. To my mind these lieder are deliberately not self-contained logical constructs. On the other hand, operas tend to have a coherent plot; and if sometimes that is not the case, I do not necessarily see it as deliberately intended by their creators. I think lieder are principally not intended to be understood in the same way as drama, which is why the comparison with opera would be particularly wrong. I believe rather that Mahler's lieder in particular often do not say what one might as a listener at first assume they do. This means that they are not 'real'; they are pretend romances, pretend humoresques, pretend narratives, pretend scenes and even perhaps *seeming* mini-tragedies. If I may be a little pompous, which this music is to a certain degree, I might term them 'associative epiphanies', phenomena born of memories that have congealed into presentiments that can fit together only as allusions, not in a finite and coherent way.[3]

Wo die schönen Trompeten blasen
Gustav Mahler: *Des Knaben Wunderhorn*

Wer ist denn draußen
Und wer klopfet an,
Der mich so leise wecken kann?

Das ist der Herzallerliebste dein,
Steh' auf und laß mich zu dir ein!
Was soll ich hier nun länger steh'n?
Ich seh' die Morgenröt' aufgeh'n,
Die Morgenröt', zwei helle Stern'.
Bei meinem Schatz da wär' ich gern!
Bei meinem Herzallerlieble!

Das Mädchen stand auf und ließ ihn ein,
Sie heißt ihn auch willkommen sein.

Willkommen, lieber Knabe mein!
So lang hast du gestanden!

Sie reicht' ihm auch die schneeweiße Hand.
Von ferne sang die Nachtigall,
Das Mädchen fing zu weinen an.

Ach weine nicht, du Liebste mein!
Auf's Jahr sollst du mein eigen sein.
Mein eigen sollst du werden gewiß,
Wie's keine sonst auf Erden ist!
O Lieb auf grüner Erden.

Ich zieh in Krieg auf grüne Heid';
Die grüne Heide, die ist so weit!
Allwo dort die schönen Trompeten blasen,
Da ist mein Haus von grünem Rasen!

Who is just outside
And who knocks the door,
Who can so quietly waken me?

It's your most loved darling,
Get up and let me in!
Why should I stand out here any longer?
I see the dawn rising,
The dawn, two bright stars.
With my love, there I would like to be!
With my dearest sweetheart!

The girl got up and let him in,
And also bade him welcome.

Welcome, dearest lad of mine!
Such long time you have waited!

She gave him her snow-white hand.
From far away sang the nightingale,
The girl began to weep.

Oh, do not weep, my dearest one!
A year from now you will be mine.
Mine shall you be quite certainly
In a way no other is on this earth!
O love on the green earth.

I go to war on a green heath;
This green heath is so far!
Where the beautiful trumpets blow,
There is my house of green grass!

The lied *Wo die schönen Trompeten blasen* ('Where the Beautiful Trumpets Blow') is sometimes performed with male and female performers singing in dialogue, even though as well as the two 'protagonists' there is a narrative voice that needs to be assigned presumably to one of two singers, which does not, of course, make sense. For me this artistic practice implies a desire to clarify the apparent narrative – something we also find in the literature about this song. The double semiquaver and demisemiquaver notes are thus interpreted as knocks at the door or as military fanfares – at first in the distance, then closer, then heard by the girl . . . Some commentators attempt to document punctiliously every detail of the narrative. I find this bewildering. This approach seems desperate to me – as if it can't be that there is no consistent story at all; that the information provided and the dialogue format do not in themselves create a real connection; that this might not in fact be a ballad – which is what happens to an art song when the lyrical is abandoned in favour of narrative or drama.

The entirely lyrical ethos that characterises Mahler's *Rückert-Lieder*, for example, where the chronological and interpersonal developments typical of the ballad are not at all apparent,[4] also reveals itself to me in the *Trompeten*, albeit only at the end, with the utmost retrospective consequence. There are plenty of ballad-like situations and characteristics here but they are not causally bound together in a narrative arc; instead they form a kind of collage, an associative gathering together of a variety of fragmentary situations. The suggestion of a narrative remains illusory, and the structure in itself is entirely lyrical. This is a direct consequence of the identities of the two speaking characters not being discernible through sound or in relationship to each other.

Mahler's friend Siegfried Lipiner (and supposedly Goethe too) was of the view that in the underlying poem the ghost of a fallen soldier returns to his beloved and speaks to her[5] – this must refer specifically to the poem *Bildchen* ('Little Picture') from *Des Knaben Wunderhorn*, which Mahler took as the basis of his 'libretto'. However, I feel (as Mahler also did[6]) that a man of flesh and blood is knocking here, at least at the beginning. On the other hand I am unsettled by the fact that the man first says that the girl will be his within the year, and then prophesies that he will lose his life on the battlefield. This macabre prediction of a shared death within twelve months is however not the result of Mahler combining two poems which do not semantically fit into each other. Instead, in the poem *Bildchen*, all the elements are already present and Mahler introduced the second poem, *Unbeschreibliche Freude* ('Indescribable Joy'), essentially only in order to adapt some of the tropes. Here, the verses omitted by Mahler are included in brackets.[7]

Bildchen

[Auf dieser Welt hab ich keine Freud,
Ich hab einen Schatz und der ist weit,
Er ist so weit, er ist nicht hier,
Ach wenn ich bei mein Schätzgen wär!

Ich kann nicht sitzen und kann nicht stehn,
Ich muß zu mein Schätzgen gehn;
Zu meinem Schatz, da muß ich gehn,
Und sollt ich vor dem Fenster stehn.]

Wer ist denn draussen, wer klopfet an?
Der mich so leis aufwecken kann;
Es ist der Herzallerliebster dein,
Steh auf, steh auf und laß mich rein!

[Ich steh nicht auf, laß dich nicht rein,
Bis meine Eltern zu Bette seyn;
Wenn meine Eltern zu Bette seyn.
So steh ich auf und laß dich rein.]

Was soll ich hier nun länger stehn,
Ich she die Morgenröth aufgehn;
Die Morgenröth, zwey helle Stern,
Bey meinem Schatz, da wär ich gern.

Da stand sie auf und ließ ihn ein,
Sie heißt ihn auch willkommen seyn;
Sie reicht ihm die schneeweiße Hand,
Da fängt sie auch zu weinen an.

Wein nicht, wein nicht mein Engelein!
Aufs Jahr sollst du mein eigen seyn;
Mein eigen sollst du werden gewiß,
Sonst keine es auf Erden ist.

Ich zieh in Krieg auf grüne Haid,
Grüne Haid die liegt von hier so weit,
Allwo die schönen Trompeten blasen;
Da ist mein Haus von grünem Rasen.

[Ein Bildchen laß ich mahlen mir,
Auf meinem Herzen trag ichs hier;
Darauf sollst du gemahlet seyn,
Daß ich niemal vergesse dein.]

―――

[I find no joy in this world,
I have a darling and he is far away,
He is so far away, he isn't here,
Oh if I were with my darling!

I cannot sit and cannot stand.
I must go to my darling;
To my darling I must go,
And should I stand outside the window.]

Who is outside and who is knocking?
Who can wake me up so quietly?
It's your dearest love,
Get up, get up and let me in!

[I won't get up, won't let you in,
Until my parents are in bed;
When my parents are in bed,
Then I'll get up and let you in.]

Why should I stand out here any longer,
I see the dawn rising;
The dawn, two bright stars.
With my love, there I would love to be.

The girl got up and let him in,
And also bade him welcome;
She reaches out her snow-white hand,
And then she begins to weep.

Don't weep, don't weep, my little angel!
A year from now you will be mine;
Mine you will be, quite certainly,
Which no one else on this earth is.

I go to war on a green heath;
The heath is so far from here,
Where the beautiful trumpets blow,
There is my house of green grass.

[A little picture I will have painted for me,
I carry it here on my heart;
You will be painted on it,
That I shall never forget you.]

Unbeschreibliche Freude

Wer ist draussen und wer klopfet an?
Der mich so leise wecken kann?
Das ist der Herzallerliebe dein,
Steh auf und laß mich zu dir ein.

Das Mädchen stand auf und ließ ihn ein,
[Mit seinem schneeweissen Hemdelein;
Mit seinen schneeweissen Beinen,]
Das Mädchen fing an zu weinen.

Ach weine nicht, du Liebste mein,
Aufs Jahr sollst du mein eigen seyn;
Mein eigen sollst du werden,
O Liebe auf grüner Erden.

[Ich wollt, dass alle Felder wáren Papier,
Und alle Studenten schrieben hier;
Sie schrieben ja hier die liebe lange Nacht,
Sie schrieben uns beiden die Liebe doch nicht ab.]

———

Who is just outside and who knocks the door,
Who can so quietly waken me?
It's your most loved darling,
Get up and let me in.

The girl got up and let him in.
[With his snow-white shirt;
With his snow-white legs.]
The girl began to weep.

Oh, do not weep, my dearest one!
A year from now you will be mine.
Mine shall you be
O love on the green earth!

[I wish that all the fields were paper,
And that all students wrote here;
They wrote here the whole night long,
But they didn't write our love away.]

So what might it mean for the beloved – literally being told that in the coming year she will lie in the grave with her lover?

In St Peter's cemetery in my home town of Straubing there is a Gothic 'dance-of-death' chapel that is completely covered with baroque painting – except these are dance-of-death themes, unique in art history. In my parents' house I also grew up with a set of four baroque paintings of a dance of death. The most striking thing about it for me was the farmer harvesting the ripened wheat with his scythe, while the skeleton, also armed with a scythe, is busy cutting off his leg from behind.

The young man who speaks in the last verse of Mahler's song seems to me to belong within this tradition of death foretold. This would also fit with the strange way of describing their union within the year: 'Mine shall you be quite certainly / In a way no other is on this earth! / O love on the green earth.' 'Like no other' – for who is the lover of death? It's as if the speaker himself were not on the green earth, but only in his house of death. In the last verse he doesn't say that he himself will fall – after all, death itself would not have to lie in the grave, in the 'house of green grass'. At least that is how things would seem only in Mahler's song, because in a final verse of *Bildchen* – not set to music – the young man speaks, as a soldier, of wanting to take a picture of his beloved around his neck onto the battlefield, which would doubtless push the supposed prediction of death into the background. In a year, in fact, the 'little picture' would be with him as a substitute for his beloved if he didn't return home and instead ended up lying in the grave beneath the grass. The last word about the 'little picture' that the soldier has brought with him unproblematically rounds off the original poem with a fleeting vision of the death of the beloved within a year.

In Mahler's song, however, the macabre prediction probably is not simply an oversight resulting from a variation of the original folk song.[8] The fact that the man speaks of being reunited with his beloved within a year, and then about his own grave, might be deemed a casual slip in the folk song. But in my view Mahler deliberately lets it stand – in line with other artistically deliberate distortions.

The macabre curtailment of the end of the poem in Mahler is strange and unambiguous enough. Even stranger is that in the setting the man speaks initially as the lover and then, in verse 6, the second occurrence is characterised by a *Ländler* that is peaceful, cheerful and not particularly masculine or demanding. This contrasts with the martial tone of the soldier leaving for battle in the final verse. So here we encounter a manifold inconsistent depiction of character: in terms of sound and music the man's first two verses (Mahler's verses 1 and 6) are comparable, while in textual terms this applies even more to the last two (Mahler's verses 6 and 7).

We are given an even less consistent sound-world for the girl than we are for the soldier. If she speaks first questioningly, almost anxiously, but at least in a voice that is bright and high, what she says next is quite different, certainly in Mahler's musical interpretation of these words, which he wrote himself (this second piece of direct speech appears in neither of the two poems[9]): they sound dark, deeply erotic and much more seductive than the young man's words ever are, and almost take on the 'male' part of the dialogue. After a descent in the bass line, which produces an agogic and dynamic calmness, the girl utters her 'welcome' in an unexpectedly confident and relaxed way, which is only partially surprising in retrospect, because the following line – 'You have been out there for so long!' – sounds almost as if the man has left himself enough time to satisfy his beloved's needs (see music example 9).

This is followed by a return to the conventionally vulnerable girl of the *Wunderhorn* poems: she begins to weep, for no discernible reason. If it is because she realises that death has shown itself to her, then this change is not semantically embedded in Mahler's song, any more than the first 'willkommen' five lines previously, which, with its melodic and declamatory emphasis, sounds almost like a

9 Gustav Mahler: *Wo die schönen Trompeten blasen*,
bars 88–99

quotation, but contrasts in its brightness with the deep and dark direct speech in the following line – I attempt to stress direct speech with a brighter voice than the one I use for the narrative text.

So in this song, which at first seems to pose few major problems for the listener, there are a number of strange shifts in perspective, although they are not immediately apparent, as their transitions are so smooth. Like clouds, they overlap each other, nonetheless producing a homogenous effect. After all, we soon become aware of one thing – that the two protagonists do not have consistent identities. This is why *Wo die schönen Trompeten blasen* is a seeming ballad with pseudo-narrative traits. This has less to do with the incompatibility of two poems than with the way in which they are integrated and set. The sham narrative quickly grips us, however, because it acts as if this were an exciting little story with a narrator. I think that only the strong, ringing, martial impact of the drastic, shattering ending, with the death foretold of both on the battlefield, blocks all the questions that the song ought to raise, as its unspokenly promised narrative is ultimately missing.

Der Abschied
Gustav Mahler: *Das Lied von der Erde* (6)
(text as for the piano version)

Die Sonne scheidet hinter dem Gebirge.
In alle Täler steigt der Abend nieder
Mit seinen Schatten, die voll Kühlung sind.

O sieh! Wie eine Silberbarke schwebt
Der Mond am blauen Himmelssee herauf.
Ich spüre eines feinen Windes Wehn
Hinter den dunklen Fichten!

Der Bach singt voller Wohllaut durch das Dunkel;
Die Blumen blassen im Dämmerschein.
Die Erde atmet voll von Ruh und Schlaf;
Alle Sehnsucht will nun träumen.
Die müden Menschen geh'n heimwärts,
Um im Schlaf vergess'nes Glück
Und Jugend neu zu lernen.

Die Vögel hocken still in ihren Zweigen.
Die Welt schläft ein!
Es wehet kühl im Schatten meiner Fichten;
Ich stehe hier und harre meines Freundes;
Er kommt zu mir, der es mir versprach.

Ich sehne mich, o Freund, an deiner Seite
Die Schönheit dieses Abends zu genießen.
Wo bleibst du? Du läßt mich lang allein!

Ich wandle auf und nieder mit meiner Laute
Auf Wegen, die von weichem Grase schwellen.
O kämst du! O kämst du ungetreuer Freund!

HANS BETHGE, after MONG-KAO-JEN

STRAUBING, NOVEMBER 2017

Er stieg vom Pferd und reichte ihm den Trunk
Des Abschieds dar. Er fragte ihn, wohin
Er führe und auch warum, warum es müßte sein.
Er sprach, seine Stimme war umflort: Du, mein Freund,
Mir war auf dieser Welt das Glück nicht hold!

Wohin ich geh'? Ich geh'; ich wandre in die Berge.
Ich suche Ruhe, Ruhe für mein einsam Herz.
Ich wandle nach der Heimat! meiner Stätte!
Ich werde niemals in die Ferne schweifen.
Still ist mein Herz und harret seiner Stunde!
Die liebe Erde allüberall blüht auf im Lenz und grünt
Auf's neu! allüberall und ewig blauen licht die Fernen,
Ewig, ewig!

HANS BETHGE, after WANG-WEI

The sun fades behind the mountain.
In all the valleys descends the evening
With its shadows, which are profoundly cool.

O see! Like a silver barque the moon
Floats up in the blue sky's lake.
I feel a faint breeze's draught
Behind the dark spruce trees.

The brook sings euphoniously through the dark;
The flowers turn pale in the twilight.
The earth breathes full of peace and sleep;
Now all yearning wants to dream.
The weary people go homewards
To, while sleeping, relearn
Happiness and youth.

The birds perch quietly in their branches.
The world is falling asleep!
It blows cool in the shade of my spruces;
I stand here and wait for my friend;
He comes to me who promised me.

I yearn, O friend, by your side
To enjoy the beauty of this evening.
Where are you? You leave me alone for a long time!

I walk up and down with my lute
On paths cushioned with soft grass.
If only you would come! If only you would come,
    disloyal friend!

He climbed from his horse and offered him the drink
Of farewell. He asked him where
He was bound and also why, why must it be.
He spoke, his voice was veiled: You, my friend,
Fortune was not good to me in this world.

Where I am bound? I am going; I am going into
    the mountains.
In search of peace, peace for my lonely heart.
I am going homewards, to my dwelling place.
Never shall I roam abroad.
Still is my heart, and awaits its hour.
The dear earth all-everywhere begins to bloom in spring
    and green
Returns, and all-everywhere the far land grows brightly blue,
Eternally, eternally!

A similar thing happens in *Der Abschied* ('The Farewell'), although even more radically, given the sheer length of the lied (just under half an hour). It forms the last movement of *Das Lied von der Erde*, a six-movement orchestral work for tenor (movements 1, 3, 5) and mezzo-soprano or baritone. Its six movements are comparable to the four movements of a nineteenth-century symphony (1: *Allegro*; 2: *Largo*; 3, 4 and 5: three-part *Scherzo*; 6: *Finale*), and therefore invite us to view this work as a prime example of a 'vocal symphony'.

In *Der Abschied*, as in *Wo die schönen Trompeten blasen*, two poems by different poets are combined – as it happens, in this case the poets were friends. In the first, by Mong-Kao-Jen, a lyrical self speaks throughout, while in the other, by Wang-Wei, Mahler introduces a narrator. Wang-Wei's first line is 'I climbed from the horse and handed him the drink of farewell'; Mahler replaces the 'I' with a 'he'. The first person appears only in the last two paragraphs, in direct speech – and is probably a response to what is anticipated in the first half of the song. So the two selves of *Der Abschied* are probably not identical, and the self that speaks at the end even seems to be divided, since it is differs in sound quality from that of the girl in *Trompeten*. In a piece of direct speech, in which the departing figure provides a brief self-explanation after his voice has been described as *umflort* ('veiled, misty'), again we encounter an extended play of colour: first a submersion in rich depths of sound ('Where am I bound . . .'), which then contrasts with his last words ('I am going homewards . . .').

Musically, these last words are an extended quotation of the early section, 'Der Bach singt voller Wohllaut' ('The brook sings euphoniously'), with the calm serenity of its contemplation of nature, and could, therefore, give the discontented farewell to a failed life a conciliatory turn before entering into the carefree state of eternal return. When it comes to observable identities, however, this melodic quotation creates an uncertainty – here the figures whose stories are apparently being told definitely lose their distinctive outlines.

At any rate, the ethereal brightness with which this end of intrinsic reality is described represents a turning away in terms of tone colour from the outspoken sadness of the departing figure as originally formulated. Such things are not unusual, of course, and for the singer this last, almost euphoric flash of brilliance is highly compatible with the *pianissimo* instruction towards the conclusion. Only one thing strikes me: this quiet, brightly spoken brilliance prompts the impression of a resolute development, although one that occurs unexpectedly quickly in spite of the epic length of the song. Thus the illusion of a narrative is conveyed though colour. Much the same is true at the beginning: essentially here the beginning of a night is described as if something were stirring, as if something were happening, which is not the case. The great illusion of a narrative gesture is spread out with colour, but without anything actually happening.

In the orchestral version the instruments (particularly the woodwind instruments) are responsible for most of this colour. On a basis of the rhythmic variation of small and large duplets, triplets, quadruplets and quintuplets, they spread out a shimmering texture within which the vocal line can develop. But particularly in Mahler's (earlier) piano version the voice is able to discover, indeed reclaim, this colour, without taking the dynamic risks that might easily arise from an orchestral performance. In fact, if colours are sung while they are changing in the orchestra, the voice may forfeit its presence and consequently go into something of a 'decline'.

The greatest possible intimacy of projection of the text can be realised more easily, but also more radically, with the piano. Here what would be competition with the orchestra becomes collaboration, which of course offers less density and, above all, in the great interplay, a considerably smaller dynamic and colouristic range than the impressive oil painting that is the orchestral version. Through the quality of *semplice*, which in my view applies to almost all lied literature, in almost every style, with almost every composer, and not only according to the content, the piano presents the equivalent of a deep-focus woodcut to be coloured in by the singer.

At any rate the effect of the piano version is quite sufficient: in Straubing, and later in the concerts on our tour of the USA, it was always extremely powerful. The audience was gripped; comparison with the orchestral version was never made, not even in the conversations afterwards, unless it was people saying they didn't miss it. Perhaps this effect has something to do with one detail that I've become practically addicted to hearing: at the end of *Der Abschied*, when the famous 'ewig, ewig' is repeated an octave lower (because this is no longer really sonorous singing), the well-known and well-loved, wonderfully extravagant glissandi with harps, strings, celesta and mandolin is represented on the piano by chords that, all of a sudden, at the third 'ewig' are almost paradoxically frozen by groups of six quavers – alternating thirds, a repeated movement of two notes a third apart (see music example 10). 'Paradoxically'

10 Gustav Mahler: *Das Lied von der Erde*, piano score, bars 535–46

because the chords, although without rhythmical movement, advance harmonically, while those quaver movements remain static, even though they are moving.[10] For me this is a unique impression: like a pulsation of the infinite, as if the eternal were suddenly showing that it is not dead, but in motion. In this way I came to understand what Schoenberg might have meant when he said composers weren't allowed to write more than nine symphonies, because after that they start saying things that people mustn't say. *Das Lied von der Erde* was indeed Mahler's ninth symphony. In renaming it he was plainly trying to outwit fate.

DRAMA OF THE MOMENT

FRANKFURT, APRIL 2014

[. . .] zwischen Vergangenem und Zukünftigem
Als schwere Wolke [. . .]
Denn ich liebe dich, oh Ewigkeit!

FRIEDRICH NIETZSCHE[1]

[. . .] between past and future
as a heavy cloud [. . .]
For I love you, oh eternity!

One day in the spring of 2014, when I wasn't quite forty-five, I went to the ticket office at Frankfurt station to buy a travel card. The previous evening I had played Don Giovanni, a role that I hadn't necessarily envisaged for myself. Not because I don't nurture any Don-Juan-esque ambitions, but because the role involves a few things to which I can't lay claim – a powerful voice, coming more from the bass range, or the profile of a tanned, slim, tall young man. Bernd Loebe, the intendant of Frankfurter Oper, had offered me Giovanni. And with Christof Loy as director, I thought it might work; he might find something new in the part, something that even I could deliver. I originally thought of a wheelchair, but Loy didn't want to go that far. Instead he put a grey wig on me, with long greasy hair – I became an ageing man. And I did as I so often do with strong parts: I didn't try to fill it with my simple life and communicate it. Instead it took hold of my simple existence.

So I wasn't very surprised when the woman at the ticket desk asked if I was sixty, because in that case the travel card I was after would be considerably cheaper. Either the previous evening could still be read on my face or the woman at the ticket desk had attended the performance and thought that my voice had aged rather. The really wounding thing was that it would mean that I had missed out on fifteen years of life. I wouldn't have experienced those years; there would be a blank sheet of paper between the relatively young man that I still was and the near-pensioner – a decade and a half of forgetting, fifteen inactive years after Giovanni's descent into hell the night before.

What strikes me about this character, whether one sees him as old and weary of his life or, on the contrary, as young, virile and unshakeably libidinous, is the explosive power of the moment, lived to the extreme, but not really experienced. In this sense the momentary is so central to the character of Don Juan that I think Mozart's vision of music theatre attains perfection with this figure, as already in considering other, earlier works by Mozart, one has to talk about the aesthetic of the moment. Don Giovanni thus becomes the archetype of Mozartian stage drama, because that drama is absolutely explained by his character. Don Giovanni lives and demands dominance in the present in a paradigmatic way, excluding his integration in past and future, a temporal continuum, indeed any kind of development.

His fellows call him immoral – 'scellerato', 'perfido', 'indegno', 'mostro! fellon! nido d'inganni' ('scoundrel', 'treacherous', 'unworthy', 'monster! criminal! birthplace of deception!'). He himself knows why. He also knows what morality means and even acknowledges it, but he resists it. He lies cynically when he asks Donna Anna why she is weeping and who has caused her distress: 'Ma voi, bella Donna Anna, perché così piangete? Il crudele chi fu che osò la calma turbar del viver vostro?' ('Why do you weep so? What cruel man could dare to disturb the peace of your life?') Shortly afterwards he reveals himself as a sly tactician when he conceals his deeds with the words 'Se men vado, si potria qualche cosa sospettar' ('If I go now, I might arouse suspicion'). Don Giovanni's awareness of morality is without consequence, either now or in the future. He does not plan strategically, for the longer term; and when he thinks ahead, it isn't for more than the next few minutes. His order to Leporello to lodge and entertain the peasant folk in his castle follows only the spontaneous desire to possess Zerlina for himself, here and now. Planning the festivity is a matter of indifference to him. (It will later take place, but not as planned, expected or desired.)

So Don Giovanni lives and acts only in the here and now. He doesn't think of the past or the future. He doesn't plan on the basis of experience, he doesn't want to achieve anything, he doesn't want to do anything better than before, he regrets nothing. His contempt for any kind of morality as a basis for his own existence results from precisely this. Don Giovanni does not simply despise the ethical – that would presuppose a sophisticated argument – he just ignores it (or not even that). Why should he abandon the absolute immediacy of his life, which he lives according to his own will and his own imagination, according to his individuality, but without planning it? For that, if necessary, he has his servants. Leporello already hints at this in the first scene when he says, 'non voglio più servir' ('I no longer want to serve'). That service means planning Giovanni's deeds as well as cleaning up after him. Consequently, Leporello also has to assume the necessary ethical authority in Don Giovanni's stead.

Giovanni's insistence on living in the moment, freed from any temporal continuum, finds its ideal equivalent in sexuality, which in this character type embodies libido much less than it does absolute immersion in the present. In being so radical, Giovanni effectively joins a triumvirate of creative atheism in the eighteenth century, which appears sometimes sardonic (La Mettrie's *L'Homme machine*), sometimes diabolical (*Don Giovanni*), sometimes perverse (the Marquis de Sade).

Apart from his nobility (as a social and material precondition for his way of life), he is the anticipated figure of the wild, free human being that we encounter in Nietzsche.[2] Living free of any external or internal value system, entirely according to the reality of his own idiosyncrasies, that is the essential nature of Don Giovanni;[3] seduction is merely his *métier*.[4] The fact of his being entirely himself is something that he perceives and lives out as a phenomenon, but he does not reflect on it, any more than he reflects on his role among his fellow humans.

For that reason the last exchange with the Commendatore in the second-act finale takes place not as a conversation or an argument, but is merely the juxtaposition of irreconcilable realities: 'Pentiti, scellerato' – 'No, vecchio infatuato' ('Repent, scoundrel' – 'No, you old lunatic'). In the face of the normative power of a god-fearing world, the dimensionlessness of the amoral man can bring out all the mockery that the world of ethics fears. Conversely, there is the pity of the believer for the unbeliever, for whom life without the prospect of the plenitude of the eternal and hence an already wretched earthly existence is prophesied, as a perpetuated but by no means appropriate self-reassurance – in the face of the impertinently free agnostic or anti-Christian. The opposition of the two dramatic protagonists, Don Giovanni and the Commendatore, which also gives the drama as a whole its framework, is finally apparent in the ultimate concluding back and forth of 'No!' and 'Sì!' ('No!' – 'Yes!'), which never occurs on a common harmonic basis, but requires a different key for each interjection.

But what is the source of the eponymous hero's serenity – compelling or stifling, according to one's religious or non-religious point of view – when facing the end? It may be explained by his temporal independence in feeling and action. Just as – as a living person – he rules out all retrospection and the regret and repentance that go with it,[5] he cannot be unsettled in the face of death and the inevitable judgement of his earthly sins, because he refuses to gaze into the future. The horrific vision of eternal torture and pointlessness, like that held up before the eyes of James Joyce's Stephen Dedalus during his spiritual exercises,[6] would just bounce off such a person – with an eruption of mocking laughter. Because the ordinary image of hell is so banal: while the eternal joys are only rarely presented in concrete terms, so remote are they from earthly experience, so impossible to speak of, in their timeless and limitless abundance, hell is usually illustrated through negatives, from the denial of everything terrestrial, as an infinite continuation of earthly restriction. Everything earthly is eternalised in a dull way, most impressively in the description of eternal pointlessness.[7]

Because of his nihilistic nature, Giovanni does not seek personal happiness – unlike the entirely opposite figure of Donna Anna, for example. Unlike Giovanni, she never shapes the plot, but only accepts developments. So she seeks her happiness in a lifelong continuum of relationships, with her father as representative of her past, of retrospection, then – and Don Ottavio as the incarnation of her future, of prospection. Giovanni's world of the present, however, does not even erase happiness as the goal of a reality that is within his power to shape; he doesn't know it at all, as he doesn't know sadness. This explains the radical otherness of these two figures, not least in musical terms: if Donna Anna's arias are idealised observations that feed on reflected and planned, but never on shaped presence, Giovanni's solo numbers are the opposite.

Curiously enough, attentive listeners often say that the figure of Giovanni is naturally strong and compelling, but has nothing of substance to say. They say that of a role that involves more than an hour's singing. At least he has no arias, they argue, while the other characters have such beautiful ones. In fact, however, Don Giovanni sings three aria-like pieces, which is not really nothing. Yes, they say, but the *Ständchen*, the serenade, is more like a lied, and the 'Champagne aria' is far too short. And none of these listeners even thinks of 'Metà di voi qua vadano', the third 'aria' in the second act, with their intuitive yet understandable judgement. Because in fact these three pieces lack precisely what is usually the essence of an aria: taking a pause, a slowing down, a breathing space in the plot, which develops chiefly through recitative.

In their different ways, however, all three of Don Giovanni's 'arias' defy convention (how could it be otherwise) by driving the plot forward. The last does so in a completely comprehensible and intelligible way. More dramatically than in the foregoing recitative with Masetto, which is only about identifying the staff, here Giovanni is organising the collision of the real and disguised antagonists, and risking Leporello's life in the face of the growing, bloodthirsty mob. In the second part of the aria he keeps Masetto alone with him so that he can finally beat him up. Things could hardly be more dramatic, and Giovanni's powerful, pleasure-seeking nature is revealed here in its entirety.

It even seems to me that this way of plotting – stirring people up, setting them against one another and injuring them – gives him greater pleasure than the 'service' he performs to women. Or organising and experiencing aggression and cruelty is a welcome relaxation after his actual occupation, his 'job', one might say, of conquering women. Just before the aria he explains this 'job' very impressively as his calling, which he cannot escape. He does say of women that they are more necessary for him than his daily bread and the air he breathes: 'Sai ch'elle per me son necessarie più del pan che mangio, più dell'aria che spiro.' But essentially they 'only' constitute his occupation. His essence, on the other hand, is different. But if women do not understand him, his nature, they call it deception: 'Le donne poi, che calcolar non sanno il mio buon natural, chiamano inganno.' Of course, nothing in his life is love – 'È tutto amore', 'everything is love', is one of his many lies – but quite the opposite. Everything is pure, egoistic self-realisation. His self is the amoral pleasure of the moment.

One of the peculiarities of this work is the fact that the title character does not embody the amoral principle in an unadulterated form, but with characteristic fractures along the lines of his being the negative inversion of superman (*Übermensch*). (Of course, Giovanni is not a prophetic *Übermensch* with a mission *à la* Nietzsche.) One such fracture, for example, occurs in the first and second recitatives of the first act, where Don Giovanni and Leporello experience the murder of the Commendatore as an elemental catastrophe: immediately after the chromatically falling end of the opening scene comes the first, almost absurd communication between Giovanni and his servant, which develops as if from a paralytic stupor: 'Leporello, ove sei?' 'Son qui per mia disgrazia, e voi?' 'Son qui.' ('Leporello, where are you?' 'I'm here, to my shame, and you?' 'I'm here.') They are in fact standing side by side. And then: 'Chi è morto, voi o il vecchio?' 'Che domanda da bestia, il vecchio.' ('Who died, you or the old man?' 'What a question, like an animal's, the old man.') Here, in this situation of unconditional guilt – reminiscent of Raskolnikov's catatonic horror after committing murder – Giovanni has to call his very being into question: the wild, free man assures himself of his existential foundations. Clearly one of these is that no human being can murder another – at this point Giovanni is not necessarily what we might imagine a radical nihilist to be.[8]

Another example: when Giovanni cynically captivates Elvira in the trio in the second act, bringing her close to Leporello and thus allowing him to conquer her maid, the first few sentences sound quite routine and deliberately tactical (mean and scheming, a moralist would say). But when he quotes in anticipation his canzonetta for the maid in the theatrical sequence 'Discendi, o gioia bella!' ('Come down, fair joy!'), all of a sudden he loses track of his routine and diverges: in the unplanned repetition of 'o gioia bella!'[9] it becomes clear that the cynical anti-hero, unexpectedly stirred by Donna Elvira's beauty and singularity, loses himself in amorousness, culminating in the confession 'pentito io son già' ('I already regret'). I can hear and sing this only as the awakening of genuine passion – and the same applies to his thrice-repeated suicide threat.[10] This alteration of meaning and expression, which is not recognisably the intention of Da Ponte's rather unequivocal text, and yet sensed by Mozart (hard to prove, but equally hard to dismiss), ends with 'Idolo mio, vien qua!' ('My darling, come here!') and makes way for Don Giovanni's well-known cynicism: 'Spero che cada presto!' ('I hope she gives in soon!')

However, the anticipatory quotation ('Discendi, o gioia bella!') of the main theme of the 'serenade' that follows – to return to the function of Giovanni's 'arias' – indicates something else. This serenade, the canzonetta, is not the theatrical realisation of spontaneous desire and momentary impulse; it is not amorously inspired by the singularity and particularity of Elvira's maid. On the contrary, in the first recitative of the second act Giovanni even compares her to an object: 'Non hai veduto qualche cosa di bello' ('You haven't seen anything beautiful'). In my view this vocal showpiece is more the result of two thousand wooings, a highly refined substratum of conquest. The four ideas in the two verses (the appeal to the idea of healing and the care of womanly love – the threat of suicide if left unheard – the glorification of feminine charms – the lament over supposed feminine cruelty) reveal themselves to be always readily accessible, polished, perfectly attuned to one another, irresistible and ultimately effective.

That this 'aria' as well, then, contains no profound reflection, no serious argument or even recognition is apparent in the music. Instead, it follows the course of that pattern of conquest that was given a strangely contemporary life in the preceding trio with Elvira, once again an embodiment of the pressing Don-Juanesque type. None of this serenade is honest, and the plot continues by deploying this well-tested and unfailingly effective seductive miracle weapon. Christof Loy showed this in Frankfurt with an impressive *coup de théâtre* – or tried to, because the task was clear but so difficult that right up to the present day I still don't see myself as being equal to it. Giovanni, continuing to exercise his calling as a seducer, is in fact no longer interested in seduction and everything that goes along with it – and after over two thousand amorous adventures who wouldn't be bored by it? So the task was – in Loy's fascinating idea – to take off the mask of the ever-pressing, ever-desiring figure for the duration of this mask-like, content-free performance, tormented by waiting and boredom, and hence to adopt a mask-like expression of waiting and boredom – while allowing no expressive deficits to appear in the music. I didn't really succeed, and every time I've tried since, I haven't managed to produce this dichotomy of musical and facial expression.[11] (The best thing would be to let Don Giovanni simply set up a speaker below the maid's window, from which the perfectly animated-sounding serenade would issue while he stood around being bored.) However, in that way Don Giovanni's serenade would not represent an aria-like pause in the plot, but would rather mean only a painful deceleration of it, for the sake of some uninteresting and unimportant stage business, an image of terrible boredom – almost, in fact, a terrestrial manifestation for a moment of the Joycean vision of infinite pointlessness from the standpoint of human finiteness.

Finally, the aria in the first act, known to Germans as the 'Champagne aria': 'Fin ch'han dal vino'. The fact that this cannot be seen as a slowing moment devoted to reflection must be immediately obvious. The one-part form of the aria also shows that there is not an imaginative idea or a plan for the coming feast, but rather only a thought, a momentary image of a prospective situation being materialised. Just as a thought as it comes into being is not yet captured in language, this idea is like raw meat to me, set down in language in the libretto, but characterised only by the simplest, well-known attributes: wine, new seductions, dancing, flirting, the list of the women seduced – all the various facets of Don Giovanni's occupation, in fact. But there is no thought needing to be developed or explained; it is only a one-dimensional idea, like a geometric point, albeit one carrying a great deal of weight. Or perhaps an extremely condensed musical manifestation of a massive imagination lasting less than a minute and a half. In my vision of the appropriate performance, it is not a matter of elegance, but rather a breathless expression of raw power. No aria is as demanding over such a short length of time as 'Fin ch'han dal vino'; for me it is the most extreme expression imaginable. This unique eruption of power, desire, violence and scorn sounds to me like the audible form of a heavy, dark star, a black hole: the mass and potential significance of whole worlds is held in a single hand. That is what I mean by the dimensionlessness of the Don Juan character: maximum concentration of sensuality, but minimal extension of present significance; simultaneity, but timelessness in the moment.

Of course there are other arias that are not reflective, even before *Don Giovanni* and before Mozart. But formally characterising an entire individual figure through such arias and allowing the idea of an aesthetic attitude to culminate in it is new, and a peak in the development of drama.

In his nihilism, Don Juan is a type who differs from the historical figure of Giacomo Casanova, a true lover carved out of passion and enthusiasm, between devotion and desire. If we ignore later additions to the subject matter – Donna Anna's affection for the malefactor,[12] for example, or a modern psychoanalytic questioning of Don Juan's masculinity, which finds a compensatory explanation in his urge to seduce women – if we ignore those, Giovanni is a seducer who has no interest in the woman that he is currently taking. Her appearance and significance are entirely indifferent to him, because he is essentially uninterested in having any kind of confrontation with a woman. That is the only way I would interpret Leporello's testimonies in his first aria.[13]

As old age and waning attractiveness approached, Casanova's fifteen years as a travelling and writing amorous adventurer came to an end. Don Giovanni, on the other hand, as a comparatively demonic character, does not allow his age to affect him. And, in passing, I should add that his lack of success with women in the course of the drama, as frequently suggested, doesn't hold water: Zerlina lies helplessly at his feet, only external circumstances prevent anything else from happening, and he effortlessly conquers Donna Elvira for a second time in the second act trio. But he does not actually seduce, he just takes – unscrupulously, until the attempted rape of Zerlina in the first-act finale. The only thing he doesn't succeed in doing is escaping the consequences of the murder he has committed. That alone destroys him, not his lifestyle as a deceiving womaniser.

Age suits him, although only in the form of the number of his conquests, not because of a decline in his strength of will. He carries on unbroken, and in this he resembles a type with whom he also shares many other similarities. In his fundamental estrangement from his fellow men, in his effective lack of morality and above all in his manic attempt to erase boundaries, Don Juan is . . . the other Faust. But while Faust strives for matter, which he attempts to understand, including the past and the future, and finally even ends his existence on earth with a kind of ascension, Don Juan's expansive nature is bound to collapse in on itself in the end. Faust strives for plenitude; Don Juan ends up in the void.

INTERMEZZO

ELMAU, SEPTEMBER 2019

> Perhaps it is one of music's particular charms that it [. . .] addresses us like reasonable speech but without having to base itself on concrete meanings. It escapes the obligation of relevant statements and yet it speaks with a meaningful voice.
>
> FLORIAN MEHLTRETTER[1]

To the question of what the lied might be, I would spontaneously answer: it is a vocal form of chamber music and it represents – as opera does drama and the oratorio the epic – lyric poetry in sung music. Such distinctions are of course deliberate, and there is no shortage of examples of plot, presented and narrated, also playing a part in the lied, for example in the form of the ballad, or even in whole cycles such as Brahms's *Die schöne Magelone* or Schubert's *Die schöne Müllerin* (in his prologue the poet Wilhelm Müller calls the unfolding plot a 'monodrama'). And yet, although here, as ever, academic categories are not always entirely reliable, an attempt at classification strikes me as inevitable, as the style of interpretative performance by singer and pianist is influenced by it, downright depends on it.

Not only do I disagree with the throwaway description, which I often come across, of a lieder evening as a sequence of many 'mini-dramas'; it also makes me want to find clarity on the subject. Lieder are based on poems, and both tend more to an abstraction of lived reality. To perform them as 'mini-dramas' or as an attempt to narrate something that cannot be narrated (who could narrate Goethe's poem *Über allen Gipfeln ist Ruh'*?) would relegate crucial aspects of both sound and text to the background. For example, here I would like to introduce a certain intimacy that is admittedly not excluded from opera and oratorio. But in the lied, in the sense of shared absorption, this intimacy often retreats along the path of expression to the interior of the creator of the lied, of its performer, and hence also of its audience. So we might say: in the lied expressive intimacy is programme and attitude, while in the course of an opera it arises entirely out of the situation and is explained only by its dramatically meaningful place within the structure of the plot.

Aside from the particular role played by the two performers, the lied recital is distinguished by the positioning of the performance on a concert platform that does not adjoin a hall but stands within it and is hence a part of it. In this way it is fundamentally different from an operatic stage: the fiction that occurs there, behind a proscenium arch, separate from the reality of the audience, does not exist in vocal chamber music. So a lieder evening is even spatially different from an illusionistic narrative or the representation of a dramatic plot. The latter takes place to a greater extent in interpersonal exchange, and appears within a network of roles. The plot of an opera seeks in the end to be understood.

In the lied, on the other hand, inner life is crucial. Events are defined by realities that resist clear definition, often and in principle – realities that occur frequently and have their effect within the pre-linguistic realm of inner life, even though they are paradoxically expressed in language: through words and notes. The pre-linguistic immediacy, on the other hand, is manifested in sound, which arises and has an effect through situation. Sound that, in opera and oratorio, attempts to assume concrete qualities, in the lied remains in that pre-linguistic sphere, although mediated via the abstraction of everything real.

The lied (like the poem on which it is based) is thus a construction whose purpose lies much less in unambiguous representation (drama) or in the retelling (oratorio) of a generally comprehensible plot than in the communication and stimulation of ideas that define our life and experience to perhaps a greater degree than our busy everyday reality, and which in turn tend to be reflected artistically in dramatic and narrative forms. These lyrical ideas need not be assembled into a whole; they are often apparent only in threads that are not spun together into strands of plot. In many instances they simply hang loosely, without beginning or continuation. They do not have to bend to the criteria of a logical, hypotactic, consecutive or causal connection.

These lyrical intimations do unfold in a space that is shared by everyone present – the audience, the performers and, in imagination, also the poets and their composers. In this space the imaginary gaze on the many different artworks of a lieder evening is slightly different from each spot in the room; the 'angle of understanding' is always slightly different. This spatial difference alone may explain why it is that the contents of the lied are different everywhere and for each individual – and that this follows a principle. Of course an opera-goer will perceive many things in a different way from the person sitting next to them as well, but essentially the situation is the same for every member of the audience: I see the proscenium as a screen that ideally facilitates reception independent of perspective, and tells a consistent story. The lied, on the other hand, tries out effects that remain in the individual, effects that are conjured by the same thing, but unfold in an intimate variety.

Added to this experience of the lied, more personal than collaborative and for that very reason relatively resistant to universalisation, there is also the fact that words are not always what they seem to have been chosen for, namely reliable representatives of a precise meaning. That, however, was the view of Eduard Hanslick, leading critic of the nineteenth century, who writes in his essay *On the Beautiful in Music*, a sentence that strikes me as actually absurd: '[. . .] in the *logical* (we almost said "legal" [he was a jurist himself by training]) sense, the text is the main thing, the music an accessory [. . .].'[2] Finally the widespread and well-intentioned, beautiful-sounding description, that music begins when language ceases to work, is reduced to absurdity by the phenomenon of the art song. The semantic approach underlying this essentially helpless demand is clear: where words are no longer unambiguously able to represent what is to be depicted, musical notes should convey it. But whether the particular object depicted in sound can possess an unambiguous content is extremely doubtful. At any rate this difficult task led Hanslick, in this influential essay, to the fatal conclusion that 'feelings' in music were simply non-existent, or at the very least not worthy of consideration.

I think it would be a false conclusion to take ambiguities as evidence of the inevitably pure self-referentiality of artistic forms of expression. Quite the contrary – it is a criterion of the lied that everything cannot – and doesn't need to be – summarised unambiguously in a communicable way. This is something that I especially like and find interesting about the lied: apprehensions become realities, become something effective, something that can be described and profitably discussed, albeit not unambiguously – not the word, not the accompanying music, and definitely not the connection between the two.[3]

Because of the impossibility of deeply understanding either of these, avoiding the connection between lyrical text and lyrical music in the lied would be one approach. Another would be leaving ambiguities in content and meaning untouched beside unambiguities of form and performance. This is how I would like to understand Wittgenstein's beautiful phrase: 'Where our language suggests a body and there is no body, there, we should like to say, there is a *spirit*.'[4]

In a sense the performer's quest for meaning, which must be open and experimental, is like a process of scientific research: 'artistic' experiences with the phenomenon of the lied are used as empirically valuable, interconnected, and expanded into constants and regularities through extrapolation. But falsification is thus very much closer to the performer than to the researcher, and actually his daily bread, because the inevitable underlying basic assumptions are much more uncertain than they are for a scientist, who must only assure himself theoretically that a microscope shows what he thinks he sees.

Here I should like to name what I see as the two most important, prototypical contents of the lied: on the one hand there is the 'serenade', sung to the beloved below her window at night, then the 'message of love', which is conveyed to the absent beloved via natural phenomena (stream, birds, wind, stars, etc.). Neither of these is particularly dramatic (this does not, of course, apply to the 'serenade' in Mozart's *Don Giovanni*, which has the clear dramatic function of seduction), because they are primarily the expression of a subject, and do not expect a direct answer in terms of an argument. It is almost like the passage in Eichendorff's novella *Das Marmorbild* ('The Marble Statue'), in which it is said of the song that the character Florio sings across the river, 'He couldn't help laughing at himself, as in the end he didn't know who he was serenading.'[5] The fact that none of the potential recipients knows what the origin of the moving phenomenon – the sung serenade or the mediating natural phenomenon – might be, makes both types of poem somewhat lyrical to my mind, because they awaken surmising emotions. And they belong together like a pair: one is spoken before and the other after the shared realisation that both parties are meant for one another. But both are uttered by a subject, and first and foremost for this subject himself, without the other having the opportunity to react.

As regards the history of the lied, and the German-language lied above all, here I would like to mention some pioneering representatives. Chauvinism aside, the development of the German-language lied is probably the most interesting because, since the transition from Classical music to Romanticism, it has lasted the longest.

In Viennese Classicism the lied had already played a major part, particularly in the work of Joseph Haydn and Ludwig van

Beethoven. But it was yet to develop as a genre – that began with Schubert. At the transition from one era to another, from the Classical to the Romantic, he created a form that would henceforth be typical, and indeed to a degree central, a form that had not previously enjoyed such a status but had been used none the less. In this way he was able to establish for the first time the artistic freedom of the lied against the inconsequential bits and pieces (probably born of formal helplessness) of the Second Berlin Lieder School of the late eighteenth century. Therefore he would set his chosen poems to music in a way that was, in the best sense, 'naive', and hence relatively true to the text.

Robert Schumann represented a more strongly interpretative approach, aiming at a meaning that went beyond language and sound. In his work, in my opinion, incongruence of the possible meanings of literature and music is particularly pronounced, and in a conscious, indeed in a deliberately conceived way. The result is a 'shimmer' between these two bearers of meaning, which may represent, in a perhaps ideally and formally completely appropriate way, ambiguity as an essential quality of the lied.

On the threshold from the Romantic to the modern, this associative freedom appeared in a particularly radical form in the music of Gustav Mahler. The combination of free-standing and unmeant-for-one-another poems into single songs shows on the one hand his scepticism towards clarity of content, and on the other his artistic desire to make use of that supposed deficit.

In between stand two almost contrary exponents: Johannes Brahms, who more or less imposed his somewhat instrumental, particularly sensual, musical ideas on the texts (when I sing his lieder, concentrated in terms of both sound and form, I feel not like a viola player, but like the viola itself); and Hugo Wolf, who in his extremely developed skill at textual interpretation and clarification made music his servant, the servant of his textual declamation.

Other national schools of art song were established, particularly from the mid-nineteenth century, in the heyday of Romanticism. At that time the difficulties in form and content that Schubert had faced, and which in his wake continued to cast their inspiring shadow over German-language lied composition, ceased to be so heavy or significant. Thus, for example, Symbolist poetry opened up a wide range of free-floating, less contoured but of course no less intense or important forms of expression for composers such as Gabriel Fauré or Claude Debussy. On the other hand, the folk songs that had been collected for over a hundred years already became the chief source of inspiration for the English-language art song, and did not raise intense questions of form and content. Particularly impressive examples here might be Ralph Vaughan Williams's *Songs of Travel* or Benjamin Britten's *Folksong Arrangements*.

From the early twentieth century, following developments in lyric poetry, metaphorical concealment played an increasingly important part (e.g. Arnold Schoenberg's *Das Buch der hängenden Gärten*). Today we encounter such different approaches as Wolfgang Rihm's ideal prosody of old, conventional texts and the highly sensual, experimental works of Heinz Holliger, which pursue shades of meaning and extreme lived realities down to the tiniest detail. But these approaches are not in fact so far from each another: they are still unconditional exponents of a 200-year-long search for the meaning of sound in the interpretation of words.

HOLLIGER'S LUNAR LANDSCAPE

ZURICH, 25 MARCH 2018

> Wir falten dich und spalten dein Gesicht
>
> NIKOLAUS LENAU
(Heinz Holliger, *Lunea*, sixth leaf)
>
> We fold you and split your face

I am fortunate in my many connections with Heinz Holliger, who knows everything and can do everything, who is constantly moving forward and never misses a thing, and who certainly can conceive of idleness only in theory, perhaps from Goncharov's *Oblomov* or Haydn's song *Lob der Faulheit* ('In Praise of Idleness'). I see the way this Swiss polymath immediately took to me and encouraged me as the expression of a friendship that began at our first meeting, in Munich, at a performance of Britten's *Cantata Misericordium*. He took me forgivingly by the hand and told me it had been wonderful, even though I thought the opposite. That's how it's been ever since – I've made a mess of countless things for him, and his indulgence has been infinite, up to and including the first performance of his song-cycle *Lunea* in 2013 and the premiere of his opera of the same name five years later, both in Zurich. The songs are settings of late aphoristic texts by Nikolaus Lenau, which in their expressive radicalism and originality are reminiscent of Friedrich Hölderlin's much better-known fragmentary phrases. Holliger then incorporated the songs into his opera, where, according to him, they perform a similar function to the chorales in Bach's Passions: moments of reflection, of recognition, of generalising expression, but always freighted with emotional intensity.

In the two *Lunea* works my fearful heart was so terrified by the mere appearance of the notes on the page that I had to close the score immediately after opening it. Then, for my birdbrain, the premiere of the lieder was impossible without some practical adjustment – and here again Heinz Holliger was indulgent. And when it came to the opera itself, I refused in the end to sing most of the microtones in the manuscript because, after all, I've spent thirty years striving for precise intonation. That may be more understandable if one bears in mind the extent to which a singer's intonation is not only affected by the fundamental vibration of a sung note; the vocal colours of the articulated word, with their light and dark values, and the coloration of the voice itself, added for reasons of interpretation, change the shape of the sound and consequently the impact of its intonation. In addition, the vibrato's genuine, to some extent intentionally controlled, oscillations in intonation could do much to affect the reception and aesthetic classification of a deliberately 'wrongly' sung note.[1]

So I felt almost justified in not singing quarter-tones – until I was forced to admit that at a few points it was actually possible for me, within certain limits – for example in the beautiful Lenau sentence, 'Man grüßt Alte wie bald Abwesende' ('One greets old people as those soon to be absent'). Once again it was shamefully clear to me what a mind such as Holliger's is actually capable of doing and is willing to do, even though he himself holds that my anxiety was caused not least by the relationship with the overtone-rich orchestral sound, since on the tempered keyboard only the octave is in tune, and how in that case could one intuitively introduce micro-intervals correctly?[2] As if I didn't need to have before me the example of Holliger, who has immersed himself in all traditional listening and playing and perfected them and still, in spite of his having perfect pitch, shakes his head only briefly if a tuning is quite alien, and who can play 'against' the absolute memory of a note. As if he did not have to fight against his internal convictions and was even willing simply to sweep them aside out of curiosity – only for the moment, of course, because there is nothing to be lost. That became apparent to me time and again, when I was present at his performances of the music of Bach, Schumann and Zelenka, or when he was conducting symphonic music by Haydn and Mozart. One of my unforgettable memories was when he rehearsed

Mozart's *Masonic Funeral Music* in a new and unexpected way: he simply moved from one instrument to the next and made one finally and happily forget all the attempts always to turn Mozart into something new and special. Here again his mind, in response to the most traditional repertoire imaginable, showed a completely unspoiled freshness – all his skills seemed to have been dreamed up and discovered on the spur of the moment, while the style of Mozart's piece was still untouched. So I could have understood much sooner: the eternally expansive spirit loses nothing unless it stops seeking new things and seeking to make old things new.

Lunea, the opera, is divided into a prologue and twenty-three 'leaves from a life'. The aphorisms from the song-cycle are then scattered irregularly, sometimes set for several voices, and worked into the opera. One particularly impressive passage opened my eyes and granted me the simple, anxiety-free and open-minded understanding of a particular phenomenon: in Zurich, in the seventeenth leaf, my two colleagues, Sarah Maria Sun and Juliane Banse, sang with unfathomable precision and heart-stopping beauty. It was a seemingly endless passage in which their two voices wound around each another, slowly lifting the tessitura (the middle zone of the vocal range) in quarter-tones and glissandi, making one's head spin. Holliger said of this that the melodies and their meaning should, in the two 'constricted' vocal lines, squeeze themselves as it were through a needle's eye of sound. The director of our first performance, Andreas Homoki, found an exquisitely appropriate response to this in his staging: the women in Lenau's life, his long-term lover Sophie von Löwenthal, his current fiancée Marie Behrends and his sister Therese, sit on a sofa singing; behind them stand Sophie's and Therese's husbands, Max von Löwenthal and Anton Schurz, Lenau's first biographer. Now all five began slowly bending their heads left and right, synchronistically, thus demonstrating the non-standing-upright, non-unambiguous

Lunea, seventeenth leaf, Zurich. Seated, left to right, Juliane Banse, Sarah Maria Sun and Annette Schönmüller, with an extra and Ivan Ludlow behind them. Christian Gerhaher, as Lenau, stands on the right.

comprehensibility of what was being heard – in bending from the vertical they were denying themselves comprehension. Lenau, who was rocking his own personal history back and forth as he listened, was able to hear the sounds, but could find no meaning in them, though unable to escape them.

These acoasms – acoustic 'hallucinations' – are characteristic of the opera as a whole. They reflect Lenau's experience and torment him because he cannot find out what they mean. For me these passages, in their incessant spherical twists, are among the most fascinating in the entire opera, because they represent the disordered world of the tormented soul with such expressive richness and in such a hopelessly uncommunicable way, and yet reveal it to us with a sense of immediacy, even though it is universalised and translated into the medium of music. In the seventeenth leaf Lenau finally has to break off – with the palindromically treated sentence 'Dein Gesicht spalten wir und falten dich' ('We split your face and fold you').[3] It is a sentence central to this opera and to the character of Lenau, who speaks of the 'tear through my face', describing the effects of a stroke – the words also expressing the suffering caused by a splitting of the mind. From the first page of the opera this division is revealed as a main constituent element not only of its content but also of its form.

Holliger describes how the 'inkblots' of the doctor and poet Justinus Kerner, which found their way into Rorschach tests, visually influenced him.[4] They not only used symmetry and reflection as explanatory and meaningful in application, but they also produced a marked randomness in outcome. In Holliger's opera (and to a significantly lesser degree in his song-cycle), there are also repeated aleatoric moments, whole stretches that derive their curious beauty from the random auto-development of given motifs. One striking example of this occurs at the transition from the ninth leaf

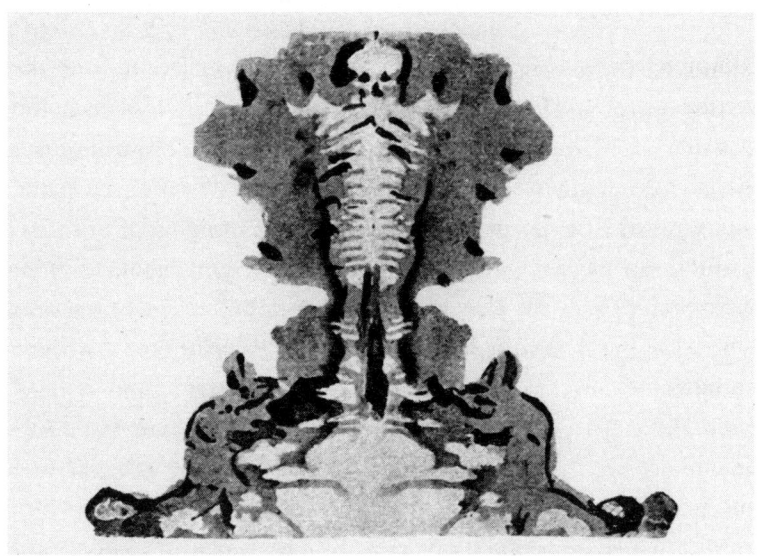

Justinus Kerner: *Todesbote*, from *Hadesbilder, Kleksographisch entstanden und in Versen erläutert* ('Den Hadesbildern noch zuvor / Erhoben aus der Tinte Nacht / (Mein Herz hat nicht an sie gedacht) / Die Todesboten sich empor' ('Even before the images of Hades / The messengers of death / (My heart did not think of them) / Rose up from the inky night')

to the tenth, where Lenau meets his former lover, Bertha Hauer, and what one has to presume to be their daughter. Here the chorus speaks the sentence 'Daß wir nicht beisammen sind bin ich selber schuldig' ('It is my own fault that we are not together'), broken down into single words and with syllables repeatedly overlaid, at the same time as the music of individual orchestral instruments is overlaid equally randomly. A ghostly scene that achieved throughout the rehearsals and the run of performances a relatively concise and ultimately not-at-all-aleatoric-seeming result – in spite of the random combination of given motifs.

Symmetry in the form of the mirror and the 'crab' has been around forever in the treatment of musical motifs, but can also be used as a form of musical time-reversal.[5] In his opera, based on the discontinuous, asynchronous experience of the suffering Lenau, jumping backwards and forwards, and even running in reverse, Holliger is attempting to play with time in music, and likewise, with his librettist Händl Klaus, to play with time in words, so the effect runs parallel in both music and libretto. That this does not entirely work, certainly not in a way that can be easily grasped, is not in fact disturbing, as it is covered anyway by the enigmatic experience of the psychopathic protagonist. In terms of literary history, the unfolding of this time-game is not blessed with nearly as much of a comparable tradition as is music: essentially it is almost only expressible as intention, since a palindrome is never perceivable without its reflection – whether in terms of sound ('schuldig' – 'gidlusch') or literal ('Grab' – 'barg', 'FEUER' – 'REUE[F]'), or sentences, words or anagrammatic fragments ('Wort' – 'oWrt') or of changes in meaning only through changes in emphasis ('Ge*bet*' – '*ge*bet'). In comparison with musical mirror images, the palindrome remains more a play of ideas – and it is used by Holliger and Händl Klaus less geometrically than in associative, fragmentary and kaleidoscopic ways. Musical mirror images, on the other hand, can be understood not necessarily intellectually but through the senses quite well.

For the opera libretto Händl Klaus used only words written by Lenau himself: letters, poems and of course fragments from the *Notizbuch aus Winnenthal*. He made virtuoso use of these sources to write an 'interior drama' – with all the palindromic and alienating verbal distortions having their origin solely in his and in Holliger's ideas. Furthermore they appear only in the main libretto, and were not used in the twenty-three interpolated songs. What impressed me most was the subtle treatment of Lenau's personal suffering – for me a counterbalance to the sensationalist, obscene presentation of Lenau in Peter Härtling's book *Niembsch oder der Stillstand: Eine Suite*. Händl Klaus is not setting out to inspire sympathy for his biographical subject, nor is he parading intimate suffering in a detached and voyeuristic way. He is concerned with the paradigmatic connection between soul torment and creativity – a theme that Heinz Holliger has addressed throughout his life (with reference to Hölderlin, Schumann, Robert Walser, etc.)[6] – and he is concerned with generalising private matters concealed in Lenau's life and writing. Händl Klaus manages not to stir the audience with a voyeuristic contemplation of a tormented individual, but instead to animate their associative reflections. Holliger views the resulting text so highly that he dignified it with these words: 'One might even say: the language is a character on stage.'[7]

As the focus on the discontinuous aspect of Lenau's life, the mirror concept – Holliger repeatedly speaks of Lenau's Janus-headedness with regard to his literary and human unpredictability – is taken in this opera to its limit, almost becoming a theme in its own right. Apart from the palindromes, the musical mirrors and 'crabs', it can sometimes be relatively fanciful. At the beginning of the seventh leaf, for example, the enigmatic text 'Wir falten dich / und spalten / dein Gesicht' ('We fold you / and split / your face') – the original of the reversal quoted above – is represented not only by the palindrome sung by the chorus, 'chid netlaf riw / netlaps dnu / tchiseg nied' (which would be translated: 'uoy dlof ew / tilps dna / ecaf ruoy'), but also associatively expressed by an almost synaesthetically mad musical structure: a horn sounds, and after the text is heard, there is a figure that is notated not in musical pitches but in weird vertical jagged lines. Holliger explained the figure to us as a graphic and musical representation of an electro-encephalograph reading, first of one hemisphere of the brain, then of the other.[8] Of course this cannot be perceived solely by listening, impressive as the orchestration sounds at the first hearing after the long rehearsal period with 'only' a piano.

Or: from the middle of the twelfth leaf everything goes backwards – even the headings of the leaves are printed in mirror writing in the libretto. And that was indicated by the staging as well: through the lighting of the stage and the colour of the costumes, play was made with the impression of a photo-optic negative as a symbol of complementarity, of reflection. And the wall that, in the first part, kept moving from right to left in front of the square area of the main stage to lead from one leaf to the next, from now on abruptly ran in the opposite direction, as an image of the symmetry around the middle of the opera.[9]

This and the fact that at the end of the twenty-second leaf Lenau sat down in the wing chair to die might almost give the impression that the opera now has a direction, that there is something resembling a plot, ending in the death of the protagonist. However, in my opinion that is not the case. In essence the structure of the opera is no different from that of Schubert's *Winterreise*. In that cycle from the first lied (*Gute Nacht*, 'Goodnight' – entrance, retrospect and prospect) to the last (*Der Leiermann*, 'The Hurdy-Gurdy Man' – open-ended conclusion) a frame is formed that admittedly indicates a sequence of events. But within that framework the individual lieder, as images along the way, actually do not claim a fixed place in this sequence. Similarly, Heinz Holliger left the order, the placing of the already existing lieder in the opera as a whole, entirely up to the librettist. Even so, the work has an arc that leads, over about a hundred minutes, from image to image, creating the impression of a substantial, quasi-traditional, operatic work.[10]

The anagrammatic title *Lunea*, concealing the name Lenau, is certainly an example of the multi-mirrored structure of the work, but it can also imply a resonance with the 'moonstruck' – *lunatic* – character of the protagonist and the world of his experience. I might add that in my opinion the moon (*luna*) appears in the work in another way related to landscape. In order to explain that, I need to go back a little: the diversity of intonation, the use of different kinds of microintervals, discussed above, is fundamentally characteristic of Heinz Holliger's work. In choral works (in conversation he refers to the choir as his actual, his core 'instrument') he even uses third tones.[11] Rhythmically, too, one can discern a similarly manic search for a subdivision in sound. He calls a rhythm of five (notes) against four (beats) the 'most natural', since virtually everyone has five fingers and toes on four extremities. In the song-cycle *Lunea*, in the fifth song (*Weit griff sein Schatten am Boden hin* – 'His shadow stretched far across the ground') he even writes quintuplets in the vocal line against 7/4 in the right hand on the piano and triplets in the left (see music example 11). In the sixteenth leaf of the opera there is a big triplet in the vocal line, the last quaver of which is tied with the last quintuplet-quaver (the quintuplet replaces the first two triplet-quavers) on the same note (see music example 12). According to my calculation the delay caused by singing this high E omitting this 'triplet-quintuplet-quaver', that is, by singing only four duplet quavers and a crotchet above the minim below, would be only a fortieth note. I told Heinz beforehand that it was impossible to sing it with such precision; he knew that (and still knows that), but he has evaded the issue. I, though, have the feeling his evasiveness reveals that the goal of his perhaps exalted-seeming notation is not mathematical precision in performance,

11 Heinz Holliger: *Lunea* (song-cycle), no. 5, bar 1

but a rhythm and style that arises out of insecurity and agitation caused by this apparently unnecessarily complicated notation.

This is similar to another pattern that occurs frequently in Holliger's work: a large triplet dotted on its first beat, which in my view seems much more energetic than for example the notation – easier to write and understand – of a crotchet followed by a small triplet over a semiquaver and a quaver. Or the frequent use of duplets or quadruplets, usually over three quavers of a 4/4 bar – objectively, this complication in performance is almost impossible for the

12 Heinz Holliger: *Lunea* (opera, piano score), sixteenth leaf, p. 150

listener to discern (see music example 13). I would describe these rhythmical finesses as Heinz Holliger's attempt to make life difficult for the singer – as difficult as life itself.

Surprisingly, there are also many unconventional rhythmical figures in Robert Schumann's settings of Lenau for solo voice, which then reappear in Holliger's work. For a long time Gerold Huber and I considered it impossible to programme the four *Husarenlieder* ('Hussar Songs'), op. 117, because of their over-enthusiastic militarism. But the hussar theme appears in Holliger's Lenau opera as a curious biographical detail – it seems that Lenau enjoyed dressing up as a hussar. So we took another look at Schumann's lieder and saw that they were musically strong and effusive, with something fascinatingly mad about them, something carnivalesque. They no longer struck us as militaristic so much as grotesque. And

13 Heinz Holliger: *Lunea* (opera, piano score), *Einklang (Nachwort)*, p. 9

14 Robert Schumann: *Husarenlieder*, op. 117 no. 4, *Da liegt der Feinde gestreckte Schar* ('There lies the enemy, strewn in piles'), bars 19–21

I find rhythmical peculiarities here in remarkable profusion: dotted triplets, for example, appear in the piano part of the *Husarenlieder*: over a basic pulse of 12/8 the dotted triplets are given a very unusual rhythmical counterpoint as if with a stress on the fourth or eighth beat. As a dialectical method, this recurs in Holliger in a generalised form – a lack of ambiguity is to be avoided (see music example 14).

15 Robert Schumann: *Lieder und Gesänge IV*, op. 96 no. 2, *Schneeglöckchen* ('Snowdrop'), bars 19–28

16 Robert Schumann: *Sechs Gedichte und Requiem*, op. 90 no. 6, *Der schwere Abend* ('The Oppressive Evening'), bars 1–9

Another example is the exuberant use of duplets or quadruplets against a fundamental triplet rhythm in the fourth *Husarenlied*, or in the second song of opus 96, the enigmatic *Schneeglöckchen* (see music example 15). *Der schwere Abend* (the sixth of the

Lenau-Lieder, op. 90) even combines both features. Here, in bars 1–6, Schumann overlays two melodic lines with duplets and dotted triplets, stripping both rhythmic figures of their clarity to such an extent that the vocal line can only hesitantly join in with the eruption of the triplets, in bars 7 and 8, with a lingering memory of the duplets. This is expressed by the attempt – probably only conceptual rather than singable – to transfer the stress from 'bang' to 'so' (see music example 16).

This rhythmical-dialectical play is also richly apparent in *Meine Rose*, op. 90 no. 2, in which I see other parallels with Holliger's opera: in bars 9, 22 and 45 there is a simply unsingable melisma – an unsingable distribution of a single syllable over several notes. Three demisemiquavers are attached to the first crotchet (followed by the fourth demisemiquaver over the next syllable); it is scarcely possible to perform this precisely, without *rubato*, within the quiet *legato* flow of this lied. In bars 9 and 45, a diphthong must also be accommodated within these three brief notes, further complicating matters. The second vowel sound of a diphthong simply cannot be sung on the final note – it needs to be the complete diphthong (see music example 17).[12] It is impossible; at least it is for me. (I cannot help making the last demisemiquaver too loud, as if accented, when I manage to accomplish vocalising the diphthong in the right way over this short note, because of the enormous effort required.) I can't remember ever managing to

17 Robert Schumann: *Sechs Gedichte und Requiem*, op. 90 no. 2, *Meine Rose* ('My Rose'), bars 8–10

do it. In my head, however, I do have a very clear idea of what it should mean and how it might sound to add a rapid *volte* quietly performed to this quiet lied.

This figure also appears in Holliger's Lenau opera, in the fifteenth leaf. In his grief over his friend Alexander von Württemberg, Lenau sings one more wonderful, particularly beautiful aphorism, which it would be worth adding retrospectively to the song-cycle: 'Bin ich eine Alpenlerche ode rein Kondor – ein singender Punkt am Himmel oder eine jauchzende Weltenkugel? Gehn wir oder fliegen wir nach dem Himalaja?' ('Am I an alpine lark or a condor – a singing dot in the sky or a rejoicing globe? Are we walking or flying to the Himalayas?') Here, on 'Alpen–', Holliger writes a very similar figure to Schumann's in *Meine Rose*. And yet because of the greater, more operatic expressiveness (and because, in this instance,

18 Heinz Holliger: *Lunea* (opera, piano score), fifteenth leaf, p. 146

of the absence of a diphthong) it is not as difficult to perform as in Schumann's lied (see music example 18).

But why does Holliger use the expression of naturalness (or 'the most natural thing of all') as an argument for what he does? Even his argument that language in its individual diversity, words in their phenomenological specificity, could be better represented by music that is not limited to semitones and bars made of crotchets, points in the same direction. I should however add that the experience of the limits of psychological extremity, which is the central theme of Holliger's opera, can be only inadequately represented by language, and that the intense experience of those suffering from psychological issues often cannot be captured in words.[13] But Holliger's representation of words through music, which far outstrips comparable works in its wealth of detail, is more than a symbol of the will. I feel this repeated fragmentation and complication runs counter to any classicistic vision of art or of the creative process.

I would compare works that correspond to such a vision of art with houses conceived and built according to the golden section. Their facades, divided by windows and floors, are placed in a formally defined relationship, and seem to present themselves expressively to a large extent by virtue of that fact.[14] Holliger's *Lunea*, on the other hand, strikes me as being entirely the opposite, and highly Romantic for that very reason. The singularity of each moment, in terms of thought and emotion, is not represented through immersion within a formal structure, but through the development of appropriate technical features. And the medium for this phenomenological bas-relief is just language. The finely wrought corners and curves of a collapsing Classical or neo-Renaissance building are treated with a big grater. Bits are broken off and broken up, roughened, bent and twisted until a manmade edifice turns into something approaching a work of nature.[15]

Lunea seems to me like a landscape seen under a magnifying glass. At first this landscape is – and here I return to my starting point – due to its daunting complication, repellent like the silvery grey moon, before unfurling into bluish-brown, even sometimes greenish-red, shimmering nature. The moon may remain silver grey, as embodied in the costume design (Klaus Bruns), set design (Frank Philipp Schlößmann) and lighting design (Franck Evin), congenially inherited from Homoki's first production, but as one approaches Holliger's lunar-landscape music more closely, the opera becomes more multiform, more gripping, more inspiring, more *colourful*.[16] But this colourful impression is rooted above all in the work's haunting instrumentation. The composer – again in line with his concept of the metamorphic-particular – describes it as being designed to prevent the listener from immediately being able to assign a sound to an instrument or a particular combination of instruments. Here, too, we have an attempt to avoid any conceptual lack of ambiguity.

Heinz Holliger's uniquely wide-ranging and profound knowledge acts on his artistic environment as a living reproach but also as an inexhaustible fountain of encouragement. Musical events organiser Tuula Sarotie in Helsinki once made the mistake of asking him, after a concert in which we had performed together, whether he could recommend an interesting post-war violin concerto. After three-quarters of an hour our weary faces were dropping into our midnight soup. He discussed countless works by composers I had never heard of, the duration of each one, where and when and by whom they had first been performed, what their stylistic peculiarities were and what practical difficulties they presented for performers – there was no end in sight. So it is scarcely surprising that, if we are looking for influences on his compositions, Holliger continually quotes not only the work of other composers, loved or even to some extent scorned, but also absorbs influences from poetry and science, etc. This is not eclecticism, where the composer's own creative work finds itself only in the constant recombination of alien material. Rather it is the joy in discoveries, a wealth of knowledge and the constant thrill of making connections that can be heard in his work.

Thus, in *Lunea* there are quotations from, for example, Schumann's *Lenau-Lieder*,[17] Liszt's *Nuages gris*, and the *Veni creator spiritus* from Mahler's Eighth Symphony.[18] In the eleventh leaf Holliger caricatures the styles of Swiss composers from the 1930s, and Lenau's fiancée Karoline Unger sings a parody (Holliger terms it a 'distortion') of Handel's *Lascia ch'io pianga*. Memories of Mahler's First Symphony are awakened in the twelfth leaf . . . and it is impossible not to think of Othmar Schoeck's *Notturno*, in which the fourth poem in the first movement, *Blick in den Strom* ('Gazing into the Stream'), is by Lenau:

Blick in den Strom
Othmar Schoeck: *Notturno*, first movement

Sahst Du ein Glück vorübergehn,
Das nie sich wiederfindet,
Ist's gut in einen Strom zu sehn
Wo Alles wogt und schwindet.

O, starre nur hinein, hinein.
Du wirst es leichter missen,
Was dir, und soll's dein Liebstes sein,
Vom Herzen ward gerissen.

Blick' unverwandt hinab zum Fluss,
Bis deine Tränen fallen,
Und sieh durch ihren warmen Guss
Die Flut hinunterwallen.

Hinträumend wird Vergessenheit
Des Herzens Wunde schliessen;
Die Seele sieht mit ihrem Leid
Sich selbst vorüberfliessen.

NIKOLAUS LENAU

If you saw a happiness expire
Never to be found again,
It is good to gaze into a stream
Where everything surges and vanishes.

O just gaze into it, gaze,
You will easily miss it
What, even if your dearest love
Has been torn from your heart.

Incessantly look down at the river
Until your tears fall
And see through their warm cast
The flood flow down.

As you dream away, oblivion
Will close the heart's wound;
The soul with its suffering
Sees itself flow by.

In the Schoeck setting, this poem ends with the most beautifully declaimed sentence that I can think of: 'Die Seele sieht mit ihrem Leid / Sich selbst vorüberfliessen' ('The soul with its suffering / Sees itself flow by'). The word 'vorüberfliessen' forms a spectacular conclusion to the almost 18-minute first movement, which begins quietly and remains quiet – and allows only a glimpse of temperament in an instrumental intermezzo. It ends with these quiet, slow lines, descends melodically more and more, until it disappears with a gleaming sonority, but even more quietly – like a downwardly inverted flageolet. In my view the slowness and the duration of the piece constitute its particularity. Schoeck has written so many lieder, so many beautiful lieder, especially to texts by Lenau. They are all, I think, significant, some entirely comparable with the ultimate Lenau work, Schumann's *Sechs Gedichte und Requiem*, like the *Elegie* for baritone and chamber orchestra. But for me one special charm of the *Notturno* is the mere duration of the movements, particularly of the first and third, demonstrating a defiance against coming to an end, as if rebelling against the inevitability of all lives' ending.

Ein Herbstabend[19]
Othmar Schoeck: *Notturno*, third movement
Heinz Holliger: *Lunea*, nineteenth leaf

Es weht der Wind so kühl, entlaubend rings die Aeste.
Er ruft zum Wald hinein: Gut' Nacht, ihr Erdengäste!

Am Hügel strahlt der Mond, die grauen Wolken jagen
Schnell übers Tal hinaus, wo alle Wälder klagen,

Das Bächlein schleicht hinab, von abgestorb'nen Hainen
Trägt es die Blätter fort mit halbersticktem Weinen.

Nie hört' ich einen Quell so leise traurig klingend,
Die Weid' am Ufer steht, die weichen Aeste ringend.

Und eines toten Freunds gedenkend lausch' ich nieder
Zum Quell, er murmelt stets: wir sehen uns nicht wieder!

Horch' plötzlich in der Luft ein schnatterndes Geplauder:
Wildgänse auf der Flucht vor winterlichem Schauder.

Sie jagen hinter sich den Herbst mit raschen Flügeln,
Sie lassen scheu zurück das Sterben auf den Hügeln.

Wo sind sie? ha! wie schnell sie dort vorüberstreichen
Am hellen Mond, und jetzt unsichtbar schon entweichen;

Ihr ahnungsvoller Laut läßt sich noch immer hören,
Dem Wandrer in der Brust die Wehmut aufzustören.

Südwärts die Vögel ziehn mit eiligem Geschwätze;
Doch auch den Süden deckt der Tod mit seinem Netze.

Natur das Ew'ge schaut in unruhvollen Träumen,
Fährt auf und will entfliehn den todverfall'nen Räumen.

Der abgeriss'ne Ruf, womit Zugvögel schweben,
Ist Aufschrei wilden Traums von einem ew'gen Leben.

Ich höre sie nicht mehr, schon sind sie weit von hinnen;
Die Zweifel in der Brust den Nachtgesang beginnen;

Ist's Erdenleben Schein? – ist es die umgekehrte
Fata Morgana[20] nur, des Ew'gen Spielgefährte?[21]

Warum denn aber wird dem Erdenleben bange,
Wenn es ein Schein nur ist, vor seinem Untergange?

Ist solche Bängnis nur von dem, was wird bestehen,
Ein Widerglanz, dass auch sein Bild nicht will vergehen?

Dies Bangen auch nur Schein? – so schwärmen die Gedanken,
Wie dort durchs öde Tal die Herbstesnebel schwanken.

NIKOLAUS LENAU

The wind blows coolly around, defoliating the branches,
It calls into the forest: goodnight, guests upon the earth!

The moon beams on the hill, the grey clouds chase
Swiftly across the valley, where all the woods lament.

The brook creeps down, faded groves'
Leaves being borne away, with half-choked weeping.

I never heard a spring sound so soft and sad,
The willow lines the bank, the soft branches wringing.

And remembering a friend deceased I listen down
To the spring, still murmuring: we won't see each other again!

Listen! Suddenly in the air a cackling chatter:
Wild geese fleeing winter's chill.

They hound, autumn behind them, with swift wings
They leave behind the dying on the hills.

Where are they? Ha! How quickly they pass
In front of the bright moon, and now vanish, already
    invisible;

Their foreboding sound can still be heard,
Stirring melancholy in the wanderer's breast.

Southwards migrate the birds, with hasty prattle;
But the south as well is covered by death with its net.

Nature sees the eternal in fidgety dreams,
Starts awake and wants to flee the death-filled spaces.

The torn call with which migrating birds soar
Is a confused dream's outcry of eternal life.

I can hear them no longer, they're already far away;
The doubts in the breast begin their nightly song:

Is life on earth only illusion – is it merely
An inverted Fata Morgana only, eternity's playmate?

But why then is earthly life getting scared
Of its doom, when it's just mirage?

Is such fear of what will persist
Only reflection that also its image does not want to pass?

This fear is but a shadow too? – so thoughts rave about,
As through the bleak valley the autumn mists waver.

For me, the other truly unusual thing about Schoeck's *Notturno* is the curious declamation realised most impressively in the third movement. While the first movement is divided relatively clearly, with two poems, followed by the big instrumental section and then another two poems, a permanent articulation develops throughout the third movement, drifting like the 'autumn mists' staggering in thoughts. A pessimistic metaphysical tirade, manic at its conclusion, is the result of an incessant argumentative inventory of the pointlessness observable in nature. Leaves fall, quiet and mute; birds flee the pointlessness; the stream mercilessly replies that everything is only ever a passing by and never a return. These terrible images follow each other relentlessly. They spill from Lenau's text exactly as they do from Schoeck's music, in a single outpouring, which, after nine minutes, plunges into an echoing silence of hopelessness and nothingness.

In Holliger, these two characteristics come together in the nineteenth leaf of the opera *Lunea*. In a work lasting only around a hundred minutes, of course, there cannot really be room for anything approaching Schoeck's lengthy exposition of the poem *Herbstabend*. But the choral voices, singing similarly almost without pause, fugally staggered and interwoven, produce on the one hand the impression of the most intense, unrelenting density of cause and expression (as in the third movement of the *Notturno*), and on the other an impression of timelessness, which, prompted by a 'dislocated' simultaneity of the text in the choral canon, comes close to the expansiveness of Schoeck's third movement – or is at least reminiscent of it. At any rate the librettist, in a gesture both tasteful and reassuringly beautiful, chose the same poem as Schoeck, which, with its acceptance of the universal earthly destiny of transience, introduces a sense of peace to this torment-driven opera, if only for a brief moment.

Otherwise, it is impossible to ignore the kinship of music and motif. Heinz Holliger does not deny these associations, but asserts

19 Heinz Holliger: *Lunea* (opera, piano score), second leaf, pp. 20–22

that they weren't introduced deliberately.[22] The 6/8 rhythm of the third movement of Schoeck's *Notturno* may contrast with a 4/4 beat in the nineteenth leaf of *Lunea*, but the way in which the suffering flows straight ahead in quavers gives the two pieces a very similar fundamental character. Because the quotation is not intentional, some of Holliger's motifs are not precise mirrorings, but they are unmistakably related to Schoeck's.[23]

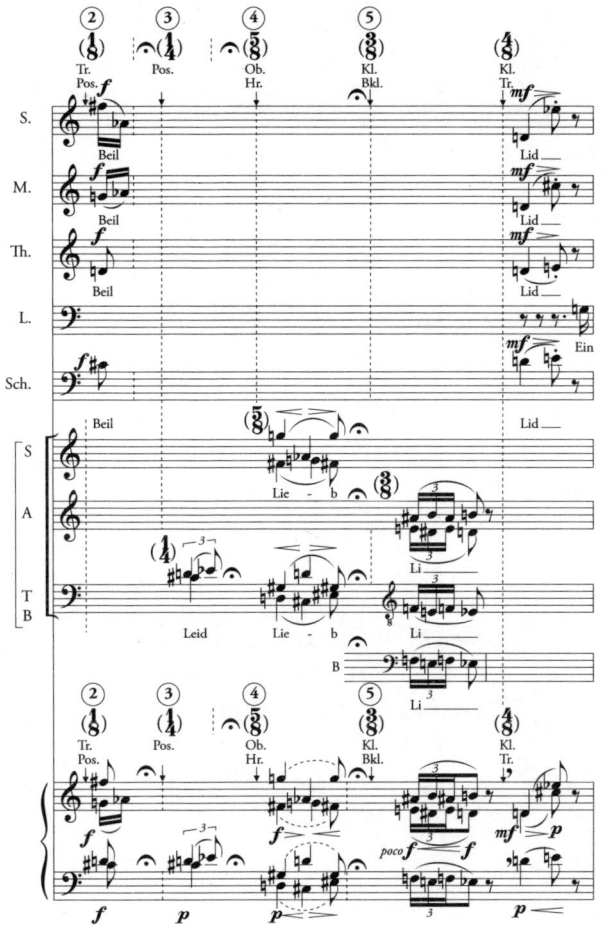

After suggestions of inner peace, there are moments of horror scattered through Holliger's very dense canon: the flow of serene melancholy is repeatedly disturbed by sudden explosions. The canon begins with only strings and choir, and almost entirely eschews melismas (several notes sung over a single syllable[24] – Schoeck's setting of the same poem avoids melisma completely). At first these moments contrast strongly, then push the choral setting more and more towards, with Lenau's unique experience, its fragmented post-stroke world, its less and less continuous, pathologically

20 Heinz Holliger: *Lunea* (opera, piano score), nineteenth leaf, p. 186

diachronic perception.[25] This occurs for the first time with the appearance of a crack in Lenau's world, which is already afflicted by syphilitic paralysis, in the second leaf (bars 8–9, most clearly in the chorus's soprano line): here the last three semiquavers of a crotchet rise to a high note that breaks off or falls downwards in a glissando (see music example 19). This striking motif, which defines the event, central to the opera, of the apoplectic 'crack', then appears obsessively and with increasing frequency in the nineteenth leaf,

21 Othmar Schoek: *Notturno*, third movement, last two bars before fig. 8

22 Othmar Schoek: *Notturno*, second movement, two bars at fig. 9

until after the massive corresponding bass passage on 'Vergessenheit' (Oblivion) when Lenau's experience of reality is expressed in these terms, shattering in their helplessness: 'lausch ich [–] wein ich' (see music example 20). We find a similarly 'crashing' motif in Schoeck's third movement, when the sudden chattering of the

23 Othmar Schoek: *Notturno*, second movement, final bar of fig. 11

wild geese frighten the listener with all the explosive power of a memento mori. It then recurs several more times (see music examples 21–23).

Heinz Holliger has spoken several times of his 'not uncritical' reverence for both the writings and the personality of Nikolaus Lenau. But the interweaving of the opera *Lunea* with Schoeck's *Notturno* – which I have described here, and which I find moving – shows me that Holliger too is in thrall, consciously or not, to the epistemological and ontological struggle towards the understanding and acceptance of transience, an aesthetic theme of Lenau's life, focused in Schoeck's *Notturno*.

For me, Holliger's use of a multiplicity of interweavings (of nature, soul, spirit, history) goes far beyond the illustrative or even the merely random. It is part of his far from apodictic nature (even though he sometimes expresses himself in harsh terms) that he does not wish to commit himself to provable regularities in his highly diverse material. Consequently, his fascination with all the sensually, intellectually and emotionally unique impressions available to a human being allows me to perceive the regression from culture to nature, from formal achievements and possibilities to a tonal exploration and a performative understanding of individual phenomena as anything but an abandonment. For me it is the expression of an Apollonian serenity and generosity, an affirmation of life utterly free of ego.

HOPE – LOVE – FAITH

MUNICH, 3 FEBRUARY 2017

Der Mensch

Empfangen und genähret
   Vom Weibe wunderbar
Kömmt er und sieht und höret
   Und nimmt des Trugs nicht wahr;
Gelüstet und begehret,
   Und bringt sein Tränlein dar,
Verachtet, und verehret,
   Hat Freude und Gefahr,
Glaubt, zweifelt, wähnt und lehret,
   Hält nichts und alles wahr;
Erbauet und zerstöret
   Und quält sich immerdar;
Schläft, wachet, wächst und zehret.
   Trägt braun und graues Haar.
Und alles dieses währet,
   Wenns hoch kommt, achtzig Jahr;
Dann legt er sich zu seinen Vätern nieder,
   Und er kömmt nimmer wieder.

                    MATTHIAS CLAUDIUS

Conceived and fed
   Wonderfully, by woman,
He comes and sees and hears
   And is not aware of the deceit;
He yearns and desires,
   And sheds the occasional tear;
Despised, and revered
   He has both joy and danger;
Believes, doubts, imagines and teaches,
   Holds everything and nothing to be true;
Builds and destroys
   And constantly torments himself;

> Sleeps, wakes, grows and feeds,
>   Has brown and grey hair.
> And all of this goes on,
>   If all goes well, for eighty years.
> Then he lies down with his forefathers,
>   Never to return.

Gerold Huber and I have only recently got to know Schumann's *Drei Gesänge*, op. 83, in its entirety. From our student days, we had performed only *Der Einsiedler* ('The Hermit'), one of only four solo lieder to texts by Eichendorff that Schumann wrote alongside the twelve famous songs of the *Liederkreis*, op. 39.[1] The evocation of peace and fear of God – or perhaps, more accurately, world anxiety – are incomparable. Many felt as if all of the motifs that run through the entire lyrical work of this poet seem to be given their ideal presentation and combination in this single song: nothing seems to be missing, from the wandering to the rustle of the forest, all in three quiet verses easily performed on the recital stage. And the singer's most mysterious interpretative tool – more than intonation, vocal colour, vocalisation, dynamics and rhythm (listed here in decreasing difficulty of comprehension) – namely vibrato, can be appropriately deployed here. At least that is the idea, because in practice there is much that is intended but that cannot be heard – perhaps it cannot be realised at all. At any rate, the use of vibrato in this song should ideally clarify the structure of the text, which is declaimed over the same musical verse three times and also demonstrates three times a comparable structure in terms of content – a real but exceptional advantage among strophic songs. On the other hand, I would tend to entrust concrete sensualisation of the words and their meaning to the simpler vocal tools: vocalisation, dynamics and colouring.

Der Einsiedler
Robert Schumann: *Drei Gesänge*, op. 83 no. 3

Komm, Trost der Welt, du stille Nacht!
Wie steigst du von den Bergen sacht,
Die Lüfte alle schlafen,
Ein Schiffer nur noch, wandermüd',
Singt übers Meer sein Abendlied
Zu Gottes Lob im Hafen.

Die Jahre wie die Wolken gehn
Und lassen mich hier einsam stehn,
Die Welt hat mich vergessen,
Da tratst du wunderbar zu mir,
Wenn ich beim Waldesrauschen hier
Gedankenvoll gesessen.

O Trost der Welt, du stille Nacht!
Der Tag hat mich so müd gemacht,
Das weite Meer schon dunkelt,
Laß ausruhn mich von Lust und Not,
Bis daß das ew'ge Morgenrot
Den stillen Wald durchfunkelt.

JOSEPH VON EICHENDORFF

Come, comfort of the world, you silent night!
How you climb from the mountains gently,
The breezes all are sleeping,
The boatman only, weary of wandering,
Sings across the sea his evening song,
To God's praise in the harbour.

The years like the clouds do pass
And make me here stand alone,
The world has forgotten me,
Then you came to me, amazingly,

> When I by the rustling forest here
> Was sitting full of thoughts.
>
> O, comfort of the world, you silent night!
> The day has made me so worn,
> The wide sea is already darkening,
> Let me rest from joy and hardship,
> Until the eternal light of dawn
> Comes sparkling through the silent woods.

In my imagination, the three heavy crotchet upbeats in the first, fifth and seventh bars (at the beginning of the poem's first, third and fourth strophes) require a deliberate use of vibrato – not least to keep the lied from sounding too much like a folk song. I often find folk songs, as they are generally performed, genuinely rather undifferentiated – detail and emotional subtlety are repeatedly homogenised, as if individuality were subordinate to the supposed protection of tradition, buoyed up by the prospect that the Lord will sort everything out in the end.[2] In Schumann, on the other hand, I think I can discern an attempt to achieve emotional honesty. Not least because of the piano's unconventional tremolo, almost frowned on in lied literature, which – surprisingly and contrary to all expectations – brings this lied to a close. *Der Einsiedler* does not have what it takes to be a folk song. In this lied every attempt to cancel and codify human adversity runs up against the disarming simplicity and clarity of the musical interpretation.[3] Here the same structural and interpretative precision can be applied three times, in a kind of meditative repetition, since the themes are strophic and also repeat line to line from verse to verse, as the stanzas represent variations of an isolated figure's complex of thoughts about night and comfort.

I now feel that the upbeat to each of the first two lines of each verse should vibrate extremely slowly, with a very narrow variation in pitch, almost like a non-vibrato seen through a magnifying glass.

That should immediately make it clear that nightfall is not only an image of the dimming of the speaker's own life, but at the same time a vivid event in itself – a celebration of sleep announcing itself. Hence the elevated expression of almost-not-vibrating, which, from a technical point of view, is actually a very restricted and controlled vibration.

This is very different from the third line of each stanza, in which the state in which the individual finds himself and with which he has come to terms is described: 'Die Lüfte alle schlafen' – 'Die Welt hat mich vergessen' – 'Das weite Meer schon dunkel' ('The breezes all are sleeping' – 'The world has forgotten me' – 'The wide sea is already darkening'). Paradoxically I find that these sentences, almost fatefully static, need a more agile upbeat, expressed in a rather unsettled, slightly faster vibrato. This is also due to the fact that the downward jump of a seventh (E to F) from the leading note to the main key's relative major, dominating the following five bars, requires a sufficient degree of vocal precision and definition; that can successfully be achieved only with a deftly sung upbeat. So Schumann has actually 'built it in', so to speak. On the other hand, the final upbeat, leading to the last three lines of each stanza, always establishes a connection to the individual, the self. The inverted paradox here would be a quiet oscillation of the leading note, and this too is implied by Schumann: the rising fifth at the beginning of the first line and the fall of a seventh in the third are now replaced by a simple whole-tone step. Perhaps these contrary ideas of the formation of the upbeat to the third and to the last three lines (I admit yet again that I might never plausibly succeed in achieving this) is also explained by the fact that in the third line the general state of affairs might seem static but is felt as a threat, and therefore vibrates uneasily, while on the other hand the last three lines of each stanza seek the solution within the self, bringing relief for existential distress, and therefore oscillate quite quietly on the upbeat.

It seems to me impossible to overlook the fact, however, that the yearning and foreshadowing of Eichendorff's *Der Einsiedler* is aimed not towards the universal – for example, a Catholic religious concept – but towards isolation. Perhaps Schumann feels the same, at least I hope he does. The art song as a musical incarnation of a poem in particular and of the lyrical in general cannot lead to communality but seeks embodiment in the singular. The person of the singer is of no interest, of course, but the individual uniqueness of the sounds his voice produces encapsulates the principle of the essential communicative language of an individual.[4] Hence *Der Einsiedler* is not a polyphonic, religiously unifying song, but the univocal paradigm of a human being – a human being who seeks expression and consolation in his solitariness, and entrusts both to art.

This song is the last in a row of three serious songs. It is a song that bears out the possibility of connecting simplicity of expression with meaningfulness – a pure and ideally successful strophic song. There cannot be many cases of such a poem, in which the structure of the lines is repeated twice, representing a threefold, almost trinitarian thought;[5] that seems like a meditation on transience and its resolution. And thus the lied can be an ideal depiction of the text. One might describe it as the ideal musical paraphrase of the underlying words.

Die Blume der Ergebung
Robert Schumann: *Drei Gesänge*, op. 83 no. 2

Ich bin die Blum' im Garten,
Und muß in Stille warten,
Wann und in welcher Weise
Du trittst in meine Kreise.

Kommst du, ein Strahl der Sonne,
So werd' ich deiner Wonne
Den Busen still entfalten
Und deinen Blick behalten.

Kommst du als Tau und Regen.
So werd' ich deinen Segen
In Liebesschalen fassen,
Ihn nicht versiegen lassen.

Und fährest du gelinde
Hin über mich im Winde,
So werd' ich dir mich neigen,
Sprechend: Ich bin dein eigen.

Ich bin die Blum' im Garten,
Und muß in Stille warten,
Wann und in welcher Weise
Du trittst in meine Kreise.

FRIEDRICH RÜCKERT

I am the flower in the garden
And must wait in silence,
To see when and how
You enter my circles.

If you come as a ray of sunlight,
I will quietly to your delight
Unfold my breast
And hold your gaze.

If you come as dew and rain,
I will capture your blessing
In bowls of love,
And not let it run dry.

And if you pass swiftly
Over me in the wind,
I will bend to you,
Saying: I am your own.

MUNICH, 3 FEBRUARY 2017

> I am the flower in the garden
> And must wait in silence,
> To see when and how
> You enter my circles.

When we return to the second of the *Drei Gesänge*, we see the necessity of setting more restless poems in a different way from the pure form of the strophic song. The middle lied, *Die Blume der Ergebung* ('The Flower of Submission'), can be seen as a version of the typical hybrid form of the art song, as a varied strophic song. The text, which, as in a number of Rückert's poems, might seem a little formal and dry, is brought wonderfully to life by the musical setting; all of a sudden it seems light and vibrant, even a bit humorous. And that is entirely in line with my sense that, compared with Rückert's relative unpopularity among readers, a disproportionately large number of his poems appear in the best musical settings.[6]

The first and last verses, with an identical text, constitute the frame within which the three middle verses unfold through contrasting variations. At first the connection arises out of the melodic mirroring of the first line of the song along a horizontal axis, but then three musically different illustrations of different states of mind appear. In their melodic uniqueness, they are each given a very specific depiction. The piano interludes formally separate them into distinct verses. At the same time a development occurs, extending from the second verse, which describes an erotic approach by the lovers, to the fourth, in which the relationship cools and turns into subordination. In between, the third verse – the middle two lines in the middle verse of the middle block and hence the middle of the work as a whole – contains the climax of the song: the depiction of the realisation of mutual fecundity: 'I will capture your blessing / In bowls of love'.

This verse too is a high point of innovative musical setting, in that important words or thoughts are stressed by being coarsened in the piano part, in an intensifying, unsettling or sensualising manner. This is, however, not affirmative in the sense of providing a concise meaning: I'm thinking of the massive bass trill under 'Kommst du' ('You come') and the carousel-like accelerating semiquaver triplets under 'Ihn nicht versiegen lassen' ('And not let it run dry'). As a method, this break with the underlying semiquaver structure is reminiscent of similar passages in *Requiem*, op. 90 no. 7, with its triplets and quintuplets.[7] Between these two passages there is one of the most beautiful and most sensual vocal phrases that I know. Separated from the rhythmical structure of the lied – even in the piano the clear three-crotchet focus is partially blurred – this is in every sense the middle, central sentence (of the verse, of the poem, of the work as a whole). 'So werd' ich deinen Segen / In Liebesschalen fassen' ('I will capture your blessing / In bowls of love') is able to expand freely in a declamatory and agogic way. It is as if between the two framing lieder, which both in their different ways express resignation – the first to the impossibility of terrestrial love; the last to the impossibility of earthly peace in solitude – there is a chance of happiness in this world: the ephemeral illusion of meaningful procreation. In this sense the *Ergebung* ('submission') of the title could be viewed more as impatient waiting than as surrender to fate.

This impatience, incidentally, is given an exquisite evocation when, in the closing verse, which repeats the opening text unchanged, the last line, 'Du trittst in meine Kreise' ('You come near to me'; literally, 'You step into my circles') is not presented in the subdominant as it is in the first verse but as a (dynamically emphasised) sequence in which the tonic, extended to a seventh chord, appears before being resolved into the subdominant for the repeat of the first two lines of the poem. This impatience is no longer related to the arrival of the lover, but to perfection in shared offspring. But in the nature of 'submission', it must calm itself auto-suggestively, and that is the reason why the first two lines of the poem reappear – *pianissimo*: not to represent peace, but to compel, to demand peace. This attitude of disciplining oneself also extends to the musical composition, when the last word of the second line, 'warten' ('wait'), has a duration of three beats, not just a crotchet as in the first verse and in the concluding reprise. I do not choose to see this as a melodic broadening towards the end of the lied – as a meticulously composed *ritardando* anticipating the piano postlude – but as an instruction, annotated in the *pianissimo*, to remain calm. So it is not a relaxed, fading *pianissimo*, but a forced and sustained withdrawing of the self, against itself and the desire that lies within the essence of the lyrical 'I'.

Resignation
Robert Schumann, *Drei Gesänge*, op. 83 no. 1

Lieben, von ganzer Seele,
Lieben herzinniglich,
Daß nimmer ich's verhehle,
Heiß lieben muß ich dich!
Wie's kommt? wie kann ich's wissen?
Wohl höher schlägt mein Herz.
Wenn deine Augen grüßen:
Gehst du, erbebt's im Schmerz,
Erbebt im heißen Glühen,
Im still verschwiegnen Rausch,
Und Tränen überziehen
Den Blick im Wechseltausch.
Lieben, von ganzer Seele, muß ich dich!

Du wirst mich nie umschließen,
Nie wird dein Aug' mir glühn!
Der Sehnsucht still Vermissen
Wird nie dich zu mir ziehn!
So hoffnungslos mein Lieben?
Gewiß! doch trostlos nicht!

Will Gegenwart nicht trüben,
Zukunft? kenn' ich ja nicht!
Will auch der Trennungsstunde
Schmerz düster mich umwehn,
Lächle mit bleichem Munde:
Jenseits ist Wiedersehn!

> JULIUS BUDDEUS

To love, with all my soul,
To love fondly from the heart.
May I never make a secret of it,
I must love you passionately!
How does it come? How can I know?
Higher beats my heart
When your eyes are greeting:
When you go, it trembles with pain,
It trembles in a hot glow,
In silently concealed ecstasy,
And tears are overlaying
The gaze in change-exchange
Love you with all my soul I must!

You will never embrace me,
Never will your eye glow for me!
The yearning's quiet missing
Will never draw you to me!
So hopeless my love?
Certainly! But not bleak!
Do not want to spoil the present,
The future? I don't know it!
And does the parting hour's pang
Want to dimly swathe around me?
Smile, pale-mouthed:
Beyond there is meeting again!

Finally, the beginning of opus 83, in which the unique quality of Schumann's treatment of the text is absolutely clear. Nikolaus Harnoncourt once said, during rehearsals for Schumann's *Das Paradies und die Peri*, with his inimitably convincing, yet apodictic illusionary powers, that there must have been one person genuinely pleased when Schumann died in 1856 – Richard Wagner, by then the only composer left who could give vocal music and music theatre a new kind of the words' sounding declamation.

The instruction above the song reads, 'Not quickly, freely performed'. In my view this applies not only to the first six bars but to the whole lied, with the exception of more formal passages such as bars 18–23 and 35–8. I would see the *forte-piano* (*fp*), which recurs twelve times up to the first double bar after bar 17 (the end of the first verse) as a musical correlative of this instruction – it is a highly unusual and striking accretion of this particular dynamic marking. An *fp* is not a purely dynamic accent; because of its lengthy extension over time I believe it to have an agogic value. Giving a phrase an initial energy that slowly ebbs away is expressed not only in diminishing volume but also, each time it occurs, in a subtle slowing of the tempo, which draws attention to itself through dynamic effect. This is certainly true in this lied, in which these revitalisations (apart from once, in bar 4) never happen simultaneously in the piano and voice parts. Instead they generally appear either in one part or in the other, and are often laid over each other – for example, in bar 15: first the voice has the *fp* and then, two beats later, when its intensity is already declining, the piano. So this is plainly not a matter of always giving precedence to the voice, its volume making it dominant over the sound of the piano. Rather it is repeatedly submerged in a complex of sound; it melds with the piano without any claim to acoustic hegemony, despite every effort to enunciate the words. Here the consonants and the intelligibility of the articulated text in general are – extremely progressively, pioneeringly – tried out in utmost reduction. This strikes me as a conscious admission that the meaning is not carried only by the musical structure or the words that have been set, but by the resulting sound: the meaning of a sung word is not conveyed only by linguistic articulation but by the immersion of the particular aural quality of the word into a totality of sound.

Beginning with Schubert, who provided particularly few dynamic instructions for the singing voice, an approach that has been accepted as almost universally valid was established, with the voice following the dynamics for the piano. I think that's a fairy tale. What is being indicated here – balance of sound as a supreme commandment – does not truly correspond to a sonically and semantically open concept of the lied. As if the meaning of a work of art could be produced so clearly! Here I am happy to acknowledge that all my efforts to pin down the meaning of lieder, as documented in this collection of essays, are in the end experiments that often only turn the seemingly obvious characteristic of one work or another into more of a problem. Gerold Huber and I attempt to replace this 'Schubert' convention – that the singer must dynamically follow the instructions for the piano when, as is almost always the case, there aren't any for the vocal line – which is basically a simplifying method used by teachers, with a quest for a sound appropriate to the context, as far as reality allows.

In *Resignation* the agogical exhaustion of the individual *fp* instructions, which accumulate through the whole of the first part of the lied up to the first double bar, continues until in its middle part it finds a completely new, slower tempo. So the initial energy gets simply lost during the first part. This could be achieved with other, more conventional means. But here the prehistory of a one-sided love is given vivid form: in the ebbing of musical energy, parallel to the muting of amorous enthusiasm, for a single metaphorical *forte-piano*.

The next phase of resignation (bars 18–24, the first four lines of the second verse) can then spread through the suddenly ponderous semiquaver figures with a very idiosyncratic sense of oppressive realisation. The rhythmical structure of the piano setting in these bars has already appeared in a similar form in bars 9–12, although still impulsively, but then, following the spectacular word *Wechseltausch* ('change by exchange'), it effectively robs itself of its power. The poet probably intends the word to imply only a switch from good to bad, from duped (*getäuscht*) to disappointed (*enttäuscht*). But the second part of the word (*-tausch*) prompts the idea of a dialectical interrelationship between the two poles similar to that at the conclusion of the poem. Schumann's melodic development eloquently expresses this when the power of the vocal line actually runs out with 'Und Tränen überziehen / Den Blick' ('And tears obscure my gaze'), and then 'im Wechseltausch' ('in change-exchange') is added as an explanatory bonus. In vocal terms the switch of mood can be realised particularly effectively if the first part of the phrase is still vibrating normally, while the last two quavers ('Wechsel–') introduce a vibrato with breath support (in order to avoid becoming too weak) that concludes this first part with a new colour redolent of resignation.[8]

After the middle part, with its recognition that this love is not mutual, there are several bars of recitative. The dynamics in bars 25–30 seem musically special to me: first a *pianissimo* as an expression of the nadir of the song ('So hoffnungslos mein Lieben? Gewiß!' – 'My love so hopeless? Certainly.'), then a small crescendo to *piano* ('Doch trostlos nicht!' – 'But not comfortless.'). But this is followed by a repetition of the text, probably for purely musical reasons, in order to support the form generated by the text and its meaning. Here, though, the antithesis 'hopeless [. . .] not comfortless' is not reflected in the dynamic. It turns out that the direction of the lied is a peculiar one, that it does not simply follow the text. And here a development in the through-composed lied, the third classic form of the art song, becomes clear: in this form it cannot be only a matter of composing 'with the text'. Ideally, even through-composed lieder are not freely rhapsodising forms but, rather, have their own individual rules and formal structures.

It might seem a trivial matter, but this is the reason I refuse to encourage the acquisition of a universal singing technique and to use vocalises – vocal lines consisting mainly of vowel sounds – to train the voice in such a way that challenging tribulations occurring in the vast repertoire are no longer too difficult or come as a surprise. I prefer training with the pieces to be performed in order not only not to call the individual identity of those pieces into question, but to do them justice as far as possible, hence avoiding putting technical generalisations in the way of the realisation of specific idiosyncratic sounds and imposing a homogenous vocal quality on what are fundamentally distinct, discrete lieder.

Finally, in the last six lines, the resolution of the poem becomes apparent: earthly disappointment (the present) cannot be healed, and what the future brings cannot be intuited.[9] In passing: the way in which this is musically articulated I can describe only as perfectly realised declamation: the question 'Zukunft?' ('The future?') as a slow, rising, slightly tightening line, is answered after an extendable pause that embodies reflection, as if with a dismissive gesture, relaxing melodically downwards: 'kenn' ich ja nicht!' – 'I don't know it!' These words are almost spoken on the note, without vibrato (not to be confused with non-vibrato, which requires an effort), a sonic statement that is not song so much as speech. At any rate, the promised consolation is in the afterlife, towards which the death-pale lips smile on the lifelong deathbed. The eternity, the eternal present that is the future of the subject and in which the better past, namely unclouded love, can live and be lived out. This ending thus realises the dialectic hinted at in the 'Wechseltausch' of the first verse.

The power of three recurs frequently in this short song-cycle: as a dialectical threefold step of present–future–past in the first lied, *Resignation*; in the triangular form of the varied strophic song in the middle lied, *Die Blume der Ergebung*; and as a hinted trinity in the three verses of the closing piece, *Der Einsiedler*. Perhaps one could in fact interpret the composition of this cycle to the point where this triadic idea is even fundamental to the overall structure. Then we could speak of a triptych of existence: in the through-composed first lied we find love and being; in the modified strophic second lied, procreation and becoming; and in the strophic third lied, transcendence and having-been. This would extend the temporal triplicity of the first lied to the work as a whole. Even if the development present–future–past is not as obviously goal-oriented as the simplification of the lied form from the first song to the third (unless we see the past as an eternal return of earthly existence once it has come to an end), this little cycle could claim to be something approaching a depiction of human existence. At any rate it would not be a random collection of variably beautiful songs.

RIHM AND GOETHE:
BUILDING A PROGRAMME

WEIMAR, NOVEMBER 2018

Aber den Einsamen hüll
In deine Goldwolken,
Umgib mit Wintergrün,
Bis die Rose wieder heranreift,
Die feuchten Haare,
O Liebe, Deines Dichters!

JOHANN WOLFGANG VON GOETHE,
Harzreise im Winter, lines 60–65

But wrap the lonely one
In your clouds of gold,
Encircle with ivy
Until the rose matures again,
The damp hair,
O Love, of your poet!

In the first recital Gerold Huber and I ever performed together, Schumann's *Dichterliebe* was the only work. Ever since our second joint performance, however, we have tried to come up with coherent overall conceptions for lieder recitals. If we ignore rarities such as Ernst Krenek's *Reisebuch aus den österreichischen Alpen* ('Journey through the Austrian Alps'), which consists of 24 lieder, the privilege of singular splendour goes almost solely to Schubert's *Winterreise*. Even the special relationships between Wilhelm Müller's 25-part sequence of poems *Die schöne Müllerin* and Schubert's setting of 20 lieder or between Tieck's novella and its setting in Brahms's *Die schöne Magelone* call for serious thinking about the best way to present these works in performance.

This is no minor undertaking, as the selection of lieder – their tiny individual formats and the context produced by their combination – is an essential part of the interpretation, not unlike the selection and hanging of paintings by the curator of an exhibition. Of course, over time, techniques, habits and aversions creep in.

For example, I have become aware that programmes based around similar content or mere assemblage are becoming ever more alien to me, and I actively rather dislike them. Musical motifs and symbolic connections tend to get lost: given programmes with titles such as 'Flowers, Blooms and Blossoms' or 'All about Sheep and Duckponds', the content on offer doesn't usually mean much to me.

I also realise that the three lied composers I consider the most important – Schubert, Schumann and Mahler (and finally I was glad to find a kind of mature respect and equal love for Brahms's songs as well) – require my utmost respect: I could never combine them in a single recital and perform them side by side. Their idiom and habitus are too idiosyncratic. They would not enrich each other but rather get in each other's way, even if we bear in mind how closely they are connected, and how tempting it might be to combine them. Schubert and Schumann differ only in degree in terms of the weight and relative autonomy they accord the piano part, and in the new importance given to prelude, interlude and postlude. Schubert and Mahler both lean towards folksong and the artfully musically reconstructed sounds of nature. Here again the difference is only one of degree. With the later two, Schumann and Mahler, the relationship with Schubert is obvious: a deliberate, almost epigonal development of the genre of the art song, which had, effectively, only just been invented. But uniquely – I can't say this of any other lied composer – the two are connected through the development of the art song away from mere pleasantness to a quest for meaning, from the accidentally and contingently entertaining to a substantial and compelling discernment. They are united in their radical claim to artistic freedom in setting poems to music in this way, to this end, practically behind and stretching them and thus turning a sound into a postulate.

I can find only some of the programmes that Gerold Huber and I assembled and performed over thirty years, and I haven't kept count of them. I have fond memories of some, for example our various *Schwanengesang* arrangements or 'Vienna Schools', when we combined Beethoven's *An die ferne Geliebte* and Schoenberg's *Buch der Hängenden Gärten* with a few lieder by Haydn to both German and English texts, Berg's *Altenberg-Lieder* and in conclusion Beethoven's *Adelaide*. Or a programme of folk songs: Haydn's lieder for piano trio and voice, which he wrote – back again in Austria – for various London publishers without access to the texts, only to the melody of the folk songs. The poems were added later in London. Fritz Wunderlich made inimitably beautiful recordings of these trio lieder to poems by Hermann Löns, so we thought we could perform them in the same format, as a homage to perhaps the greatest singer of all time. We added to this selection some of Britten's *Folksong Arrangements* for piano and voice, Shostakovich's Second Piano Trio with its quotations from Jewish folk music, and in conclusion – once again for violin, cello, voice and piano – English-language folksong arrangements by Beethoven. (It was important to me to maintain my distance from Brahms's concept of folksong, which strikes me as a bit overly sentimental, even kitsch.) I have a particular memory of some programmes containing lieder only by Schubert (one of these was issued as a CD, entitled *Nachtviolen*), and finally many exclusively Schumann recitals, which Gerold Huber and I conceived primarily as part of our plan to perform the entirety of Schumann's lieder and by doing so to get to know them inside out. We also wanted to achieve our life's ambition, a recording of all the Schumann lieder, without it becoming a hotchpotch of rehearsed material and sight-reading.

For many years, apart from our pleasure in devising new programmes, creating largely new combinations, not just incorporating freshly learned songs, there was also the thrill of a bet: whoever weighed less at the turn of the millennium would claim a case of champagne from the other. I was far ahead for years, but in the end I lost the wager. Two years later I was the first to give up smoking completely and I became a father – dams were beginning to break. Gerold Huber said he would eventually give up cigarettes, and then the extent of our pollution would be restricted to the visual. He did it too, quite often in fact, just like Mark Twain, who said giving up smoking was easy, he'd done it hundreds of times. After my last and final cigarette, I was left – to quote Goethe's *Harzreise im Winter* – with 'overflowing measure'. The fact that most good singers – this was my impression, my anchor, my hope – weigh rather more than strictly necessary is simply inexplicable to me for physiological reasons: the fatty tissue does vibrate as well, just not in a way that noticeably affects the frequency of the notes being sung.

The last word on the subject was spoken by a Berlin critic after a lieder recital in December 2018. He rightly praised Gerold Huber as incredibly wonderful (for example I could never tire of listening to his six perfect quick yet soft turns in Schubert's *Lachen und Weinen*, D. 777). The critic didn't think I was that good – and that was fine too. But my performance that evening did make me stop and think. It was the sixth concert of a tour involving a lot of travelling; it was probably the longest programme we had ever performed, and because of a change in repertoire in Berlin we needed to schedule extra exhausting rehearsals on the day of the concert. So perhaps my voice was a little tired – of course critics and the audience can't know that, and neither do they need to. But that rationalisation didn't make things any easier, because I'm the one responsible for the conception and practicability of an evening. But you don't need to bring the house down every time; every performance is different and not one is perfect. Sure, but this time I decided once again to follow Gerold Huber's maxim: because it's somehow nonsense not to read any reviews at all, he thinks it's a good idea to read only the good ones.

However, this particular review took a turn for the better as far as I was concerned. Gerold Huber is a passionate jogger, football player, even marathon runner, while I've always hated sport, indeed movement of pretty much any kind. I think that if life can be made bearable only by tormenting yourself running, bending, stretching and sweating, then I can manage without that kind of bearability. In principle, addiction to physical activity is no less problematic than my addiction to those wonderful cigarettes. The review spoke of Huber's 'baroque appearance',[1] and I was described as 'ascetic' in comparison. 'Asceticism' really does describe me to a T: if I manage to abstain from Gummy Bears; if I'm in the supermarket and I heroically walk past one of those beautiful one- or two-kilo plastic boxes containing the brightly coloured little animals, dummies, cherries or devils with a cool smile on my face, then I'm Siddhartha to the life. So I must say that in the most scathingly accurate review of a performance there is also usually a morsel of consoling truth.

So I'm constantly working on these things, just as I constantly have to rethink *Winterreise* and *Dichterliebe*, contexts and assemblages – as I have to reconsider my relationship to sweets and beer.

A few years before the Berlin event, in 2012, I met the composer Wolfgang Rihm at the award of the Siemens Music Prize. He said I should sing something by him again. In fact until then all I had sung of his were the *Hölderlin-Fragmente*, first as a student in my home town of Straubing, actually in his presence, and the short *Stilles Stück* (for baritone and eight string instruments). I had had to withdraw from a performance of the *Wölfli-Lieder* in 2001 because of illness. Then I asked him, without really thinking about it, what he thought of setting the *Sturm-und-Drang* hymns of Goethe (his genius era) that Schubert had left unset. He answered that he liked to choose his own texts, but in fact *Harzreise im Winter* ('Winter Journey in the Harz') arrived through my letterbox two or three weeks later. The first performance didn't occur until two years later, at the Würzburg Mozart Festival in May 2014, and then it was far from straightforward. We finally managed to make it possible, almost forced it to happen, squeezed in between two *Don Giovanni* performances in Frankfurt. I was a little ill at ease with this very difficult work, and perhaps my voice had been affected to some extent by *Giovanni*. In addition, the Imperial Hall of the Residenz in Würzburg is somewhat overwhelming as a building, and it also has too much reverberation – every sound seemed to overlap and blur at the edges. Then Gerold Huber's page-turner kept turning too quickly. A lot of things didn't go as we would have wanted – and as Wolfgang Rihm would probably have wanted as well. Later we had better luck with the piece, and I have good memories of the two most recent performances, at the MelosLogos Festival in Weimar in 2014 (which is also where we gave the first performance of Rihm's *Tasso-Gedanken* in November 2018) and in Munich at the Bavarian Academy of Fine Arts. That last performance was part of a lecture recital with all of Goethe's hymns thus far set as lieder: Schubert's *An Schwager Kronos*, *Ganymed*, *Prometheus* and the first fragment of *Mahomets Gesang*, as well as Rihm's *Harzreise im Winter* and Gerold Huber's *Seefahrt*.[2] Wolfgang Rihm was present in person, and that evening, luckily, it was only Schubert's *Ganymed* I messed up, not Rihm's work.

Goethe's *Harzreise im Winter*, impenetrable at first sight, is about an episode in his life – a kind of pilgrimage to his own roots and the prospect of his future life at the end of his 'genius' period before he took up his responsibilities at the Weimar court. The comfortably established poet leaves a hunting party and finds himself in immediate danger: he turns away from the security of the path to climb the snow-covered Brocken, the location of Walpurgisnacht. And he sympathetically follows in the steps of the unfortunate imitator of Werther, Friedrich Plessing, who had degenerated into a world-hater.[3] Here we see the fundamental theme of this last and perhaps least demanding, least radical of Goethe's dithyrambic hymns (one can sense his estrangement from *Sturm und Drang*): it is love that shall now reconcile happiness and suffering. The journey ends at the summit of the Brocken, and the promising view becomes the occasion for and expression of euphoric thanks.

This curiously spontaneous journey puts one in mind of a purifying path. Goethe himself spoke of a 'cure' to which he subjected himself and also proposed to Plessing.[4] I now see this journey as being captured in an ideal form by Wolfgang Rihm's setting: no longer as in a lied, almost more as in a cantata, with narrative and dramatic elements merged with meditative qualities, entirely in the service of illuminating the text – a highly sensual illumination, however, more or less as a fulfilment of Goethe's proposition: 'Wem die Natur ihr offenbares Geheimniß zu enthüllen anfängt, der empfindet eine unwiderstehliche Sehnsucht nach ihrer würdigsten Auslegerin, der Kunst.' ('Should nature begin to reveal her obvious mystery to someone, he will feel an irresistible longing for her most worthy interpreter, art.')[5] Goethe's nature, then, interpreted by Rihm's art.

Wolfgang Rihm: Harzreise im Winter
(first verse)

Dem Geier gleich,
Der auf schweren Morgenwolken
Mit sanftem Fittich ruhend
Nach Beute schaut,
Schwebe mein Lied.

JOHANN WOLFGANG VON GOETHE

Like the vulture who,
On heavy morning clouds

Resting with soft wing
Seeks his prey,
Float my song.

To my mind, Rihm's elevated, metaphysical tone, beginning with the almost pure melody in the prelude, makes him stand out among his contemporaries. This melody is repeated and the seemingly endless vocal line stretches across the whole of the first verse. Rihm is demonstrating what *legato* can mean in song: not a chain of sounds technically placed one after the other in the right order and held in place by superglue but rather a malleable stretch of diverse sound – an idea connected by content. A stretch that consists of individual vowel sounds that in turn separate and define themselves through consonants, by the ends and beginnings of words. It is a dialectical play of broad, dark vowels and short, sharper consonants, all grouped around the underlying meaning of the text and in the service of a self-explanatory language of sound.

Wolfgang Rihm: Harzreise im Winter
(last verse)

Du stehst mit unerforschtem Busen
Geheimnisvoll-offenbar
Über der erstaunten Welt
Und schaust aus Wolken
Auf ihre Reiche und Herrlichkeit,
Die du aus den Adern deiner Brüder
Neben dir wässerst.

JOHANN WOLFGANG VON GOETHE

You stand with bosom unexplored
Mysterious and revealed
Above the astonished world
And look from clouds
Upon their realms and magnificence
Which from the veins of your brothers
You water nearby.

Goethe's pantheistic tone[6] runs through Rihm's work. It peaks in the inspired view from the summit of the Brocken across the lower mountains of the Harz range, stretching ahead of Goethe, already opened up by mining, just as the *vita activa* as a State's Councillor lies before him, replacing the contemplation of his own genius with mundane, real activity. Present throughout the whole poem is the openness of lyrical thought, which can gather together many different elements but then release itself once more into the freedom of intellectual diversity, divorced from meaning. (Plessing's journey here is also a depiction of the nature of the poem: 'Ins Gebüsch verliert sich sein Pfad, / Hinter ihm schlagen / Die Sträuche zusammen' – 'His path disappears into the undergrowth, / Behind him / The bushes crash together.') What astounds me is Wolfgang Rihm's almost unique ability to transpose this lyrical openness into music by leaving the end of the lied, with two terse concluding chords, just as open as Goethe's vista: eleven bars without a single pause and breath end in a happy, relieving inhalation of breathless ecstasy – an evocation of the breathlessly celebrated experience that even pantheism does not exclude a personal sense of the Divine (see music example 24).

Four years later this was followed by a new song-cycle, Wolfgang Rihm's four *Tasso-Gedanken* ('Thoughts on Tasso'). They are not a chronological distilling of Goethe's tragedy, the first drama in world literature about a poet and in effect a psychopathogram of the artist. I had long been surprised that no musical adaptation existed of this particular work, as it is such promising material, for music makes practically everything usable at some time or another. Goethe's work is a drama of words, a conversation, and for that reason it admittedly might not desperately cry out to be staged in the theatre. It might be considered more as a drama to be read – Goethe himself thought so, and for the late Weimar premiere he wrote a more performable version. In spite of the non-chronological text selection, which denies any approximation of dialogue, Rihm does not allow us to forget that these *thoughts* unfold in a structure akin to drama: we recognise psychological developments of a kind that seldom exists in a poem, the usual textual foundation of an art song.

That applies, for example, to the third lied, when Tasso's thought advances rhapsodically in recitative-like declamation, expressed in the volatile disposition of dynamism and rhythmic emphasis. It also applies to the replacement of neurotic, hypochondriac, indeed misanthropic, irresolution in the second lied with Tasso's ingenious text on the metamorphosis of the silkworm, which spins itself 'to death' in its cocoon (implying the end of one way of life, before the same creature transforms from pupa into moth). In the fourth lied Tasso finally recovers from what he himself sees as the catastrophic misstep, returning to rational, no longer self-referential, accounts, such as that of the shipwreck and the reorientation that it rendered necessary – even though, given the artist's mental incapacity with regard to the demands of everyday life, this is barely conceivable.[7]

The four Rihm *Gedanken*[8] are neither a summary of all the motifs in Goethe's play nor even a precis of its plot. Rather, the composer has been at pains to remove any dialogue and, where reference to another character is implied, to remove those words and phrases – in my view to re-emphasise the brilliant artist's struggle for life and creativity as the theme of the musical work. Rihm put the two crucial dramatic developments, the only authentic ones that are not only recognisable through words and thoughts, as a frame around the imagination of Tasso's existence and poetic reality: at the beginning (in the first lied) Tasso's reflection on his own impulsive attempt to duel with his antagonist Antonio, which is not permitted at the absolutist enlightened court (in the Goethe this is the first scene of the fourth act), and at the end (in the final lied) we have

24 Wolfgang Rihm: *Harzreise im Winter*, bars 179–91

Tasso's despair over his uncountenanceable spontaneous embrace of Princess Leonora d'Este (the last scene of the final act in the Goethe) – completely against etiquette. In between, Rihm's portrait of Tasso as an artist leaps back and forth through the text of the play, appropriating passages from the fifth and the second act.

Wolfgang Rihm, *Tasso-Gedanken* (1)

Bist du aus einem Traum erwacht, und hat
Der schöne Trug auf einmal dich verlassen?
Hat dich nach einem Tag der höchsten Lust
Ein Schlaf gebändigt, hält und ängstet nun
Mit schweren Fesseln Deine Seele? Ja,
Du wachst und träumst. Wo sind die Stunden hin,
Die um dein Haupt mit Blumenkränzen spielten?
Die Tage, wo dein Geist mit freier Sehnsucht
Des Himmels ausgespanntes Blau durchdrang?
Und dennoch lebst du noch, und fühlst dich an,
Du fühlst dich an, und weißt nicht, ob du lebst.

JOHANN WOLFGANG VON GOETHE,
Torquato Tasso, Act IV scene i

Have you awoken from a dream, and has
The fair illusion you suddenly abandoned?
Has sleep, after a day of greatest pleasure,
A sleep tamed you, holds and frightens now
In heavy fetters your soul? Yes,
You wake and dream. Where went the hours
That played around your head with floral wreaths?
The days in which your spirit with free longing
Permeates the sky's spanned blue?
And yet you live still, and feel yourself,
You feel yourself and know not if you live.

The physical clash that almost occurred between the pragmatic, slippery, icy privy councillor Antonio, who fancies himself a poet, and Tasso – brilliant, quick-tempered but unable to cope with life – precedes the first lied. Tasso's imprisonment in radical subjectivity matches Hölderlin's phrase about Empedocles: 'Unendlich trifft es den Unendlichen' ('Infinitely the infinite is struck').[9] It is Tasso's personal tragedy that, as an uncompromising, subjective idealist, not only does he not desire to think and act pragmatically; he cannot, because nature has not granted him the will to do so.

In this brief song of reminiscence (pp. 7–9), mythological Arcadian motifs, such as the laurel wreath previously awarded to Tasso and the princess's shepherdess costume, symbolise the essence of poetic creativity. Also reflected in Tasso's familiarity with mythical primal states, however, is his evasive unease in social environments – to Caroline Herder, Goethe identified the attitude of his protagonist as a 'disproportion between talent and life'.[10] And also reflected among the Arcadian motifs in this text chosen by Wolfgang Rihm for the first lied is his flight from dealing with the failed duel.

The music for these emphatic but also escapist lines receives its immediately engaging effect by virtue of the fact that, in its serene tone of voice, it describes Tasso's aura paratactically; it doesn't attempt to explain it. Tasso's inescapable emotional state conveys itself to me in Rihm's vision as a sensorily tangible phenomenon and not as a logically unfolding argument. Gerold Huber and I thought we might represent that by drawing the manic flow of ideas like a long elastic continuum. The great textual dynamic of this flow of ideas finds musical expression in a power that surges back and forth, that pulls forwards and compensatingly backwards, giving the lied a physical cohesion as if in the equilibrium of forces exerted on a large block of rubber.

For example, we were struck by an intensified agogic stress and excitement at the words 'Wo sind die Stunden hin [. . .]

Blau durchdrang?' ('Where went the hours [. . .] spanned blue'), lines 6–9, which finally – 'Du fühlst dich an, und weißt nicht, ob du lebst' ('You feel yourself and know not if you live'), line 11 – falls back into a melancholy astonishment, an astonishment at the incomprehensibility of the protagonist's own identity, characterised by a repeated paralysis of performative expressiveness. But on the smaller scale as well, many elastic compensatory oscillations in activity and energy can constantly be observed, even if Wolfgang Rihm does not indicate them specifically with his sparse agogic and dynamic instructions. In their breath-like recurrences they strike me as resembling the movements of a living body (lines 4–6): they often rear up in the high passages ('höchsten', '–bändigt', 'ängstet nun') before relaxing again as the melody falls away ('Lust', 'hält und', 'mit schweren Fesseln') (see music example 25). But these oscillations, this lying down, rearing up and calming again are not compellingly linked to pitch, as the conclusion of the music example shows: 'deine Seele' loses expressive energy in the melodic rise. Astonishing to me, however, is the fact that the oscillations in Rihm's lyrical adaptation seem so unconsciously physical; they act like a breathing, moving mass of flesh, even though Goethe's work is quite unambiguously – not least in the artistic effect of the composition – a work of the highest consciousness and shimmering intellect.

Wolfgang Rihm, *Tasso-Gedanken* (2)

[. . .] Ganz
Ruht mein Gemüt auf diesem Werke nun.
Nun muß es werden, was es werden kann.
[. . .] ich bin gesund,
Wenn ich mich meinem Fleiß ergeben kann,
Und so macht wieder mich mein Fleiß gesund.
[. . .] mir ist nicht wohl

25 Wolfgang Rihm: *Tasso-Gedanken* no. 1, bars 7–13

In freier Üppigkeit. Mir läßt die Ruh'
Am mind'sten Ruhe. [. . .]
Wenn ich nicht sinnen oder dichten soll,
So ist das Leben mir kein Leben mehr.
Verbiete du dem Seidenwurm zu spinnen,
Wenn er sich schon dem Tode näher spinnt,
Das köstliche Geweb' entwickelt er
Aus seinem Innersten und läßt nicht ab,
Bis er in seinen Sarg sich eingeschlossen.
O geb' ein guter Gott uns auch dereinst
Das Schicksal des beneidenswerten Wurms,
Im neuen Sonnental die Flügel rasch
Und freudig zu entfalten.

JOHANN WOLFGANG VON GOETHE,
Torquato Tasso, Act V scene ii

[. . .] Entirely
My mind is now at rest upon this work.
Now it must become what it can become.
[. . .] I am well,
When I myself to my industry can devote.
And so my industry makes me well again.
[. . .] I do not feel well
In free luxuriance. Rest gives me
The least respite. [. . .]
If I am not allowed to think or write,
Then life for me is life no more.
As you would forbid the silkworm spinning,
When it is already spinning close to death.
Its precious fabric, it builds
From its inside and does not stop
Until it closes itself into the grave.
O may a benign God some day grant us
The fate of this most enviable worm,
In this new sunlit vale quickly and with joy
To spread our wings.

This lied is not an organically breathing body like the first one. Arguments are voiced only briefly, often somewhat unconvincingly, even apologetically, in order to justify the unorthodox wish that the Duke may return the poem that Tasso has already dedicated to him for revision.[11] But the desire to be cured far from the court in Ferrara is also voiced. However, the multiple attempts at justification take the form of a series of unpredictable neurotic self-mirrorings (lines 1–11), switching between complacency ('Ganz / Ruht mein Gemüt' – 'Entirely / My mind is now at rest'), euphoria ('Nun muß es werden, was es werden kann' – 'Now it must become what it can become'), submissiveness and defiance ('ich bin gesund' – 'I am well' – a reaction to the Duke's demand that he be cured before returning to Ferrara), hypochondria ('mir ist nicht wohl / In freier Üppigkeit' – I do not feel well / In free luxuriance') and fear of the artistic freedom that he has just extracted from him ('Mir läßt die Ruh' / Am mind'sten Ruhe' – 'Rest gives me / The least respite'). After Duke Alfons's demand that he moderate himself ('Ich bitte dich, entreiße dich dir selbst / Der Mensch gewinnt, was der Poet verliert' – 'Please escape yourself / The man gains what the poet loses') Tasso even lapses into childishness: 'Wenn ich nicht sinnen oder dichten soll, / So ist das Leben mir kein Leben mehr' ('If I am not allowed to think or write / Then life for me is life no more').

Duke Alfons, who plainly (and hardly surprisingly) has no sympathy for Tasso's problematic take on his life, refers in the quoted demand to Goethe's central motif of 'disproportion between talent and life', and particularly to the political dimension of this disproportion, by not enquiring into Tasso's state of mind. The question is, in fact, to what extent the prince even has to respond to the artist's talent. An artist cannot simply abandon the fact of being an artist, once developed, to return to the normality that he has just fled. This would represent a far greater danger than the characteristic danger to the artist himself. Dieter Borchmeyer impressively describes this dichotomy with the words of Thomas Mann in *Tonio Kröger*: 'Kein Blatt läßt sich pflücken "vom Lorbeerbaum der Kunst, ohne mit seinem Leben dafür zu zahlen"' ('One may not pluck a leaf "from the laurel tree of art without paying for it with one's life"'), and Franz Grillparzer's phrase about the 'malheur d'être un poète' ('the misfortune of being a poet').[12]

But in the unexpected, safe, creative peace of genius Tasso suddenly turns his attention to a more objective thought (lines 12–20), which leads to an artistic work – the poem of the silkworm, which ends the lied with a justifiably euphoric prospect: the idea of a directed metamorphosis of the artist, which develops into an aria, finally replacing the self-referential stammering of the first part.

Wolfgang Rihm, *Tasso-Gedanken* (3)

[. . .] Gedanken ohne Maß
Und Ordnung regen sich in meiner Seele.
Mir scheint die Einsamkeit zu winken, mich
Gefällig anzulispeln: Komm, ich löse
Die neu erregten Zweifel deiner Brust.
Doch werf' ich einen Blick [. . .], vernimmt
Mein horchend Ohr ein Wort [. . .] –
So wird ein neuer Tag um mich herum
And alle Bande fallen von mir los.
Ich will [. . .] gestehn, es hat [. . .]
unerwartet [. . .], nicht sanft.
Aus einem schönen Traum mich aufgeweckt;
[. . .] Wesen, [. . .] Worte haben mich
So wunderbar getroffen, daß ich mehr
Als je mich doppelt fühle, mit mir selbst
Aufs neu in streitender Verwirrung bin. [. . .]
Doch ach! je mehr ich horchte, mehr und mehr
Versank ich vor mir selbst, ich fürchtete,
Wie Echo an den Felsen zu verschwinden,
Ein Widerhall, ein Nichts mich zu verlieren.

JOHANN WOLFGANG VON GOETHE,
Torquato Tasso, Act II scene i

[. . .] Thoughts without measure
And order stir within my soul.
Loneliness seems to wave to me, and
Pleasantly whisper: Come, I free
Your breast of these fresh doubts.
But when I cast a glance [. . .], hears
My listening ear a word [. . .] –
So a new day dawns around me

> And all my bonds fall from me.
> I will [. . .] admit that [. . .]
> Unexpectedly [. . .], not gently,
> It woke me from a lovely dream;
> [. . .] Nature, [. . .] words have struck me
> So wondrously that I more
> Than twice feel my double self, that with myself
> I am again in quarrelsome confusion. [. . .]
> But oh! The more I listened, more and more
> I sank before myself, I feared,
>
> Like an echo disappearing at the rocks,
> A resonance, a nothing, to lose myself.

This lied is best suited to the requirements of the theatre: with its abruptly interrupted and then rising thoughts, some of which initially line up, recitative-like, and then dissolve into declamatory conclusions, as well as with the impressive psychological development of Tasso, which still occurs in the context of the earlier laurel-wreath crowning. This is basically the dramatically concrete counterpart to the opening, rather abstract, lied.

In addition, Tasso's memory of two contradictory encounters in the very recent past demonstrates in exemplary fashion what a musical setting can do in terms of interpretation: Tasso reflects briefly on his inspiring meeting with the princess (lines 6–9). Its sensuality reappears, and assumes form in two musical antecedent phrases (lines 6–7). Each of these begins deeply and richly, embodying Tasso's amorous response ('Doch werf ich ei–', 'vernimmt / Mein hor–') to the princess's glance and words, which then find their own shape in light, high melodic ends ('–nen Blick', '–chend Ohr ein Wort'). The two antecedent phrases finally conclude with a cheering consequent phrase (lines 8–9) (see music example 26).

The second memory is of the depressing meeting with Antonio (lines 13–16), whose 'essence' and 'words' have struck Tasso 'so wondrously'. This 'wondrous' (literally, 'wonderful') should be understood in the sense of 'strange, confusing, destructive'. For me, Rihm's triplets in this passage should be clearly taken as defiant – they do not form a rounded, descending line, but with a rather syncopated third beat they form the destructive counterpart to the two phrases that characterise the princess. Tasso has been deliberately duped by Antonio. He openly praised Tasso's rival Ariosto's poetry to the skies and not his. As a result he again aroused, even provoked, Tasso's self-tormenting fear that the significance of his work might crumble to ashes (lines 17–20). That shows what a delicate flower Tasso is – the smallest breath of wind knocks him over (see music example 27).

26 Wolfgang Rihm: *Tasso-Gedanken* no. 3, bars 24–8

27 Wolfgang Rihm: *Tasso-Gedanken* no. 3, bars 49–54

Wolfgang Rihm, *Tasso-Gedanken* (4)

Die Träne hat uns die Natur verliehen,
Den Schrei des Schmerzens, wenn der Mensch [in Goethe:
    'Mann'] zuletzt
Es nicht mehr trägt – Und mir noch über alles –
Sie ließ im Schmerz mir Melodie und Rede,
Die tiefste Fülle meiner Not zu klagen:
Und wenn der Mensch in seiner Qual verstummt,
Gab mir ein Gott, zu sagen wie ich leide.
[. . .] du stehest fest und still,
Ich scheine nur die sturmbewegte Welle.
Allein bedenk und überhebe nicht
Dich deiner Kraft! Die mächtige Natur,
Die diesen Felsen gründete, hat auch
Der Welle die Beweglichkeit gegeben.
Sie sendet ihren Sturm, die Welle flieht
Und schwankt und schwillt und beugt sich schäumend über.

In dieser Woge spiegelte so schön
Die Sonne sich, es ruhten die Gestirne
An dieser Brust, die zärtlich sich bewegte.
Verschwunden ist der Glanz, entflohn die Ruhe.
Ich kenne mich in der Gefahr nicht mehr,
Und schäme mich nicht mehr, es zu bekennen.
Zerbrochen ist das Steuer, und es kracht
Das Schiff an allen Seiten. Berstend reißt
Der Boden unter meinen Füßen auf!
Ich fasse dich mit beiden Armen an!
So klammert sich der Schiffer endlich noch
Am Felsen fest, and dem er scheitern sollte.

JOHANN WOLFGANG VON GOETHE,
Torquato Tasso, Act V scene v

The tear was given to us, by nature
The cry of pain, when man at last
Can bear it no longer – to me more than any –
It left in pain me melody and speech
The deepest richness of my hardship to lament:
And when man is rendered silent by his torment,
A god gave me the ability to say how I suffer.
[. . .] you stand solid and silent,
I only seem to be the storm-tossed wave.
But think and do not overreach
Your power! The mighty nature
That formed these rocks has also
Given the wave its nimbleness.
It sends its storm, the wave flees
And rocks and swells and foaming falls to shore.
In that wave splendidly reflected.
The sun, the stars rested

On this breast that moved so tenderly.
The gleam has gone, the peace has fled.
I no longer know myself in this peril,
And feel no longer shame when I admit.
The helm has shattered and crashing
Is the ship on every side. Bursting open
Is the deck beneath my feet!
I grasp you with both arms!
So finally clings the helmsman after all
To the rock where he was due to founder.

In view of the consequences of the fatefully unhappy embrace of the princess – which was not an expression of Tasso's desire but rather of his sense of having been understood – which makes a future for him at the court of the Duke of Ferrara practically impossible, the fourth lied begins with the expression of despair: 'Den Schrei des Schmerzens, wenn der Mensch zuletzt / Es nicht mehr trägt' ('The cry of pain, when man at last / Can bear it no longer'; lines 2–3). At least, the artist immediately finds in that an opportunity for creativity – and relief: 'Und wenn der Mensch in seiner Qual verstummt, / Gab mir ein Gott, zu sagen wie ich leide' ('And when man is rendered silent by his torment, / A god gave me the ability to say how I suffer'). But this art is only a sublimation; it springs from Tasso's own subjectivity, the history of his own life,[13] his own genius, and not from his universal, supra-personal work, *Gerusalemme liberata*.[14]

At last, however, Tasso overcomes this excessive subjectivity, which has already become apparent in the second song and now resurfaces, as well as the delusions that develop in the fifth act, and that border on the absurd: with sudden self-knowledge he describes and concludes what has happened with the image of the wave[15] and shipwreck (symbolising his creativity and his life as an artist) on the rock (representing Antonio and his pragmatism). The fallen

Tasso clings to the rock, thus pragmatically (!) extending his hand to his former enemy Antonio. Rihm's gripping and immediately graspable setting of this rescuing clasp is the culmination of a long-developed escalation into an ultimately thrilling fire.

At the same time, however, Tasso's growing recognition of his own incapacity for living feeds into his destiny as a poet,[16] thus confirming once again the impossibility of reconciling his existence as an artist with life at the court of Ferrara, governed as it is by reason. Tasso's personal tragedy thus embodies the failed union of worldly reality and the poetic ideal. This recognition makes Rihm's *Tasso-Gedanken* end in dull silence – for me this is the melancholy perception of the artist in both Goethe and Rihm.[17]

At some point Gerold Huber and I had this new work in front of us and, estimating a running time of about thirteen minutes (only three *Tasso* lieder reached us initially, before Wolfgang Rihm sent us a fourth), we tried to find a programme to build around it. All we knew was that we didn't want to do a recital solely of Goethe settings, as we had planned for the premiere of *Harzreise*.

We had long been intending to work on Alban Berg's *Vier Lieder*, op. 2. And I was uneasy about having sung so little Hugo Wolf. Until then I had always got somehow stuck with my favourite lied composers, Schubert, Schumann and Mahler – and also Debussy and Berg. But for years, quite rightly, our good friend and adviser Dieter Borchmeyer had been feeding my bad conscience with reminders of Wolf. But since there was already so much difficult new material in the programme to learn, we included Wolf's *Harfenspieler* lieder, which we had often performed, and in the last group a number of Mörike settings, concluding with the Goethe lied *Grenzen der Menschheit* ('The Limits of Mankind'). So, finally, Wolf again! Last of all, for ease of learning (not singability) we planned to add Schubert's five great Rückert settings, which we were also scheduled to perform shortly in a programme with *Schwanengesang*. And while we were considering Schubert, there were also the two Silbert lieder, which we particularly liked and which were very seldom performed: *Abendbilder* ('Evening Pictures') and *Himmelsfunken* ('Sparks from Heaven').

This was a programme that had been more or less thrown together: we wanted to begin with the *Harfenspieler* lieder, once again. For a long time Gerold Huber and I had been trying to include one of the three settings of Goethe's harpist songs, by Schubert, Schumann and Wolf, as a kind of preamble, since an excellent account of the role of the performer appears in Goethe's novel *Wilhelm Meisters Lehrjahre*: actors preparing a production of *Hamlet* in the theatre in a count's castle are treated badly and nastily, as though they are nothing; they are even despised by the despised domestic servants. And then we have the central figures of Mignon and the harpist, the daughter born of incest and her father, defeated by fate – she a mysterious artiste, he a dull has-been, an erratic and numb block in the midst of a *Bildungsroman*, a gloomy person of mere suffering.

But then there was also the fourth – long – Tasso lied, which increased the estimated duration of Rihm's work in the recital from thirteen minutes to twenty. So we had to delete and rearrange. I was no longer entirely confident about performing the extremely difficult Rückert group after the unknown quantity of the *Tasso-Gedanken*; placed at the end, as they were initially, they also seemed dramaturgically out of place. That meant: Rückert lieder at the beginning; that worked, as we knew. And then why not end the first half with the *Silbert-Lieder*? In terms of length that still just about worked (the first half now running at fifty minutes). Wolf now disappeared entirely from the second half. Admittedly it then seemed strange that the big Goethe setting had been shoe-horned in after the rather smaller group of Mörike lieder at the end. But it had to be in there, first because Gerold Huber thinks it's so extraordinary, and then because he wanted us to perform it together at long last. So we arrived at the following programme:

Franz Schubert
(Friedrich Rückert)
Sei mir gegrüßt, D. 741
Dass sie hier gewesen, D. 775
Lachen und Weinen, D. 777
Du bist die Ruh, D. 776
Greisengesang, D. 778

Wolfgang Rihm
(Johann Wolfgang von Goethe)
Tasso-Gedanken – Monolog-Stücke aus *Torquato Tasso*
1 *Bist du aus einem Traum erwacht*
2 *Ganz ruht mein Gemüt auf diesem Werke nun*
3 *Gedanken ohne Maß und Ordnung*
4 *Die Träne hat uns die Natur verliehen*

Franz Schubert
(Johann Peter Silbert)
Abendbilder, D. 650
Himmelsfunken, D. 651

Interval

Hugo Wolf
(Johann Wolfgang von Goethe)
Harfenspieler
1 *Wer sich der Einsamkeit ergibt'*
2 *An die Türen will ich schleichen*
3 *Wer nie sein Brot mit Tränen aß*

> In Berlin the Wolf group was replaced by:
> Wolfgang Rihm
> (Johann Wolfgang von Goethe)
> *Harzreise im Winter*

Alban Berg
Vier Lieder, op. 2
(Friedrich Hebbel)
 I *Aus 'Dem Schmerz sein Recht'*
 II *Drei Lieder aus 'Der Glühende'*
(Alfred Mombert)
 1 *Schlafend trägt man mich*
 2 *Nun ich der Risen Stärksten überwand*
 3 *Warm die Lüfte*

Hugo Wolf
(Eduard Mörike)
Begegnung
Lied eines Verliebten
Auf ein altes Bild
Auf eine Christblume II
Schlafendes Jesukind
(Johann Wolfgang von Goethe)
Grenzen der Menschheit

Encores:
Alban Berg
(Peter Altenberg)
Über die Grenzen des All . . ., Ansichtskarten-Lieder, op. 4 no. 3
– attacca –
Franz Schubert
(Karl Lappe)
Der Einsame, D. 800

I thought it would be rather an odd programme, even though it contained nothing but lovely things. But then – as if by the magic hand of chance – we became more and more aware of an overarching series of songs, interconnected in all kinds of different ways. Important motifs in Goethe's cosmos radiating out from the central work of the evening had found multiple reflections.

In the final song of the *Tasso-Gedanken*, the wave, a symbol of unleashed creative power, and a sea voyage provide the image of a response to poetic creativity and how artistic natures survive the fundamental dangers they face or else are shattered on the rocks. These symbols also decided the course of the evening in Wolf's *Grenzen der Menschheit*, in which they formulate the contingency of all human lives, as in a sea voyage. (At the end of Gerold Huber's setting of *Die Seefahrt*, Goethe's *Sturm-und-Drang* hymn, a homage to Wolf's *Grenzen der Menschheit* appears in a particularly animated and startling 4/4 rhythm divided into three plus five quavers.)

The artist's power to depict the reality of human life is the central theme of Goethe's *Torquato Tasso*, and is given exemplary expression in the last scene of the last act: 'Und wenn der Mensch in seiner Qual verstummt, / Gab mir ein Gott zu sagen, wie ich leide' ('And while man is rendered silent by his torment, / A god allowed me to express how I suffer') – with the small change from 'wie' (*how* I suffer) to 'was' (*what* I suffer), Goethe almost forty years later reused this sentence as the epigraph for his *Marienbader Elegie*. This power of the artist is also apparent in the transition from Wolf–Mörike's depiction of human passion (*Begegnung*, *Lied eines Verliebten*) to the thematisation of that very depiction, that representation (*Auf ein altes Bild*, *Schlafendes Jesukind*).

Pupation and metamorphosis into a different life-form, expressed most profoundly by Goethe in *Faust*, with the concept of entelechy, appeared in our programme in the motif of the silkworm (the second of the *Tasso-Gedanken*) and in the 'Blumenkeim' ('bud') of the butterfly (Wolf's *Auf eine Christblume*).

Sleep and dream as an image of flight from the world and healing (in the first of the *Tasso-Gedanken*) also appear in the first two of Alban Berg's *Vier Lieder*, op. 2.

The experience of the beyond – I wouldn't call it pantheistic, although it does arise out of natural phenomena – in Silbert's *Abendbilder* and *Himmelsfunken* appears in a very similar form in *Harzreise*.

The themes of genius and genuine creative force are fundamentally addressed in all four *Tasso-Gedanken* and in *Harzreise*, but also in the two Wolf lieder, *Auf ein altes Bild* and *Schlafendes Jesukind*. (This often sounds strangely as if it is about the innocent face of the new-born son of God and not his painter – perhaps also because a reflective level is rather unusual in Wolf's lieder.)

Hugo Wolf: Harfenspieler I

Wer sich der Einsamkeit ergibt,
Ach! Der ist bald allein;
Ein jeder lebt, ein jeder liebt
Und läßt ihn seiner Pein.

Ja! Laßt mich meiner Qual!
Und kann ich nur einmal
Recht einsam sein,
Dann bin ich nicht allein.

Es schleicht ein Liebender lauschend sacht,
Ob seine Freundin allein?
So überschleicht bei Tag und Nacht
Mich Einsamen die Pein,
Mich Einsamen die Qual.
Ach, werd ich erst einmal
Einsam im Grabe sein,
Da läßt sie mich allein!

JOHANN WOLFGANG VON GOETHE

He who yields to loneliness,
Ah! He will soon be alone;
Everyone lives, everyone loves
And leaves him to his pain.

> Yes! Leave me to my torment!
> And if I can just once
> Be properly lonely,
> Then I am not alone.
>
> A lover creeps along, ears pricked,
> If his beloved is alone?
> Just so, all day and night, creeps up
> On me, lonely man, the pain,
> On me, lonely man, the torment.
> Oh – only when one day
> I am lonely in my grave
> Will it leave me alone!

Loneliness, neurotically sought and then fled again (*Tasso-Gedanken*, songs 1, 2, and 3), reappears with the harpist, the central tragic artist figure from *Wilhelm Meisters Lehrjahre*. In the first harpist lied, dialectical play with the concepts of 'loneliness' and 'being alone' emphasises the set of problems attached to creative flight from, and longing for, fellow human beings: at the beginning of the poem 'loneliness' and 'being alone' are systematically given switched meanings – no judgement is attached to 'alone', while 'lonely' is given pejorative connotations (while their opposite meanings are used in the poem). Only in the third verse is the conceptual distinction restored – the loneliness of the one who has been left alone ends in the grave. He will be lonely only in the eyes of the outside world, but in fact he is alone there: the pejorative overtone of loneliness vanishes with the solitude of the grave, emotionally no longer effective, where all earthly abandonment and torment and of course all sensation are finally left behind.

Closely related to the problem of the artist's loneliness is melancholy, practically an essential property of the creative artist. Centrally important to all three *Harfenspieler* lieder, it also occurs in Rihm's work (*Tasso-Gedanken*, songs 2, 3 and 4).

Franz Schubert: Sei mir gegrüßt

[...]

Ein Hauch der Liebe tilget Räum' und Zeiten
Ich bin bei dir, du bist bei mir,
Ich halte dich in dieses Arms Umschlusse,
Sei mir gegrüßt, sei mir geküßt!

       FRIEDRICH RÜCKERT

[...]

A breath of love redeems spaces and times
I am with you, you are with me,
I hold you in this arm's embrace,
Feel my greetings, feel my kiss!

Tasso's embrace of Princess Eleonore (in the fourth of the *Tasso-Gedanken*), misunderstood but consequential, was anticipated in our programme in the last verse of Schubert's *Sei mir gegrüßt* ('I greet you').

Recovery and healing are themes in both *Harzreise* and in all four of the *Tasso-Gedanken*; they touch both Plessing and Tasso, each suffering from concepts of genius like soulmates.

Finally, the 'disproportion between talent and life' (*Tasso-Gedanken*) was a theme that ran through the evening. In Schubert's *Greisengesang* ('Old Man's Song'), the nightingale addresses it programmatically: 'Herr des Hauses! Verschleuß dein Tor, / Daß nicht die Welt, die kalte, dring ins Gemach. / Schleuß aus den rauhen Odem der Wirklichkeit, / Und nur dem Duft der Träume gib Dach und Fach!' ('Master of the house! Lock your door / To keep the cold world out of your room. / Keep out the rough breath of reality, / And give shelter only to the scent of dreams!') That is practically the reciprocal vision of the artist to the Duke's challenge to Tasso: 'Ich bitte dich, entreiße dich dur selbst! / Der Mensch gewinnt, was der Poet verliert!' ('Please escape yourself / The man gains what the poet loses.')

Of course Gerold Huber and I can never really prepare our programmes or address them contextually as thoroughly as I have described here. It was only my surprise at the many happy coincidences that gave us such a richly harmonious and interconnected programme that made me in retrospect (shortly after the start of our journey) recognise all these resonances with ever greater delight. In many respects this programme was a serendipitous one-off occurrence.

STELES IN AN ICE FIELD

LONDON, DECEMBER 2018

Ich will [. . .] durchdringen Eis und Schnee [. . .]
Bis ich [. . .] seh'.

> WILHELM MÜLLER, *Erstarrung*
> ('Numbness')

I want [. . .] to pass through ice and snow [. . .]
Until I [. . .] see.

Some people think of Franz Schubert's *Winterreise* as *the* towering song-cycle, the epitome of the form. I can accept they feel like that, but I don't actually understand why, and I'm not sure if I share this opinion – in view of so many other magnificent works.

I can trace this almost universal judgement to the coincidence of several unusual qualities. There is the arrangement of the cycle into visual images inspired by the song titles, virtually a description of a journey. Consequently, *Winterreise*, not least because of the bringing together of the 'wanderer' theme with loneliness and danger, can clearly be viewed as the prime example of a Romantic lieder cycle. Then the sheer length of the sequence – almost unique in the recital repertoire with a duration of 75 minutes – affords plenty of time for internalisation, almost a compulsion to immerse oneself. Intensified by the mystical number of 24 lieder, this immersion is required more unconditionally than is usual with other cycles. *Die schöne Mülllerin*, for example, at ten minutes shorter, is considerably less demanding. The existential urgency that appears over the course of the poems really does make *Winterreise* something outstanding and unusual, something almost incomparable. This existential urgency is related to the existential experience of hearing as well as of performing it.

As a young singer I was less concerned with penetrating the ice and snow of this unique work. The whole cycle was perfectly clear to me, I thought – at least up to the twenty-third song,

Die Nebensonnen ('Mock Suns'), in which a strange phenomenon is described: the refraction of horizontal sunlight by atmospheric snow crystals, and its focus into balls of light, which, because they lie on each side of the sun, appear to be extra suns. In the poem, this physical phenomenon is linked with the beloved's eyes.[1] In this way it finally establishes a connection with the protagonist's desire that the actual sun, a metaphor for the light of the winter traveller's life, should set not only in the evening with the accompanying mock suns, but for ever, in accordance with *Winterreise*'s omnipresent dalliance with death.

Things have changed. But even now I think that a less anguished approach to this work might not be inappropriate. Such an approach, I sense, would render unnecessary what has gradually become more widespread since Dietrich Fischer-Dieskau retired from performing: excessive emotion tending towards naturalism, expressed in sighs, verismo sound-painting and an increasing tendency to stretch and compress Schubertian rhythm – caused by the performers' emotional state and the infectious reality of the stage at that moment. That's what I feel, at any rate.[2]

As a result of this heightened emotion, some types of interpretation have become increasingly and unquestioningly universal for the presentation of *Winterreise*, both on the stage and also among the audience. The wanderer inclines to madness; he runs the risk of ending up in a mental hospital (this can be used to justify almost any over-excitable performing style). That he doesn't is due to the assumption that instead his journey takes him straight to an appointment with death. This alliance of human extremes is often and gladly combined with omnipresent irony, because it seems clear to me that *Winterreise* isn't in reality about death and the madhouse.

What isn't clear to me, though, is why the indisputable presence of cynicism and pretentious exaggeration in Wilhelm Müller's text and its setting should be labelled 'irony'. Of course there's a detachment going on here, but it isn't detachment from the audience or from the poet's own writing; it's from the despised world of conservative, bourgeois philistines who have made themselves comfortable in their houses, besieged as they are by winter. After all, Schubert was not really inclined to irony as a stylistic device, nor to the translation of that literary device into music. Here we need only consider his treatment of the six Heine poems in his *Schwanengesang* (songs 8–13), which, not just in their remarkably straightforward setting but even in their selection demonstrates a lack of interest in the irony that was so important to Heine.[3] But to my mind the setting of the *Winterreise* poems shows more a heroic than an ironic understanding of the collection of poems (Müller's verses are less drenched in irony than Heine's). And also apparent is Schubert's tendency to blunt or even to drain some of the emotion from Wilhelm Müller's often more pointed diction: in no. 17, *Im Dorfe* ('In the Village'), Schubert has the scornfully envied people in their beds 'schlafen' (sleep) rather than 'schnarchen' (snore); in no. 24, *Der Leiermann* ('The Hurdy-Gurdy Man'), the dogs don't 'knurren' (growl), they 'brummen' (hum), and many abrupt bits of punctuation (hyphens, question marks and above all exclamation marks) – exaggerations of emotion taken to the limit – are softened (into full stops and commas) or simply removed.[4]

When it is claimed that *Winterreise* is in many respects an ironic work,[5] I see that as an exaggeration. It's as if the supposedly omnipresent irony is often used to justify the fact that critics and audiences increasingly demand interpretations and performances of *Winterreise* that take it to the edge and beyond.

So, here we are. I'm behaving like a Johann Christoph Gottsched or an Eduard Hanslick of singing, and insisting on pure theory, on formality, which is not really my purpose here. But I see the beauty and authenticity of this work as being under unnecessary threat. And in March 2020, at the beginning of the Covid epidemic, when

Heinz Holliger, conducting the Basel Chamber Orchestra, and I were recording Othmar Schoeck's *Elegie* (because we weren't allowed to perform it publicly at the time), I found myself thinking how *Winterreise* must once have sounded: shattering and genuine and unburdened by the listener's experience and the history of its interpretation. Schoeck's setting of 24 poems mostly by Lenau and occasionally by Eichendorff was able to convey *Weltschmerz* in as ghostly a way as must once have been the case with *Winterreise*.

Of course there are many legitimate ways to access a work of art; if there weren't then it would just be an artistic feat. This diversity of interpretation is particularly pronounced with *Winterreise* and the history of its performances and recordings. For that very reason one might question my irritation. Except, unfortunately, as far as I am concerned it has gone beyond irritation, and I have developed an aversion to what I see as the increasingly vicarious glee with which people watch the suffering man (suffering to death), comfortably shuffling off their pseudo-empathy after an hour and a quarter of horror. I didn't want to, I couldn't, I don't want to and can't serve this desire, so I have often sung this work a little more matter-of-factly than may have been intended. I finally arrived at the point where I no longer wanted to sing it at all. My wife and Gerold Huber persuaded me otherwise. Yet . . . I would still like to solve this burdensome conundrum for myself. That's why with every new series of performances I try to grapple with the meaning of the work all over again. I haven't yet had an epiphany, but at least my pondering has produced a line of thought.

I don't see the wanderer as being insane in the morbid sense (even though the word *Wahn* (delusion) appears once in the second lied). All the reactions to abandonment, exile, cold, danger and natural phenomena such as a frozen river, a will o' the wisp, a flight of crows and mock suns are completely rational. I do not see a pathological boundary being approached by any cynicism caused by the sense of personal grievance that we encounter frequently throughout the cycle.

Neither, in my view, is death, which of course appears constantly as a theme in this work, the end of this journey, and certainly not its destination. If death appears as a subject, then it's either the real danger of hypothermia – although that danger appears only in passing, it's hardly addressed directly, as it is in 'erstarrt zu Eise' ('frozen to ice') in no. 3 *Gefrorne Tränen* ('Frozen Tears')[6] – or, in many other passages, as hyperbole, as toying with the idea of death, as in no. 9, *Irrlicht* ('Will o' the Wisp'): 'Jeder Strom wird's Meer gewinnen, / Jedes Leiden auch sein Grab' ('Every river will reach the sea, as every sorrow its grave').[7] Nowhere here do I see the wanderer seriously and deliberately advancing towards his own death. On the contrary: I have the feeling that the longer the journey goes on – and the further his pretentious attitude towards his own end moves into the foreground – that in fact it represents a flight from genuinely increasing danger.

What I do find absurd in the commentaries one frequently comes across is that the hurdy-gurdy man in the final song represents the ultimate confrontation with one's own mortality in the form of a dance of death. For me, this song on the contrary offers a possible way out of this crisis-ridden journey: in the hurdy-gurdy man we have someone who has fallen far further socially than our wanderer, and who is lost to apathy. It is an inauthentic and disrespectful suggestion on the part of the cynical traveller to join him (one does not interrupt a musician's performance) but if the hurdy-gurdy man was indeed playing his tunes for our man of sorrows,[8] then he was certainly not engaging with him in any way, and definitely not amplifying the singer's self-indulgent lament. It's an unreal picture of inequality, with no visible end in sight. In my eyes, however, a new spirit has arisen within the traveller: he has met someone who trumps him as an outsider, who actually does radically embody someone living outside society. The hurdy-gurdy man's own loss of vital energy makes him the ideal stepping stone – our protagonist is able to get back on his feet, and use him to climb up and leave his vale of tears behind. As I see it, all this hurdy-gurdy man has to do with death is that he allows our hero to escape it. (This is of course only a thesis. I wouldn't want it to be thought incontestable.)

No. 24, *Der Leiermann*, makes two things clear to me: on the one hand, the extent to which all the previous weeping and fatalism were mere play and coincidence, as is stated in no. 9, *Irrlicht*, 'Unsre Freuden, unsre Leiden, / Alles eines Irrlichts Spiel!' ('Our joys, our sorrows / All the play of a will o' the wisp!'), and on the other, that being alone was what our traveller might have been suffering from most. In this list of themes from the individual poems assembled according to association, being alone is one of the most frequent – followed by its effects: loneliness and self-pity.

1 *Gute Nacht* ('Goodnight') – address, retrospect, welcome, expulsion, loneliness, flight, bitterness, cynicism, love, innocence
2 *Die Wetterfahne* ('The Weathervane') – deception, delusion, disregard, poverty as definition, self-pity, accusation, foreignness, ostracism, humiliation
3 *Gefrorne Tränen* ('Frozen Tears') – disappointment, incomprehension, helplessness, being alone, accusation
4 *Erstarrung* ('Numbness') – searching, bewilderment, meaning, memory, grief, freezing, forgetting, self-pity, loss
5 *Der Lindenbaum* ('The Linden Tree') – home, abroad, life, temptation, death, path of life, emigration, loneliness, memory, self-protection
6 *Wasserflut* ('Flood') – dying away, forgetting, insignificance, extinction, being alone, humiliation, accusation
7 *Auf dem Flusse* ('On the River') – numbness, forgetting, extinction, mirroring, self-pity, being alone, loss
8 *Rückblick* ('Looking Back') – expulsion, accusation, ostracism, memory, welcome, pair of eyes, making things unhappen, self-pity, being alone

9 *Irrlicht* ('Will o' the Wisp') – path of life, lightness, enticement, hope, delusion, transience, insignificance, finding, redemption, dalliance with death

10 *Rast* ('Rest') – waking, rest, dalliance with death, ostracism, cynicism, self-pity

11 *Frühlingstraum* ('Dream of Springtime') – idyll, waking, persecution, childlikeness, dream, self-pity, temptation, ostracism, longing, being alone

12 *Einsamkeit* ('Loneliness') – walking, danger, resting, life, ostracism, self-pity, being alone

13 *Die Post* ('The Post') – deception, hope, heart, beloved, unease, expectation, curiosity, being alone

14 *Der greise Kopf* ('The Grey Head') – deception, dalliance with death, looking back, semblance, self-pity, enticement

15 *Die Krähe* ('The Crow') – meanness, fear of death, dalliance with death, fidelity, self-pity

16 *Letzte Hoffnung* ('Last Hope') – superstition, disappointment, fear, hope, dalliance with death, grief, self-pity

17 *Im Dorfe* ('In the Village') – ostracism, danger, helplessness, expulsion, contempt, envy, dream, hope, waking, resting, accusation, disregard, foreignness, cynicism, self-pity, being alone, humiliation, dalliance with death, deception

18 *Der stürmische Morgen* ('The Stormy Morning') – cynicism, self-pity, self-destruction, fury

19 *Täuschung* ('Deception') – deception, hope, self-pity, cynicism, enticement, loneliness

20 *Der Wegweiser* ('The Signpost') – loneliness, self-pity, path of life, flight, waking, resting, persistence, walking, fear, dalliance with death

21 *Das Wirtshaus* ('The Inn') – dalliance with death, cynicism, blasphemy, self-pity, walking, accusation, being alone

22 *Mut* ('Courage') – fear, walking, being alone, persistence, blasphemy

23 *Die Nebensonnen* ('Mock Suns') – deception, pair of eyes, foreignness, loss, cynicism, self-pity, dalliance with death

24 *Der Leiermann* ('The Hurdy-Gurdy Man') – chance meeting, contemplation, ostracism, cynicism, contempt, pity, courage, hope, conversation, presumption, new beginning

So *Der Leiermann* really does mark an ending, a turning point in the cycle. Here I see the longed-for conclusion of the strenuous journey as having been reached. This can also be observed in the altered form of address: what is being described here is no longer the situation and state of mind of the 'I'. Everything observed, felt and suffered is no longer being assessed for its meaning in relation to the speaker's own nature, and instead a phenomenon is described that lies outside his own sphere. This is the first time this has happened in the whole work, and all of a sudden the sound and declamation are different: sober and quiet. All previous intensity, or at least suppressed intensity, is blown away, and an emotional ease begins to be established.

If the cycle can be 'read' and understood by its ending, as a performer I would like to extend the aesthetic of this last song to the whole work, as a performing attitude – not as content, of course not, since in the previous 23 lieder the 'I' has been extremely emotional and highly agitated. Here I mean a sober attitude on the part of the performer, reporting on a situation without wishing to hold the audience prisoner of his own distress. I believe that such a detached attitude would be an unburdening. It would be my ideal – describing something without aiming to drag the audience into one's own empathetic emphasis.[9]

My attitude is supported by a biographical aspect I realised some time ago. I'm not looking for any specious biographical markers, and as a rule I try to avoid biographism. However, when a work is so thickly coated with the resinous varnish of the history of interpretation that one tends to see the varnish rather than the artwork beneath, a clarifying return to basics may be salutary. This biographical approach to interpretation would give me reason and justification for replacing a lachrymose emotional reaction to death with something more like reportage. The emotionally intense, gripping black of a melodrama based on identification with the protagonist would make way for something approaching the grey of a report on the banality of loneliness – for me, a much more profound and authentic horror – if one were to seek it out. The suffering of which the protagonist sings would thus be only the subject of an account and not a cause of wide-ranging but ultimately limited and imperfect solidarity. In this way the indulgent self-pity of the winter traveller would not be replaced by the pity for which he so loudly yearns. Then one might be able to look at this bountiful work without having to sink into it. The constant reference of all phenomena back to one's own state of mind, as most fully revealed in no. 16, *Letzte Hoffnung* – 'Schaue nach dem einen Blatte, / Hänge meine Hoffung dran; / Spielt der Wind mit meinem Blatte, / Zitt'r' ich, was ich zittern kann' ('Look at that single leaf, / I hang my hope upon it; / If the wind plays with my leaf, / I tremble as much as I can') – would be left with the protagonist, and would not have to be a part or even a required condition of understanding by the interpreter and the audience.

This supposed parallel would have been simply too perfect. In her fictionalised account of Wilhelm Müller's life, Erika von Borries describes how, having reached Brussels while fighting in the Napoleonic wars, Müller was dishonourably discharged for fraternisation and an extra-marital love affair, and in the winter of 1814–15 he finally had to undertake his own 'Winterreise'.[10] He had to return to Berlin, Borries recounts, possibly on foot, to continue his interrupted studies. It's very easy to conjure up a visual image: a poor, very disappointed man now forced to view from the outside a life that he would have worked hard to have – in danger, alone, lonely, filled with self-pity, someone in dire straits.

In any case Wilhelm Müller returned to Berlin and resumed his old life. He recalled the events of the recent past in a very impressive diary entry from 1815: 'The past year lies as far behind me or in front of me as if I had gone from child to old man or from old man to child' – the image of no. 14 *Der greise Kopf* provides a vivid echo.[11] Although whether everything fell out in quite the ideal form that Borries describes is questionable to say the least.

In his review, Günter Hartung furiously tore apart this attempt at reconstructing a 'Müller-Winterreise' (along with practically the rest of Borries's biography).[12] Hartung is impressively well informed about Wilhelm Müller and his historical context, but he is himself not free of speculation when, without supplying any evidence, he relocates Müller's undisputed sexual experiences from the bed of the businessman's wife Thérèse (according to Borries) to a brothel.[13] What he does not go into, however, is the interesting fact recounted by Erika von Borries that in his application for a librarian's post in Dessau he supplied all his personal testimonies, etc., but not a word about his service as a volunteer in the army.[14] His participation in the Napoleonic wars, during which he apparently attained the rank of lieutenant, would have stood him in extremely good stead. Under normal circumstances Müller would never have neglected to mention it. But there is no doubt that he did join up as a volunteer in the war against Napoleon.

That does seem to imply, albeit speculatively, something other than harmless visits to a brothel and a warning letter from his father. Müller's dishonourable discharge in Brussels – possibly on the grounds of an immoral and adulterous relationship – remains entirely feasible. Of course Borries's biography is 'fictionalised', and sometimes so emotional that one might feel, along with Hartung, that the boundary between speculation and invention has been substantially crossed. But empathetic fantasy can sometimes bear artistically useful fruit. Because – without being sensationalist – not only would the possible parallel journey sit very well with the text of *Winterreise*, but assumptions about Müller's mental state could contribute a great deal to the understanding of the work. I do not see – either in Müller's biography or in the poem and song-cycle – the desolate derelict, in a state of terminal despair, yearning for the end to come, but rather someone who has suffered severe setbacks in his planned career. I see someone who has been deeply hurt (but not 'terminally', as is melodramatically claimed in no. 21, *Das Wirtshaus*), and who now feels excluded from society, despite never wanting to be.

So in *Winterreise* I see a man who is wounded, yet still vigorous and reproachful, for me an unmistakable and astonishing analogy with the real-life situation of Wilhelm Müller in the winter of 1814–15. Volunteering for the war, with its horrendous, life-threatening terrors, and then being excluded from it (however and for whatever reason) would surely take its toll on one's ambition and self-respect, and by coming to an end so abruptly could lead to a genuine identity crisis. And that is what, to my mind, we experience so powerfully in *Winterreise*.

In this sense no. 17, *Im Dorfe*, has a key role for me: at no point in the cycle is the traveller's situation presented as vividly as it is here. In this poem, jeopardised by the freezing cold of winter, the protagonist is forced to walk past a place of emotional and physical security. Nowhere else are so many aspects that largely define other lieder in *Winterreise* simultaneously present, as my (subjective) list of the themes of the individual poems/songs may make clear. If one song in *Winterreise* can be said to be *Winterreise* in a nutshell, it is *Im Dorfe*: the physical danger is made every bit as clear as the intimation of mortality; revulsion against philistines goes hand in hand with envy for their orderly life, while the sense of being alone, the cynicism and, generally speaking, almost all the emotions found elsewhere in the cycle appear here all bound up together – it is exactly how I would imagine Wilhelm Müller on his personal 'Winterreise'. At least I do see the possibility of this actually having taken place, as Borries suggests, as more illuminating than Hartung's furious dismissal of her speculation.

Schubert captured the wanderer's crisis in music in a very special and – for the time – new way. His familiar model of a long-extended melodic line, often inclining to the retrospective and a certain *Seligkeit* (bliss), is replaced in many passages of *Winterreise* by new, often harsh, gestures. The act of remembering (still seeming to have conventional melodic connotations, for example in no. 1, *Gute Nacht*; no. 5, *Der Lindenbaum*; no. 11, *Frühlingstraum*, or no. 19, *Täuschung*) is confronted with a correlative of the present, which the protagonist finds difficult to bear, and musically therefore no longer aims for melodic resolution and form. Melodies no longer return to their beginning, and are instead an illustration of the traveller's unstable situation: 'Jeder Strom wird's Meer gewinnen . . .' ('Every stream will reach the sea . . .') from no. 9, *Irrlicht*; '. . . als noch die Stürme tobten, war ich so elend nicht' ('. . . when the storms still raged I was not so miserable') from no. 12, *Einsamkeit*; 'Fall' ich selber mit zu Boden' ('I too fall to the ground') from no. 16, *Letzte Hoffnung*; 'Ich bin zu Ende mit allen Träumen' ('I am done with all dreams') from no. 17, *Im Dorfe*; 'Die Wolkenfetzen flattern umher in mattem Streit' ('The ragged clouds flutter around in weary dispute') from no. 18, *Der stürmische Morgen* are examples of the many distortions that not only indicate a new concept in Schubert's approach to the management of mood but already present it in a finished form.

Schubert's friends noticed this immediately on first hearing: apart from *Der Lindenbaum*, they were not – especially Franz von Schober – initially impressed with *Winterreise*, as the famous account of Josef von Spaun reveals.[15] Schubert sang the songs to them himself – what a privilege! – and in their entirety (a very early and more or less irrefutable vote for cyclical lied performances). And even in *Der Lindenbaum* the first half of the poem's third verse ('Die kalten Winde bliesen . . .' – 'The cold winds blew . . .') is clearly so disturbing that Friedrich Silcher was unhappy about using it for his arrangement for men's choir. In the published editions of the Silcher treatment of which I am aware, however, the third verse is not excised (although usually it is only the first verse that is sung). Essentially this decision to ignore the complexity of the underlying poem is even greater proof of Silcher's inconceivable lack of sensibility than his transformation of a sophisticatedly modified strophic song into one entirely rigid.

Silcher retained the unspoilt description of the supposed *locus amoenus* (delightful location) by ironing out all differences. Here, once again, we find an endlessly repeated assertion of the lied aesthetic from around 1800: the greatest simplicity of accompaniment and strophic uniformity in the more or less standardised affects when poems were set to music as lieder. (In the case of Silcher, about half a century later, I would label this process desophistication or even 'dedifferentiation'.[16]) Also, the prelude and postlude are absent. Formal melodic,[17] rhythmic and even harmonic simplifications are shamelessly indulged. Obviously Silcher was aiming to produce a 'folk song', and the modification (*Umsingen*, i.e. a constant change by singing[18]) of the found material (i.e. by Schubert) led not to a further development of the original song, but to its being rendered simple, even banal.[19]

Der Lindenbaum
Franz Schubert: *Winterreise* (5)

[strophe 1]
Am Brunnen vor dem Tore
Da steht ein Lindenbaum
Ich träumt' in seinem Schatten
So manchen süßen Traum.

[strophe 1]
Ich schnitt in seine Rinde
So manches liebe Wort;
Es zog in Freud und Leide
Zu ihm mich immer fort

[strophe 2]
Ich mußt auch heute wandern
Vorbei in tiefer Nacht,
Da hab ich noch im Dunkeln
Die Augen zugemacht.

[strophe 2]
Und seine Zweige rauschten,
Als riefen sie mir zu:
Komm her zu mir, Geselle,
Hier findst du deine Ruh.

[recitative-like intermezzo]
Die kalten Winde bliesen
Mir grad ins Angesicht,
Der Hut flog mir vom Kopfe,
Ich wendete mich nicht.

[strophe 3; repeat]
Nun bin ich manche Stunde
Entfernt von jenem Ort,
Und immer hör ich's rauschen:
Du fändest Ruhe dort!

WILHELM MÜLLER

At the well by the gate,
There stands a linden tree.
I have dreamt in its shade
Many a sweet dream.

I have cut into its bark
Many a dear word;
Drawn in joy and suffering
To it I was all the time.

Today as well I had to wander
Past it deep in the night,
I have, still in the dark,
Closed my eyes.

And its branches rustled
As if calling to me:
Come here to me, comrade,
Here you shall find your peace.

The cold winds blew
Straight into my face,
My hat flew from my head
And I didn't turn.

Now I am several hours
Away from that place,
And still I hear it rustle:
You would find rest there!

Schubert's lied, on the other hand, shows a subtle sophistication increasing from verse to verse: from the account of untroubled meeting (the first and second verses of the poem), and the protagonist getting acquainted with this spot as a place of retreat, of recovery, to the mention of the site of the tree (third and fourth verses) as a place one walks past because one has to and, perhaps also because the place speaks of (eternal) rest, one runs away from it – hungry for life (!) – and then to the tree as a distant memory (sixth verse) and the bringing together of the first and second experiences. To sum up, the linden tree is peaceful but also dangerous, and above all no longer attainable, a symbol of the loss of innocence, but also of the avoidance of death, a symbol of the temptation of suicide and the will to escape that enticement. It's the same as when one steps back from the edge of the station platform to render an ultimate leap that briefly suggested itself in a moment of despair impossible. In short: Schubert's lied is a work of art that avoids both nostalgia and the longing for death that might be a radical reaction to it by bringing together both aspects of the place (of the loving and the dying, of shared and private self-collection) in the last verse – as memory and as distance.

This last verse moves this centrally significant lied away from any possibility of simple appropriation; it ceases to be fodder for either folksong devotees or listeners with a tasty death wish. Thomas Mann's phrase in the 'Fülle des Wohllauts' ('Fullness of Harmony') chapter in *The Magic Mountain* and its repetition when Hans Castorp goes into war perhaps best captures this character of the lied (and its last verse): fullness of life or quest for death.[20] This verse sets aside both grief over the loss of the idyll and also the temptation of death, by abandoning the place in favour of a different phase of life. It is a manifesto setting out the painful insight of the change necessary if one is not to endanger or lose one's identity. That being the case, this song would be a first destination for our wanderer. And to judge from experience of past concerts, after *Der Lindenbaum* one can take the first pause for breath during a performance of *Winterreise*.

From the point of view of performance and singing technique I consider this lied the most difficult in the cycle: the shadowy colour in the third verse (the sixth stanza of the poem), where the voice must sound as if it is coming from a distance, is less of a challenge, even though the singing is entirely in the foreground and only the linden tree far away. It may be dramaturgically difficult, but in my view it is not avoidable, and in fact unproblematic, like an optical illusion that doesn't upset anybody. Much more difficult, on the other hand, is the piano part in the second verse of the lied, beginning in the minor. It is entirely in the context of the melancholic performance practice of this lied, and is at least retrospectively explained by the return of the major in the second half of the verse ('Und seine Zweige rauschten . . .' – 'And its branches rustled . . .') and its now brighter sonority.

However, particularly difficult in my view is the first verse of *Der Lindenbaum*, which – uniquely in the whole song-cycle – draws a picture of unselfconscious candour – a picture not current, but immediate and lifelike.[21] Here I imagine a direct and naive accent, which gives an untroubled account of this village idyll with a linden tree, which Silcher then extended to the lied as a whole, and was later preserved in sentimental *Heimat* movies. From my own experience, this idyllic spirit can be conveyed in three ways: first of all with a tone that is not too bright and above all not sharp, a somewhat rounded tone that is intended to express insouciance; secondly by ensuring a dynamic that is not too reticent – in view of the preceding, rather dramatic *Erstarrung* ('Numbness'), this might not seem difficult, but the integration of the required round, relaxed, fading tone actually makes it more of a challenge; and thirdly, with a device very unusual in Schubert: a *portamento* (a kind of vocal slide between notes) downwards in both double leaps from the fifth to the third ('Bru–nnen', ''träumt' in') and from there to the tonic ('To–re', 'Scha–tten').[22]

Not only in Schubert, but in German music generally (and not only in the lied), this kind of intonational transition is usually considered tasteless – or at least unfashionable. For example, in the minor half of the second verse I can't bring myself to sing it (except out of negligence or inability), because the distinction between what is performed and the act of performance, typical of Schubert in my eyes, here again already assumes its particular importance. But the *portamento* does excellently convey the folkloric quality of the first verse – experience not quoted or reported but direct and authentic. It is the subject of this verse of the lied, and in reminiscence recurs in the third verse, but tends to pass without being noticed, so I sing the *portamento* again there, not least in order to maintain the difficult suppleness of the slow 3/4 rhythm.[23] I only recently discovered this function of *portamento*. It finally brings something of which I was previously aware but could never actually accomplish as a part of a deliberate and achievable performance.

At this point I should add that Gerold Huber and I are convinced devotees of the faction that resolutely rejects the instruction in *Wasserflut* to match the dotted chords in the left hand of the piano to the triplets in the right. (Ian Bostridge gives an impressive anecdotal and factual account of this phenomenon, which is why I am also happy to refer to it.[24]) In short: in Schubert's time, triplets whose first two beats are tied and, given that they are at the same pitch, sound as a single note, are not yet written in that way. This notational deficiency was sometimes compensated for by instead writing dotted duplets of the same overall duration, and hence with a proportion of 3:1 instead of the intended 2:1. For me, however, that does not inevitably – certainly not – mean that all dotted duplets should be understood as triplets (see music example 28). This would be logically a classical false conclusion. Otherwise, the first two quavers in bar 3 of *Wasserflut* could be understood as triplets. Or in 'Der Lindenbaum', after the first triplet beat, the first dotted duplet beat of the second bar could be seen as a triplet – an absurdity. So, seriously, could any sane person insist on such a thing? (See music example 29.)

One word about the lack of development within this suggested journey, though: in *Winterreise* we find very many very impressive images, both literary – Wilhelm Müller's *Winterreise* poems are surely among those that make German poetry worth reading – and

28 Franz Schubert: *Wasserflut*, bars 1–3

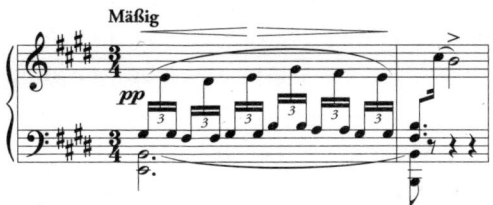

29 Franz Schubert: *Der Lindenbaum*, bar 1f.

also musical. Time and again throughout Schubert's body of lieder I find an extraordinary ability to add a visual narrative perspective in pictures to a per se lyrical form. Then, before the listener's eye, situations from a painting or a little film appear, something I am at best familiar with from truly epic works such as Haydn's *The Creation* and *The Seasons*.

A few examples from Schubert's lieder might suffice to explain what I mean: *Der Winterabend* ('Winter Evening'), D. 938; *Abschied* ('Farewell'), D. 475, and *Der Schiffer* ('The Boatman'), D. 694, have this essentially narrative quality, which might also have something to do with Schubert's overall choice of poems, particularly in comparison with other great composers who have set German-language poetry, but above all with the way he sets them to music, with the sound conjuring a visual image to an unusual degree. In *Der Winterabend*, for example, the picture he paints is of a protagonist walking up and down the room, looking out of the window, and the moonlight gliding in. In *Abschied*, I see a procession of pilgrims approaching and then disappearing into the distance. Finally, there is the fantasy of the boatman in *Der Schiffer*, in love and self-absorbed as his boat rocks gently in the moonlight. The list of Schubert songs evoking such vivid images is a long one.

But this phenomenon, I believe, also shapes the songs of *Winterreise* – in a unique way: the lyrical images are strong, if never particularly concentrated or compact, and every concrete image has more of a symbolic than a narrative value. They seem to me like steles grouped together in a thematic landscape of melancholy and isolation, while at the same time each remaining discrete in expression and content. This attractive and inspiring visual quality forges a strong bond between the poems and their settings. In comparison with many other images from Schubert lieder, however, those in *Winterreise* are more static than dynamic. That might be the crucial point and why I find the narrative drive to be so absent from this cycle, except in the two framing songs. So winter, with its frozen torpor, has a correlative of meaning not only in the coldness of the soul that our 'hero' encounters, but also a formal correlative in images that stand side by side as if frozen.

It is not my impression that Schubertian rhetoric follows in detail every turn of a poem, every shift in argument. This genuinely applies, for example, to strophic songs such as no. 1, *Gute Nacht*; no. 6, *Wasserflut*; no. 10, *Rast*; no. 11, *Frühlingstraum*, or no. 13, *Die Post*, but also to individual motifs such as the musical theme of the concretely visual first stanza of no. 4, *Erstarrung*, which is repeated in the more abstract fourth stanza and seems to me to fit much better there. Or for the musical setting of whole poems such as no. 3, *Gefrorne Tränen*, in which, at least in the third stanza of the poem, I discern a certain lack of congruence between the searching despondence of the poem and the relatively accusatory gesture of the musical setting.

But the expressive power, the downright monstrously accurate creative decisiveness, revealing itself almost sculpturally (in 24 separate steles), is unique, and I also see this expressive vividness and potency as an essential characteristic that distinguishes *Winterreise* from other song-cycles. What is crucial for me here as a performer is not so much the singularity in sound of each individual song. I would assume that in any case for any song or work being performed. It is rather the depictive strength or power, appearing not so much human as monolithic. To understand the protagonist's psychology, particularly in terms of development, is in my view irrelevant to the interpretation of the work. One must in principle understand only the nature and situation of the winter traveller, which for me, as I have said, is best captured by the term 'crisis'.

This 'field of steles', however, could be visited and approached from all angles.[25] In this sense there is (apart from songs 1 and 24 – the entrance and exit of this wintry garden) no sequential relationship between those affectively particular monuments, but there is a relatedness between them. That also fits with the field of affects, which appears in my overview of the poems, a field that is constantly varied, but not fundamentally changeable in terms of character development – or indeed of plot.

Similarly, one could also switch the order of the lieder, and indeed there are performances in which they are performed in the sequence in which Schubert set Wilhelm Müller's poems (and which is slightly different from the composer's final sequence). As far as I am concerned, this makes only partial sense, because the established sequence is so familiar, and a different order might confuse rather than add meaning. Listeners might start trying to work out what a particular song was doing in a particular position, and might miss the music in consequence.

So, I do not believe, along with Elmar Budde, that *Winterreise* – Müller's or Schubert's – depicts a nocturnal wander in any chronological sense.[26] Instead, we should perhaps see *Winterreise* in concrete terms, as we do the Stations of the Cross. Christ's humiliations would be equally meaningful in a different sequence, but the traditional one is the one that we have internalised.

This comparison also makes sense in terms of the obvious religious allusions in *Winterreise*. In Schubert's setting they are apparent in an affirmative and generally presumptuous religious attitude. Thus, for example, at the end of some songs, especially in the second part – no. 14, *Der greise Kopf*; no. 15, *Die Krähe*; no. 16, *Letzte Hoffnung*; no. 17, *Im Dorfe*; or no. 20, *Der Wegweiser* – one can become aware of a chorale-like broadening in the underlying structure of the melody.[27] And some songs might, because of their recitative-like interruptions, be understood more or less as parodies of an overall quasi-chorale structure: no. 21, *Das Wirtshaus*; no. 23, *Die Nebensonnen*.[28] These chorale associations become more frequent as the rather abstract nature of the early part of the cycle fades away. And the more concrete the images become, particularly from no. 17, *Im Dorfe* onwards, the greater – as I have regularly observed – the enthralled attention of the audience. One might conclude that this increasingly concrete pictorial nature at least contributes to the gripping quality so often attributed to the cycle.

On the other hand, there seems to be in Wilhelm Müller's verse a rather cynical use of religious allusion, its overwrought blasphemy virtually setting out an artistic programme. In no. 22, *Mut*, which might at first suggest the fearfulness of a child singing in a basement, refuge is finally sought in self-aggrandisement ('Sind wir selber Götter!' – 'Are we ourselves gods?'). In no. 15, *Die Krähe*, the desired fidelity is expected of a crow, commonly associated with meanness, because no one, whether human or divine, is willing to show fidelity. The grave addressed in this song runs like a leitmotif throughout the whole of the cycle – directly so in no. 16, *Letzte Hoffnung* ('auf meiner Hoffnung Grab' – 'on my hope's grave') and no. 21, *Das Wirtshaus*, whose titles stands for the graveyard. In that song this – yes! – blasphemy reaches a spectacular climax when the protagonist, in his world-weariness[29] and never-ending self-pity, identifies with Mary and Joseph, the parents of the Saviour. They too, of course, were cruelly refused shelter at the inn. Except that the winter traveller does not sit by the manger; his only resting place can mean no less than the final descent into the grave – not to die, however, but to display his suffering as a dying man, or, even better, as one who has been buried alive.[30]

The anchoring of *Winterreise* in a Christian vision of the world – the churches in the villages and the nearby homes that our hero walks past might not be named, but I can't ignore them – appears to me one last time *ex negativo* in the image of the hurdy-gurdy man: he is the opposite of the protagonist, a man who is disillusioned, indolent, but living entirely in the moment, at the service of the hurdy-gurdy, a figure reminiscent of the Buddhist ideal of desiring nothing. It is an ideal as far as one can imagine from that of the winter traveller, who is entirely rooted in occidental Christian thought, who cannot conceal his desires, his hopes, his longings and his reviving ambitions. Through all his hateful inciting and separations, all his vulnerabilities, his laments and his world-disgust, he has practically screamed over the course of 22 songs how much he mourns his (temporarily) lost world. The lovesickness addressed at the beginning may be nothing but a trigger to suggest the fear of losing cultural integration. The culture of the West is the almost symbolically idealised background to these diverse and multiply inter-referential etchings in sound, with the diverse grey and brown palette of an illustrated gallery of stones.

Postscript
London, October 2021

A few weeks ago, at our 'own' little Lied Biennale in Elmau, Gerold Huber and I tried out Schubert's 'original' sequence. The first publication of *Winterreise*, which Schubert had found in the literary almanac *Urania*, was only a first half of the poems' cycle, in a slightly different sequence from that when the final 24 poems were released. After receiving them (published in Müller's *Sieben und siebzig Gedicthe aus den hintlerlassenen Papieren eines reisenden Waldhornisten* – 'Seventy-seven Poems from the Posthumous Papers of a Travelling Horn-Player'), Schubert set the additional 12 poems and finally combined them with the first 12 lieder, editing the completed song-cycle in the sequence of Müller's cycle of poems. The extent to which the 'original' sequence corresponds to Schubert's composition process is not easily determined, and perhaps it is not particularly relevant. But the opportunity to dare to take another look at *Winterreise* excited us.

Something like this is easier in a smaller, intimate festival. We began the day with a performance of Schoeck's *Elegie*, to install an attuning counterweight that, with its comparably gloomy poems and the same number of lieder, should above all form a powerful parallel to the evening's fare. Othmar Schoeck is said to have spoken of the *Elegie* as being novella-like in form,[31] although (like *Winterreise*), it cannot in fact be defined in any chronological sense as it would be generally understood, or in terms of a plot. It is also comparably visual. These similarities (even though the two cycles are of course very different and very much their own) encouraged us to offer the *Elegie* as a way of opening up a receptive attitude for the work to be performed in the evening. Given the fact that the work was likely to be unfamiliar, we felt justified in hoping that the audience would approach it with an open mind.

Othmar Schoeck's biographer Chris Walton tells us that Alfred Schoeck, the composer's father, could not escape the radically depressive effect of the *Elegie* but, given the relatively secure bourgeois existence of his son, felt very ashamed of his lack of gratitude. Faced with the selection of Lenau's *Weltschmerz* poems, in hindsight he would have preferred a seat nearer to the exit so that he would have been able to leave early.[32] In other respects too, the impact of the work was huge in Othmar Schoeck's time. The *Elegie* became one of his most popular and successful works, from which, after wild nights of partying, the composer delighted in belting out the mood-killer *Herbstklage* ('Autumn Lament'), accompanying himself on the piano. We dare to conclude from this that it is permissible to perform the *Elegie* not only with chamber orchestra (as well as with strings and piano, or with flute, clarinet, cor anglais, oboe, horn, trombones and tam-tam) but also in the highly practical piano version from 1921–22 that Schoeck did not orchestrate until the winter of 1922–23. That option, we thought, might compensate for the work's meanwhile regrettable lack of familiarity.

This early cycle contains a widely divergent range of styles, from lieder that would have seemed idyllic and conservative even in Brahms's time, let alone in the 1920s – *Wehmut* ('Melancholy'), *Liebesfrühling* ('Spring of Love'), *An den Wind* ('To the Wind'), *Vergangenheit* ('The Past') – to strife-torn avant-garde songs – *Stille Sicherheit* ('Silent Safety'), *Waldlied I* ('Forest Song I'), *Herbstgefühl I* ('Autumn Feeling I'), *Nachklang* ('Echo'), *Waldlied II* ('Forest Song II') – culminating in the modernist climax, *Verlorenes Glück* ('Forlorn Fortune'). But all the songs share recurring figures,[33] which also appear in the accompaniment and not always at a lower pitch (for example, the eleventh song, *Vesper*, has a diminished chord in the descant, unchanging over 51 bars). This applies particularly to the relatively calm songs with their repetition of musical motifs, tending towards uniformity. The effect of these monotonous repetitions unites the whole work and brings out the unmistakable – even unique – melancholy that seems to have so distressed Schoeck's father.

The idea of performing the work with piano proved to be an excellent one, and it was an unforgettable concert, at least for Gerold Huber and me. Then, after the lunch break, came the preparation for *Winterreise* in the late afternoon. Here I had to husband my remaining forces as carefully as possible, and in the end I simply read through Müller's poems again in sequence. I was deeply shaken. Of course, I knew every word, but quite suddenly I saw in them an innocence and almost a lightness of which I had not previously been aware, because of the practicalities of performing, and perhaps because of the setting itself. And I took that impression with me into the recital. Admittedly the rearrangement of the songs explained above also helped me to see the cycle differently: certain stretches of the journey were deconstructed (above all the final strand of death drills from *Der Wegweiser* onwards), and as might have been expected it was possible to envisage some of the songs in a different way. The fact that *Im Dorfe*, which we consider central, moved from being no. 17 to no. 12 and opened the second part was both sensible and enlightening. But the beautiful thing for me was that I was able to seize on the impression of innocence that I had taken from my reading and convert it into sound: a lightness and brightness took hold from the outset. And that allowed me to sing the songs as I had long wished to do: unadorned, and without aiming for a potentially overstated cynicism. Something I generally seek to avoid in performance, balancing the virile darkening of the voice with the brightness of the 'mask' (a technical term describing the placement of the tone above the upper incisors), now proved possible to achieve. An innocence in the presentation (as a correlate to a vocal brightness) is actually more effective at creating genuine drama and intensity (as a correlate to a vocal darkness) without any forcing – just as an unadorned voice can summon its brightness from within, from its own flow as it were, and thus not have to be forced by squeezing. The performance gave me a *Winterreise* of the kind that I had long yearned for: essentially fulfilling in itself, without any dependence on established ways of responding to the work. And I would hope to be able to carry this approach forward in the future.

ART NOUVEAU ROSE

LISBON, 5 SEPTEMBER 2019

The Lake Isle of Innisfree

I will arise and go now, and go to Innisfree,
And a small cabin build there, of clay and wattles made;
Nine bean rows will I have there, a hive for the honey bee,
And live alone in the bee-loud glade.

And I shall have some peace there, for peace comes
    dropping slow,
Dropping from the veils of the morning to where the
    cricket sings;
There midnight's all a glimmer, and noon a purple glow,
And evening full of the linnet's wings.

I will arise and go now, for always night and day
I hear lake water lapping with low sounds by the shore;
While I stand on the roadway, or on the pavements grey,
I hear it in the deep heart's core.

WILLIAM BUTLER YEATS

Gustav Mahler's *Rückert-Lieder*, settings of poems by Friedrich Rückert, are in my view his most tricky lieder in terms of interpretation. Because the song *Liebst du um Schönheit* ('If You Love for Beauty') was not originally a part of the set and was introduced only later, there is no official sequence stipulated by the composer. My solution, which I justify below, is as follows:

1 *Blicke mir nicht in die Lieder*
2 *Ich atmet' einen linden Duft*
3 *Um Mitternacht*
4 *Liebst du um Schönheit*
5 *Ich bin der Welt abhanden gekommen*

One sometimes comes across internal cross-references in Mahler's relatively small body of work as a composer of lieder, not least in the two songs placed, in my view, to best effect at the beginning and the end of a performance of the *Rückert-Lieder*. *Blicke mir nicht in die Lieder* ('Do Not Look into My Songs') is about the creative process itself, in which Rückert employs a topos for the writing of poetry that can be traced back to classical antiquity: the collection of honey by bees. Here the composer demands a degree of privacy for himself, something that is not often granted to him. Related to this, the song *Ich bin der Welt abhanden gekommen* ('I Am Lost to the World') ends (in my sequence) the reflection on the creative process with the words 'Ich leb' allein [. . .] in meinem Lied' ('I live alone [. . .] in my song') and thus closes the sequence with a renewed demand for privacy. The two lieder *Ich atmet' einen linden Duft* ('I Breathed a Mild Fragrance') and *Liebst du um Schönheit* ('If You Love for Beauty') now also connect the 'I' with the 'you' when they are grouped around the central *Um Mitternacht* ('At Midnight') as a reciprocal internal parenthesis.

Blicke mir nicht in die Lieder
Gustav Mahler: *Rückert-Lieder* (1)

Blicke mir nicht in die Lieder!
Meine Augen schlag' ich nieder,
Wie ertappt auf böser Tat.
Selber darf ich nicht getrauen,
Ihrem Wachsen zuzuschauen:
Deine Neugier ist Verrat!
Bienen, wenn sie Zellen bauen,
Lassen auch nicht zu sich schauen,
Schauen selbst auch nicht zu.
Wenn die reichen Honigwaben
Sie zu Tag gefördert haben,
Dann vor allen nasche du!

FRIEDRICH RÜCKERT

> Do not look into my songs!
> My eyes I'm casting down,
> As if caught in evil deed.
> I myself may not even dare
> To watch their growth;
> Your curiosity is betrayal!
> Bees, when they build their cells,
> Do not allow themselves to be watched,
> Do not even watch themselves.
> Once the rich honeycombs
> They have brought to light
> You shall be the first to taste!

Throughout, the cycle continually exudes an aura of egocentricity, as is the case in most poems and songs in the first person singular, and in that way is nothing out of the ordinary. With the work of Gustav Mahler in particular, however, this egocentricity has justified a common and popular interpretation invested in the composer's life and personality. Many authors and interpreters believe they can deduce from Mahler's private annotations that egocentricity was his actual and primary aesthetic mode. Two conductors I particularly like and admire have even referred to this eternal 'me, me, me' as the main shortcoming of his work. They find it irksome, and feel fed up with this sentimentality. One of them, Nikolaus Harnoncourt, has never performed Mahler's music for this very reason, and I find that very regrettable.

Certainly I am always enthusiastic when a stand is being taken against sentimentality of this kind, an emotionally over-exuberant charging of an artwork with one's own psychological traits. But in this special instance, the case of Mahler's oeuvre, where the often encountered biographistic approach to art is truly extreme, I would maintain that there really is no need to bother with what Mahler associated with his own works and their origins. Why should these works not be granted an impersonal universality, even if the artist in question readily and quite legitimately associated them with his private concerns? Similarly, none of us is entirely innocent of associating art with our own life and experiences, whether receptively or creatively (although without overtly and immediately displaying this connection). If an author clings to a self-reference or even, as Mahler did more than once, writes it down in the score as a private exclamation (not as a performance instruction), that does not mean that one must take this on board as a performer or interpreter of a work, should one even be able to do so. Something of the kind – in my experience – actually happens only when the performer unpleasantly and (in my opinion) inappropriately introduces their own private life into a work that cannot bear the weight of it and does not need it. Who really wants that? Not me, if I may make so bold. I can tolerate a performer's tears only when offered as an illusory deception.

Liebst du um Schönheit
Gustav Mahler: *Rückert-Lieder* (4)

> Liebst du um Schönheit, o nicht mich liebe!
> Liebe die Sonne, sie trägt ein goldnes Haar!
> Liebst du um Jugend, o nicht mich liebe!
> Liebe den Frühling, der jung ist jedes Jahr!
> Liebst du um Schätze, o nicht mich liebe!
> Liebe die Meerfrau, sie hat viel Perlen klar!
> Liebst du um Liebe, o ja – mich liebe!
> Liebe mich immer, dich lieb ich immerdar!
>
> FRIEDRICH RÜCKERT

> If you love for beauty, oh do not love me!
> Love the sun, for it has golden hair.
> If you love for youth, oh do not love me!

Love the springtime, which is young each year!
If you love for treasures, oh do not love me!
Love the mermaid, who has many bright pearls!
If you love for love, then love me!
Love me for ever, and I will love you for ever!

Particularly important in this respect, to my mind, is the song *Liebst du um Schönheit*, which, as I have mentioned, did not belong to the *Rückert-Lieder* (so says the philologist). Mahler composed it as a gift for his wife, and besides did not orchestrate it himself. It is often argued that it should be omitted from the cycle on precisely the same the grounds of discreet piety that is then blithely disregarded in the unashamedly mawkish rendition of the other four songs. The circumstances of its composition tend to be taken as an ominous sign that the song was supposed to remain private. However, everything else that is private about Mahler is merrily dragged into the light of day, exaggerated and overemphasised almost at will. I am thinking here particularly of the sickeningly indiscreet 'documentary films' about him from the Jubilee Biennial of 2010–11.

The moral value of different kinds of love is the theme of this song. The worst would be to love for wealth, the next worst for beauty. That is not quite as bad, but somehow troubling and regrettable, as to love for the youth of the other person. In fact what is displayed here is grief for lost youth and innocence; it is the only verse in which the thematic gesture appears in the minor key. Then, as the fourth and final alternative, the best cause for love is finally named: love itself. A non-reason, without any need for justification.

Like a bolt from the blue, on a magically inspiring stage in Lisbon, I realised how well this insight could be applied to the performance and interpretation of art by those of us who are musicians, singers, actors and directors. One can serve art in order to become rich (verse 3), but how stupid is that? Unforgivable! Then, out of vanity (verse 1), out of narcissism, out of empty emotion and to make oneself appear attractive – not good either. But then, and this would correspond to the 'youth' of the second verse, there is the sad and hermeneutic exegete, who attempts to assign a secretly encrypted meaning to a work, however unlikely it might be, while the interpreter demands the freedom of interpretation, arguing at the same time that their vision is causally derived from the work itself. I see this as presumptuous and immature, even youthful – charming but ultimately unacceptable.

Last of all, however, we have perhaps the best and most serious kind of interpretation: one that respects the literary and musical language, emerging from unconditional love for the work to be performed. This came to me during a performance of the *Rückert-Lieder* with the Gustav Mahler Youth Orchestra under the baton of Herbert Blomstedt in the enchanting auditorium of the Calouste Gulbenkian Foundation in Lisbon, whose park is bathed in green and purple light that shines through the huge glass wall behind the stage, illuminating and inspiring the performance. What I experienced here was musicianship that was fully informed, as faithful as possible to the words, and intellectually sound. We might assume that something like this might move in lockstep towards execution, but that assumption, since I knew Herbert Blomstedt, would be wide of the mark. He makes possible the ensemble playing of the musicians, essentially of the notes themselves; he creates a basis for universal comprehensibility, insofar as such a thing is possible in the arts, but he does not attempt to suppress differences between all the participants. On the contrary: his most tolerant attitude creates the possibility of aesthetic variety in the unambiguous context of musical form. (I would place myself somewhere between verses 2 and 3, between vanity and reverent interpretation.)

Ich bin der Welt abhanden gekommen
Gustav Mahler, *Rückert-Lieder* (5)

Ich bin der Welt abhanden gekommen,
Mit der ich sonst viele Zeit verdorben;
Sie hat so lange nichts von mir vernommen,
Sie mag wohl glauben, ich sei gestorben!
Es ist mir auch gar nichts daran gelegen,
Ob sie mich für gestorben hält.
Ich kann auch gar nichts sagen dagegen,
Denn wirklich bin ich gestorben der Welt.
Ich bin gestorben dem Weltgetümmel
Und ruh' in einem stillen Gebiet.
Ich leb' allein in meinem Himmel,
In meinem Lieben, in meinem Lied.

FRIEDRICH RÜCKERT

I am lost to the world
On which I have usually wasted so much time;
It has for so long nothing heard from me,
It may well think that I have died.
And I even do not care
If it thinks that I am dead.
I couldn't even raise objection,
For really I have died to the world.
I have died to the world's turmoil
And rest in a quiet place.
I live alone in my heaven,
In my love, in my song.

There is hardly any need to point out the extent to which – almost in eschatological terms – this song is frequently taken as being concerned with death and the understanding of last things. On the other hand, the farewell to the world, in my eyes often overwrought in performance, may be considered merely as a rather more innocuous form of escapism: expressing a weariness with the world, certainly, yet at the same time being serene, almost carefree. I would therefore prefer to see this song as a humoresque, because its message is clear: no one has died – at most perhaps to another person, but only 'to the world'. Merely that 'dying', essentially an intransitive verb, should suddenly take an indirect object reveals the grotesque-humorous, no longer definitive nature of the dying to which this poem alludes. Later in the lied it becomes still clearer what it is to which the 'I' has died: 'to the world's turmoil'. Here someone is just hopping off, and he doesn't care what might be made of it. Only at the end is there something like a confession that might be intended seriously, when the 'quiet place' to which the 'I' has withdrawn is given concrete form: heaven, love, song. Only with this strange tripartite constellation is the 'I' able and willing to remain whole. It cannot stay dead to those three.

I must acknowledge a feeling of possible embarrassment in my own performances because with that final word, 'Lied' ('song'), *the* attribute of the singer, the borderline to the private seems at the very least jeopardised. That radical conditions for a bearable life are being formulated here is indisputable, but that the focus ultimately has to be 'song' . . . ! Also, these conditions are not kept universally. They are presented by possessive pronouns as the coordinates of a solipsistic vision of the world – I dare to stress 'meinem' ('my') dynamically, since this is the confession of an egoist. The risk of blurring the boundary between the presenting and the lyrical 'I' is particularly great here – but of course only from the audience's point of view. Attempts to insist on objectivity by avoiding the slightest reduction in tempo while singing 'in meinem Lied' inevitably, in my experience, are doomed to fail. As a compromise, I have found, it is possible to place the inevitable *ritardando* between 'in' and 'mei–' rather than between 'mei–' and '–nem', the more obvious location from a musical point of view. One has simply to get through it somehow. But the embarrassment, with this one-syllable word – 'Lied' – is still minor if the alternative were to be a noticeably self-indulgent revelling in a farewell to the world for a full five minutes.

The *Rückert-Lieder*, particularly the song *Ich bin der Welt abhanden gekommen*, are often interpreted as a particularly personal work of Mahler's. I see them instead as rather super-personal, as a floral, paradigmatically perfect work of 'musical *art nouveau*':[1] five petals – a rose in bloom – in a seemingly decorative arrangement that is not perfectly balanced, formally just slightly off kilter. The relative length of the individual lieder – three short songs, 1, 2 and 4, alongside considerably more substantial ones, 3 and 5 – is responsible for the danger of massive asymmetry. It seems to me, therefore, that the final half-sentence gives the cycle a confessional character in the person of the performer that is difficult to ignore, and which tends to bring the person of the singer more into the foreground – something the collection as a whole has until then been discreetly and decently avoiding. However, I don't see that placing the song anywhere other than at the conclusion of the sequence would be workable, as the sense of an ending is so obvious and too insistent to be denied. I am happy, though, to counter this effect by adding Mahler's *Wunderhorn* lied *Urlicht* ('Primal Light') – which does not belong only to his Second Symphony but also exists in both an orchestrated and a piano version – as an encore.

Urlicht
Gustav Mahler

O Röschen rot!
Der Mensch liegt in größter Not!
Der Mensch liegt in größter Pein!
Je lieber möcht' ich im Himmel sein!

Da kam ich auf einen breiten Weg,
Da kam ein Engelein und wollt' mich abweisen.
Ach nein, ich ließ mich nicht abweisen!
Ich bin von Gott, und will wieder zu Gott!
Der liebe Gott wird mir ein Lichtchen geben,
Wird leuchten mir bis an das ewig, selig Leben!

                from DES KNABEN WUNDERHORN

O little rose so red!
The man lies in greatest need.
The man lies in the greatest pain.
The more I want to be in heaven.

At once I came to a wide path.
There came an angel and wanted to turn me away.
But no, I would not have me turned away.
I am of God, and with God I want to be again.
The good Lord will give me a small light,
Will light my way to eternal, blissful life.

For me, this song shows the extent to which Mahler uses the humoresque, indeed the grotesque, to encounter the all-too-present motif of end times, with all its existential dread and hopelessness, that is present in many of his works. I even take it as an indication that Mahler was fully aware of the danger of a surfeit of sentimentality, and that he was perhaps attempting to rein it in by counterbalancing it with laughter, with the bizarre. Because how else, after the evocation of the disaster of the end of the world, are we to understand the image of the deceased briskly denied entrance to heaven by an angel and then indignantly rejecting the exclusion and insisting on forcing his fully deserved path to God? I can't help thinking of Franz Kafka's short story *Before the Law*, in which a man does not dare to go through the gate that is meant for him for fear of the guard. Only at the moment of his death does he learn that it would have been his own path. The glimpse of horror, the long wait by the 'gate of truth', is distorted into caricature by both Kafka and Mahler. We know from Kafka's friend Max Brod, who guarded his posthumous reputation, how Kafka would often burst out laughing when giving public readings of his work. This is an excellent example of what I understand by Mahler's term, 'the humoresque'.

Um Mitternacht
Gustav Mahler: *Rückert-Lieder* (3)

Um Mitternacht
Hab' ich gewacht
Und aufgeblickt zum Himmel;
Kein Stern vom Sterngewimmel
Hat mir gelacht
Um Mitternacht.

Um Mitternacht
Hab' ich gedacht
Hinaus in dunkle Schranken.
Es hat kein Lichtgedanken
Mir Trost gebracht
Um Mitternacht.

Um Mitternacht
Nahm ich in acht
Die Schläge meines Herzens;
Ein einz'ger Puls des Schmerzens
War angefacht
Um Mitternacht.

Um Mitternacht
Kämpft' ich die Schlacht,
O Menschheit, deiner Leiden;
Nicht konnt' ich sie entscheiden

Mit meiner Macht
Um Mitternacht.

Um Mitternacht
Hab' ich die Macht
In deine Hand gegeben;
Herr über Tod und Leben,
Du hältst die Wacht
Um Mitternacht.

FRIEDRICH RÜCKERT

At midnight
I was awake
And looked up in the sky:
Now star from starry host
Did beam at me
At midnight.

At midnight
My thoughts went out
Into the realms of darkness.
No thought of light
Did comfort me
At midnight.

At midnight
I took care of
The beats of my heart;
A single pulse of pain
Was stirred
At midnight.

At midnight
I fought the battle,
O mankind, of your suffering;
Nor could I gain victory

With my power
At midnight.

At midnight
Have I the might
Put in your hand;
Lord over death and life,
You keep the watch
At midnight.

Let us return to the *Rückert-Lieder*. *Um Mitternacht* ('At Midnight') is not the expression and representation of a veritable existential crisis that one might initially assume. Instead, I see it as an account of a disturbed awakening at night, when the taming of circumstantial, unbridled emotions and anxieties are finally placed in God's hands – not unlike surrendering to an anti-depressant – before one takes charge of one's own life again the following morning (i.e. not the equivalent of an anti-depressant). Because of its force and temporal expansiveness, Gerold Huber and I see *Um Mitternacht* as the central song of the cycle and place it in the middle, even if it hurts vocally to have to sing *Liebst du um Schönheit* after it – I often find the whole cycle almost impossibly difficult to perform. With its high and tender notes on the vowels 'ü' and 'i', *Liebst du um Schönheit* does not, in terms of vocal technique, follow on well from the vocally darker, broad and loud, indeed 'heroic', ending of *Um Mitternacht*.

So the consciously non-self-reflective and non-representational, even rational element flows through this cycle: *Blicke mir nicht in die Lieder* is only a reflection on the creative process, and it becomes a downright attempt to prevent the establishment of the personal as the ultimate foundation of the work's reception. Both listener and reader are challenged to understand a work of art on its own terms, and not to relate it to the personal biography of its creator. This approach is seldom associated with Mahler and his work, as I have said at some length, but it is so programmatic that I (whether I am performing with Gerold Huber or with an orchestra) deliberately open the collection of *Rückert-Lieder* with this lied, and think that it would be impossible to embark on these lieder, with their very calculated and hence particularly formal formlessness, with any other song.

Ich atmet' einen linden Duft
Gustav Mahler: *Rückert-Lieder* (2)

Ich atmet' einen linden Duft.
Im Zimmer stand
Ein Zweig der Linde,
Ein Angebinde
Von lieber Hand.
Wie lieblich war der Lindenduft!

Wie lieblich ist der Lindenduft!
Das Lindenreis
brachst du gelinde;
Ich atme leis
Im Duft der Linde
Der Liebe linden Duft.

FRIEDRICH RÜCKERT

I breathed a mild fragrance.
In the room stood
A lime branch
A bouquet bound
By a dear hand.
How lovely was the scent of lime!

How lovely is the lime tree's scent!
The lime tree's twig
You gently broke;

> I softly breathe
> In the scent of lime
> The mild allure of love.

Again, *Ich atmet' einen linden Duft* ('I breathed a mild fragrance') need not necessarily be understood as something personal, not as a revelation of something actually experienced. I see it more as something along the lines of an Indian-ink drawing from an album of sketches, a work of art from the Far East with a universal resonance, as less the expression of a personal mood than the depiction of an impersonal essence, namely nature. Connecting the scent of a blossoming tree with the sensation of love does seem slightly obscene to me, but that is not to say at all that the rational character of this very concise poem is fundamentally lost.

For the sake of internal variety and to an extent for the sake of performance practice, I hereby admit that in this song I take the liberty of articulating 'Lindenduft' at the end of the first verse in a way differently from how it is written, and thus undertake a (quite insignificant) grammatical reinterpretation. At the beginning of the second verse I stress 'Lindenduft' in the usual way and in accordance with its meaning as a single word, with the emphasis on the first syllable, but at the end of the first verse I do something else. With a broad and dynamic emphasis on the second part of the word, '–duft', I suggest that this is the actual subject with the genitive, 'der Linden' ('of the lime'), placed before it. By way of mitigation, I hope I can rely on the acknowledgement that this additional variation does not do any mischief to a poem that is already characterised by play on the words 'lind' (mild), 'Linde' (lime tree), 'gelinde' (mildly) and 'Duft' (scent), particularly since it is audible only to those who wish to hear it.[2]

To return, finally, to *Liebst du um Schönheit*, conceived as an intimate gift to Mahler's wife. The poem on which it is based, formally so severe, elevates this song into the ranks of universal attractiveness and validity. The fact that it was conceived in a personal context does not in any way call into question its status as an objectively accessible work of art. So I deliberately resist – and not only in order to complete the five-part rose-petal wreath – the prudishness of performing only the four other *Rückert-Lieder*. I think we can find enough that is interesting in this song without having to join the Mahlers in their marriage bed.

MEANING OR BEING

MUNICH, DECEMBER 2020

> Thus art no longer points towards another exemplary form of being, but is rather itself that being paradigmatic for the human: the work of art no longer seeks only to *mean* something, it seeks to *be* something.¹
>
> HANS BLUMENBERG

It was only about sixty years before the birth of Franz Schubert that the separation between the artist's creation and the creator's art gradually succeeded in German literature – with Johann Jakob Bodmer and Johann Jakob Breitinger, with Friedrich Gottlieb Klopstock and then with the poets of the *Sturm und Drang* movement.² Not only in the works the artists created, but also in their consciousness of themselves, a new self-image could grow. They realised they could achieve something beyond the recreation and imitation of nature and ideas: beyond the incorporation of all existence into the singular potential of our world. Henceforth, art was increasingly a matter of expressing the self, and no longer of merely depicting the objective world. Although the journey from Schubert to Nietzsche, who speaks of 'art as the supreme task and the actually metaphysical activity of this life',³ still seems to be a long one, the art song, groundbreaking at least during the nineteenth century, with its emphasis on the creative artist, could not have come into being as a genre without that focus on subjectivity in literature.

Schubert initially staked a claim to the mere existence of an artwork that has come into being, that is more or less depictive but has no point of reference beyond itself. It was Robert Schumann who took the next step with his desire to give that existence further artistic justification, not so much in terms of depiction (which is what Hans Blumenberg intends by 'mean'), but in the sense of interpreting itself, of *providing* meaning.

In Schubert's lieder there is much evidence that in his work – and long after – nature is being imitated: for example, in the piano figurations of *Gretchen am Spinnrade*, D. 118, in which a turn formed by six notes in the piano right hand suggests the movement of the spinning wheel and differs only in degree from the metaphorical, intensified portrayal of Gretchen's mounting agitation as the song progresses. Or, although less unambiguously, in the first song of *Die schöne Müllerin*, D. 795, in which the turning mill wheel is represented – or perhaps more specifically, given the vertical orientation of the broken triadic sequences, the transfer of power from the mill wheel to the grinding stones. There are, however, many more examples where the contrary is true, with imitation fading into the background, from *Liebesbotschaft*, the first song in *Schwanengesang*, D. 957, in which the motion of the stream mentioned in the song's lyric is merely a device to create a metaphor for the restless longing for the beloved; to the abstract *Gesängen des Harfners* ('The Harper's Songs'), D. 478–80; to the settings of Goethe's genius-hymns (for example, *Prometheus*, D. 674, and *Ganymed*, D. 544), or the Petrarch sonnets, D. 628–30. Here perhaps some fragments of the depiction of 'reality' remain, but otherwise everything is so much the expression of the thinking and feeling 'I' that I would dare to say, in retrospect, considering the whole body of Schubert's lieder, that it is an unhelpful trivialisation to understand *Gretchen* primarily on the basis of the visualisation of the spinning wheel. If anything is being depicted here, it is – although not yet the artist's self, and genius drawing on its own being – the inner life of a character and not the whirring of a spinning wheel.

So it might not be such a long journey from Schubert to Schumann. Schumann's relativisation of depiction is only more unambiguous, even perhaps more conscious. Early on, and pointing far into the future (Brahms and Wolf did not want to follow him there, and it was not until Mahler that anyone else did), Schumann made the lied into an abstract art form and thus achieved what Wagner later set as a seemingly paradoxical objective for opera: it is only when forming an alloy with language that music becomes absolute. Here it is worth considering Schumann's song *Schneeglöckchen* ('Snowdrop'), op. 96 no. 2, which resists all the picturesque sweetness that he richly conveyed in his other song of the same title, no. 27 from the *Liederalbum für die Jugend* ('Album of Songs for the Young'), op. 79, which is quite tangibly devoted to the phenomenon of spring.

Schneeglöckchen
Robert Schumann, *Lieder und Gesänge*, op. 96 no. 2

Die Sonne sah die Erde an,
Es ging ein milder Wind,
Und plötzlich stand Schneeglöckchen da,
Das fremde blasse Kind.

Und plötzlich brach mit Pomp und Braus
Der alte Winter auf,
Die Wolken eilten pfeilgeschwind
Zum dunkeln Nord hinauf.

Eisscholle lief, Schneeflocke schmolz,
Die Stürme heulten drein,
Schneeglöckchen stand gesenkten Haupts
In dem Gewühl allein.

Ei komm! Du weisses Schwesterlein,
Wie lange willst du stehn?
Der Winter ruft, das Reich ist aus,
Wir müssen nach Hause gehn!

Und was nur rings auf Erden trägt
Die weisse Liverei,
Das schürze sich, das tummle sich
Zur Abfahrt schnell herbei!

Schneeglöckchen sah sich bebend an
Und dachte halb im Traum:

'Was soll um Winters Liverei
Der grüne, grüne Saum?

Wob ihn wohl um das weisse Kleid
Des Winters rauhe Hand?
Wo komm' ich her? wo geh' ich hin?
Wo ist mein Vaterland?'

POET UNKNOWN

The sun was looking at the earth,
There blew a mildish wind,
And suddenly there the snowdrop stood,
The strange and pallid child.

And suddenly, with pomp and roar
Old winter did set off,
The clouds were rushing arrow-swift
Towards the dusky north.

Ice floe did melt, snowflake too,
The storms came wailing in,
Snowdrop stood with lowered head
In the hubbub alone.

Now come! You little sister white,
How long you want to stand?
The winter calls, his realm is gone,
We have to go homewards!

And what around all earth does wear
The snow-white livery,
Should lift the coat and hurry up,
Come quickly now and leave!

Snowdrop, did trembling watch itself
And thought, as half in dream:

> 'What means round winter's livery
> This leafy, light-green hem?
>
> 'Did it weave round the garment white
> The winter's own rough hand?
> Where come I from? Where am I bound?
> Where is my fatherland?'

This second song from Schumann's *Lieder und Gesänge*, op. 96, is a mystery. The author of the poem has not been identified, and it is not known when it was written. It is probably a metaphorical description of the end of a battle, a landscape of siege and war. An army (the rushing clouds) seems to be retreating to its kingdom in the north. The uniform ('livery') is white, but as the snowdrop reveals itself, it is surprised to notice its own green 'hem'. This could possibly be the livery of a servant, but it could also be the uniform of, for example, the Freikorps of Scheither (under the authority of the Electorate of Braunschweig-Lüneburg, 'Kurhannover') between 1757 and 1762, hence the period of the Seven Years War. In that case the text could – this is pure speculation, of course – be about the battle of Moys near Görlitz on 7 September 1757, when Prussian troops under the Duke of Braunschweig-Bevern were forced to retreat northwards by the imperial Habsburg army. A wounded irregular volunteer might not have managed to flee. And since the Seven Years War turned into something like a world war on an unimagined scale, the question of one's own national identity (in the last two lines of the poem) could perhaps be intended quite literally – does the speaker owe allegiance to Prussia or to its ally Great Britain?

But the question 'Where is my fatherland?' could as well be aporetic and might alone have aroused Schumann's interest in the poem. The question, however, cannot be answered, because the snowdrop, rooted firmly in the earth, is incapable of following the retreat and, besides, there is no one left to provide an answer. The question is unanswerable for another reason: we can only speculate about who wrote the poem, and where and why. While we might have our own opinion on the matter, it is not necessary to reach a conclusion. Much more important is the message that this poem, its selection by Schumann, and its stirring, dramatic ballad-like setting conveys. As an allegory it does not aim to give meaning to an experience (the end of a battle) by creating an approximate parallel with nature (the beginning of spring), as the snowdrop does not suggest the beginning of blossoming and growth, but only a remnant of vanishing winter. It cannot leave the earth, even though it is commanded to do so. It will not be able to escape, because the storm of a retreat will soon be followed by a fresh storm under the new ruler, which will crush the poor snowdrop. All this means that an uplifting parable, of the kind popular in the time of the literary theorist and author Johann Christoph Gottsched and then in the cosy artistic world of Biedermeier that surrounded Schumann, is hardly likely to be the intended meaning in this context. Schumann ends the song abruptly, after the many fractures and emotional reversals that befall the snowdrop, with the unanswered question about the 'where' of the fatherland – without postlude and harmonically unresolved – in darkness. The hope of not only continuing to live but also experiencing one's own identity disappears with the retreat of the comrades.

I do not believe that the 'I' that appears only indirectly in the poem serves as an expressive conduit for the expanding subjectivity we find in confessional poetry. Rather, the allegorical introduction of the snowdrop is intended to stand as a metaphor for the isolation of the human being. I think that here Schumann is attempting to establish an understanding of art that is different from Schubert's. He is concerned with subjectivity but not, however, with the subject of the artist. Instead he is focusing on the subjective uniqueness of all human existence. That is in itself something very different from pure imitation (the millennia-old principle of

This carabinier in his smart uniform would probably not have been pleased to be told that he looked like a snowdrop. The lapel and hem of his white uniform are green, as are the matching decorations on the saddle.

artistic practice), and it provides at least some illustrative material to Nietzsche's proposition concerning art as man's 'actually metaphysical activity of this life'.

Schneeglöckchen is the second song of the five-part cycle *Lieder und Gesänge*, op. 96. At its centre are three songs expressing scepticism about the possibility of earthly understanding. These songs are linked more by the astonishment at failing mutual understanding (particularly in the fourth lied, *Gesungen!* ('Sung!') to a poem by Wilfried von der Neun[4]) compared with the understanding that words are supposed to communicate comprehensively. This primal failure of language is given particularly vivid expression in the second verse of the third song, *Ihre Stimme* ('Her Voice'), to words by August von Platen ('So viele Worte dringen / Ans Ohr uns ohne

Plan, / Und während sie verklingen / Ist alles abgetan!' – 'So many words / Come to our ears at random / And as they fade / Everything is brushed aside'), and in the closing sentence of that song ('Mein Herz und deine Stimme / Versteh'n sich gar zu gut!' – 'My heart and your voice / Understand one another all too well!'), as if heart and voice could understand one another, at any rate not through language.

This inner triptych of earthly scepticism is framed by two eschatological songs: by the well-known *Nachtlied* ('Night Song') to Goethe's poem 'Über allen Gipfeln ist Ruh' . . .' ('Above every mountain top lies peace . . .') as a gloomy starting point, and its redemption in the fifth song by the merging of *Himmel und Erde* ('Heaven and Earth').[5]

> **Himmel und Erde**
> Robert Schumann, *Lieder und Gesänge*, op. 96 no. 5
>
> Wie der Bäume kühne Wipfel
> Zu des Lichtes Höhen streben!
> Wie der Berge greise Gipfel
> In des Himmels Wolken schweben!
>
> Wie im Mai der Wiesen Blühen
> Mit des Äthers Blau verschwimmet!
> Wie der Wälder herbstlich Glühen
> In des Frührots Licht verglimmet!
>
> O so seid ihr denn Verwandte,
> Himmel du und Mutter Erde!
> Freudig trag ich irdsche Bande,
> Da ich dein, O Himmel, werde!
>
> WILFRIED VON DER NEUN

As the daring trees' high crowns
To the heights of light are striving,
As the mountains' grizzled summits
Up in heaven's clouds are floating.

As in May the meadows' blossoms
With the ether's blue are mingling.
As the forests' autumn glowing
In the dawn's red light is fading.

O like them you are close kin,
Heaven you and mother earth.
Gladly bear I earthly bindings
When I yours become, O heaven.

Schumann's setting is a varied strophic song, but the middle part, whose clear musical distinction is not based on any obvious fresh thought in the second verse of the poem, contains with its return to the tonic the possibility of a massive emotional intensification: the 'solemn, intimate' instruction at the beginning of the song (interrupted only by the leap of a sixth to 'Lichtes' as the first senses-filling flash) now and finally develops a euphorically urgent tension. It does not allow the song to end in mere pantheistic sublimity, but the closing words, going far beyond this, make me think of Nicholas of Cusa's[6] 'Coincidentia oppositorum', an overcoming of all the limits of the intellect when faced with the abundance of transcendental infinity, where all opposites fall into one. In this song, however, the four exemplary pairs of opposites of the first two verses merge in art – the art of words and sounds – rather than in the divine unity and wholeness that are, for Nicholas of Cusa, the foundation and goal of thought. Based on this song by Schumann I think I can recognise the extent to which philosophical developments throughout the nineteenth century, when religion (but not of course the existence of God) is largely equalled if not actually replaced by the arts, move towards Nietzsche's conception of art as 'the actually metaphysical activity'.

As so often, then, in these five late *Lieder und Gesänge*, Schumann's metaphysically oriented art is particularly apparent in the cyclical form. And even in the individual songs the absence of any traditional imitation seems to me to be part of the aesthetic concept. Schumann tends rather not to compose an aural picture of a poem, even when doing so could be a way to bridge the boundaries between the two art forms of literature and music, together with the tools of both, which intersect only marginally and are largely incomparable. And Schumann certainly never illustrates the content-related processes of a poem through music, as far as I can see. I find something different in his work: he likes to allow poem and song to stand side by side as it were, rather than force them into congruence. He seems to be looking for the puzzling element in each, which does not allow for interpretative clarity – at least not without loss – or in fact doesn't actually aim for it. His *Schneeglöckchen* from the five *Lieder und Gesänge* is perhaps an ideal example of this. It is not that two completely different modes of expression co-exist here. The snowdrop's agitation at its awareness of violent upheaval is much reflected in the setting of the poem. Not, however, in the existentially menacing sense that the poem might well express as an allegory, but as a presentation of the impossibility of understanding a poem. The melancholy effect of feeling under threat is at best evident in the last twelve bars of Schumann's setting. Otherwise what prevails in the poem's sound is a slightly curious irritation, a musical setting that does not clearly search for meaning, like a parataxis alongside words whose meaning cannot be deciphered.

The fact that Schubert, who only slightly predates Schumann, seems to evidence less in the way of metaphysical ambition, is certainly not a disadvantage. As the initiator of the genre of the art song he transcends time. That Shakespeare and Monteverdi had brilliant successors does not in any way lessen the value of their work (we moved on a long time ago from teleologically oriented cultural history). As it does in Schumann's work, however, the dichotomy of media, of word and sound, is also sometimes apparent in Schubert's lieder – paradoxically the more so the more he tries to transform the poem and its musical interpretation unambiguously into an ideal unified construct of text and music.

The relationship between word and sound is less crucial for opera, with its dedicated libretto, than it is in the lied. And there is the manneredly overrated question of which is more important, the music or the text. There is something much more important we need to decide: if the aim is to achieve the greatest possible congruence of word and sound, the result will always be a simplification of the pre-existing text – either it will be shortened or there will be a concentration on a single aspect in the interpretation. Both these things have happened with *Die schöne Müllerin* – the text has been cut and there has been a concentration on outward events at the expense of inner ones (within the person of the miller's apprentice, whom Wilhelm Müller calls a 'monodramist' in his prologue). The advantage of this approach is a high level of consistency in terms of content. If, on the other hand, the composer can live with the fact that a song has two aspects, one rooted in sound and the other in the text, which might sometimes (or even fundamentally) differ in essence, then the autonomous life of the poem can be left more or less intact, while at the same time the essential lyrical character of openness to the text can be preserved. For me, the most important proponents of the first approach are Schubert and Hugo Wolf, those of the second Gustav Mahler (taken with a pinch of salt)[7] and Schumann.

But some settings by Schubert of poems by Johann Mayrhofer come close to Schumann's abstract aesthetic of the lied. In *Sehnsucht*

('Longing'), D. 516, or *Beim Winde* ('When the Wind Blows'), D. 669, for example, the metaphors meander restlessly, indeed incessantly, through the lines. Their impenetrability also arises from the fact that Mayrhofer – almost tragically – was obliged to work as a censor during the Restoration of the Austrian Empire. As a poet it meant that he knew all the technical tricks for the concealment of artistic freedom and insubordination at first hand, and sometimes used them to the point of indecipherability in his own works. The resulting disparity between semantics and sound, perceived in many of Schubert's gloomy Mayrhofer settings as something cryptic and enigmatic, was thus (or so it seems to me) more a matter of chance than an artistic intention.

On the other hand, I see *Die schöne Müllerin* as an ideal example of how a literary text can be concentrated, even reduced to a specific, downright simplified meaning, before this is depicted with intensely clear, near-synaesthetic vividness.

Das Wandern
Franz Schubert, *Die schöne Müllerin* (1)

Das Wandern ist des Müllers Lust,
    Das Wandern!
Das muß ein schlechter Müller sein,
Dem niemals fiel das Wandern ein,
    Das Wandern.

Vom Wasser haben wir's gelernt,
    Vom Wasser!
Das hat nicht Rast bei Tag und Nacht,
Ist stets auf Wanderschaft bedacht,
    Das Wasser.

Das sehn wir auch den Rädern ab,
    Den Rädern!
Die gar nicht gerne stille stehn,

Die sich mein Tag nicht müde gehn,
  Die Räder.

Die Steine selbst, so schwer sie sind,
  Die Steine!
Sie tanzen mit den muntern Reihn
Und wollen gar noch schneller sein,
  Die Steine.

O Wandern, Wandern, meine Lust,
  O Wandern!
Herr Meister und Frau Meisterin,*
Laßt mich in Frieden weiterziehn
  Und Wandern.

WILHELM MÜLLER

The wandering is the miller's joy,
  The wandering!
The miller has to be quite bad
Who never thought of wandering,
  Of wandering.

We learned it from the water's course,
  The water's course!
It never rests, by day and night,
Forever set on wandering,
  The water.

We also see it in the wheels,
  The mill's wheels!
Which do not like to idle stand,
And don't grow tired all day long,
  The mill's wheels.

---

* A nonce word, as it is in the translation.

> The stones themselves, as heavy they are,
>   The stones themselves!
> They join the cheerful dancing row
> And even want to overhaul
>   The stones themselves.
>
> O wand'ring, wand'ring, my delight,
>   O wandering!
> My master and my misteress.
> Let me peacefully go my way
>   And wander.

A pianist and composer in Munich studied *Die schöne Müllerin* at a young age, along with a fellow schoolboy. After long and enthusiastic preparation, it was finally time for the first performance. In the very first verse disaster befell them – the singer sang: 'Das muß ein schlechtes Wasser sein' ('That must be a bad water'). The initial giggles did not abate. They became louder and louder and eventually uncontrollable, and the performance, if I remember his story correctly, had to be abandoned after about five songs.

That is probably the worst and most consequential slip of the tongue that I know of. But it also shows that in this work, full as it is of technical hurdles, even the first, supposedly harmless and simple song can become a source of danger. This cycle of poems and lieder, which does not at first glance appear at all difficult, is in fact very complicated – a few instances from the rest of the work may be enough to make this clear. Schubert, in setting only 20 out of the 25 poems by Wilhelm Müller and, as we have ascertained, placing emphasis on the poems' outward events, was striving for simplicity, over which, however, the complexity of the texts repeatedly prevails.

In my view the opening lied plants the seed from which the miller's terrible story develops, and by which its course seems preordained. How can this be? Here we have a young man who would now like finally to embark on life. But how does one do that if one comes from a lowly background and has to earn one's living by hard manual labour? And why would one want to do that, if one is in fact already alive, through and with that work?

In pre-industrial times, after some years as an apprentice, it was customary to leave one's master and go 'on the road', drifting for a while from one job to the next, from one place to the next. The journeyman (the status acquired after having completed an apprenticeship), having been 'discharged' ('freigesprochen' – 'named free'; 'fremdgeschrieben' – 'written unknown'), was free. But that freedom came at a high price: as a wandering journeyman one was a nobody; one had nothing, no civic rights, no master, and did not even have the right to get married. But why all that travelling? Why did that period of homelessness need to be prolonged still further?

To collect experiences, to acquire other skills away from home, perhaps even to prepare for a later role as master, and to marry – but certainly also to end up with a better understanding of the world and its conditions. Travelling would help all that, perhaps particularly so in the case of Schubert's journeyman miller. His description of the conditions of his previous life also sets out all future possibilities: the water has taught him to keep going; the wheels won't pause or even grow tired, and the stones, finally, don't just join in the dance, they want to outstrip everyone else. So that in a nutshell would be the horizon of the young miller. But what is the source of the euphoria of the first four verses?

It probably has something to do with the fact that with his 'discharge' ('Freispruch') the new life that he has for so long only imagined and yearned for is about to become a reality at last. But that euphoria also certainly relates – and this is characteristic of the journeyman throughout the cycle, the actual root of his catastrophic failure – to his fervent conviction that his years of wandering are governed by a secret power and set of rules. Wandering, homelessness, the urge to move into the unknown and always wanting to go further – all in reality alien to the modest life of a settled miller – become the perpetual driving forces of his life, just as the water turns the mill wheel. And his euphoric certainty leads the miller to exclaim that any member of his guild who settles down and ceases to wander must in his eyes be a bad miller. That is how he phrases it: he does not say that such a person 'is' a bad miller, but that he 'must be' one. Here for the first time – already in the first strophe – it becomes apparent that it is the fate of this journeyman to be compelled almost obsessively to follow supposedly predetermined rules, as in a chain of causation. And the miller expresses it in such a way that this wayfaring cannot simply be a harmless evening walk once work is over; it embodies his entire world view.

What does this kind of wandering mean for the journeyman miller? The poems *Am Feierabend* ('After Work') and *Das Mühlenleben* ('Life at the Mill') demonstrate very clearly that the reality of the life of the mill-worker is lacking any cosy, idyllic flavour. They show, in fact, a fervent dreamer in the middle of a world that works functionally and runs in an organised fashion, however sweet the face it presents to the world.[8] The miller's wandering, on the other hand, represents a withdrawal from everyday life and activity. He says that he has recognised this even before the beginning of the first song, and he must experience it, since he now at last has the opportunity to do so – at least until he is obliged to live a settled life once more.

So at the very start of *Die schöne Müllerin* the listener already senses that this young man cannot exist without giving everything a meaning through which he can grasp the world – albeit only within these self-imposed limits. Every idea that he thinks he sees in something – in the water, in the wheels, in the stones – must become his unconditional reality because of his youthful impetuosity. Even though we as yet learn nothing about his work ethic and his capacity for work – it is only in *Am Feierabend* that he mentions how, regardless of how hard he tries, his colleagues usually achieve more than he does – it becomes clear that he cannot work without always thinking about the deeper significance of his actions, without constantly justifying himself and his life. So a troublesome trait becomes apparent in the very first words that we hear from him. The person singing here is one who leads a life in which everything has its secretly predetermined place and direction, or at least it must as far as he is concerned. We could call this delusional, and in this sense our hero probably only imagines his loving relationship with the miller's daughter. But we might also think that this is someone who wants to interpret the world, not as a scientist or a philosopher – for that he lacks the distance of experience and knowledge – but almost as an artist. In his youthful exuberance he identifies his daily life with his thinking, and soon enough he imbues this unrealistic experiential world with a life-defining, quasi-religious significance that he follows compulsively and superstitiously throughout the rest of the cycle.

This attitude is the cipher that characterises the artist – like the 'mark on his forehead' in Thomas Mann's *Tonio Kröger* or the 'mark of Cain' in Hermann Hesse's *Demian* – which the comrades of the young miller will certainly not notice, and which will attract the attention only of the miller's daughter – perhaps. But the associated darkness will not escape her either. In the tenth song, *Tränenregen* ('Rain of Tears') she is bound to notice that something is not quite right with this miller, and that he is in danger of losing his place in the world of lived and not only imagined meaningfulness. This is all the more likely the more resolutely he devotes himself to the life of feeling and its constant impact. The aforementioned mark of the artist becomes clearly apparent also to the reader (more so, in my view, than to the listener). And so one could actually see the 23 poems by Wilhelm Müller, framed by prologue and epilogue, as the work of a poetry-writing wandering miller, recounted by Wilhelm Müller, who expresses himself only in the words of the prologue and the epilogue – sarcastically distancing himself from this disaster.

In the last verse of the first song of *Die schöne Müllerin*, however, the supposedly barnstorming young miller who has recently been 'let go' reveals a first sign of insecurity, almost of fear. For that reason Gerold Huber and I always add a kind of awkward hesitation before it, a brief fermata. Not only is there an element of autosuggestion in the miller's claim to find joy in wandering, to find even his determination in it. He is right at the beginning of his journey, so he has certainly not yet experienced it (and as an apprentice he would never have been granted permission). But it also sounds as if he is trying to convince himself, to bolster himself now that he finally has the chance to set off. This is why he asks the master, and even the mistress – who also exercised a function within the guild, by being a kind of substitute mother for the apprentices – if they can let him go, even though he has long since been discharged. So the first poem expresses a twofold insecurity: the one that the young miller has entered into materially, and the one that a young artist enters as an ideal.

Schubert's *Die schöne Müllerin* – as I hope that this brief consideration of the first song makes clear – is thus a work that makes disproportionately greater interpretative demands than Schumann's *Lieder und Gesänge*, and not only because of its scale. It also does so because of obviously different content-related intentions on the part of poet and composer. But the attempt alone to understand, as a performer, the detailed psychological account of a suicide through twenty pictures, could be seen as an interpretative life's work, even if one focused on Schubert's music without also considering Wilhelm Müller's words.

As for Schumann, however, psychological exploration and dissection are not in the forefront of his song-writing. The decisive issue for his work, it rather seems to me, is what meaning his songs could have, indeed why and for what end they were actually created. They are works that grow together, by an arrangement of impressions that creates connections into a world-interpreting system – whose chapters and volumes are Schumann's forty or so song-cycles.

SCHUBERT'S LIED LEGACY

HELSINKI, JANUARY 2021

> Komm' beglücke mich!
> LUDWIG RELLSTAB, *Ständchen*

> Come, make me happy!

In the autumn of 1988 Gerold Huber and I left Straubing for Munich – he for music, me for a bit of philosophy, and later medicine. In November I heard an impressive song recital performed by Hermann Prey and Wolfgang Sawallisch consisting of Schumann's *Kerner-Lieder* and *Dichterliebe*. It had the effect of an initiation and has inspired me ever since. We immediately began studying the latter cycles (in private). Six months later came the first performance, although the example of the philosopher dabbling amateurishly as a singer in Woody Allen's *A Midsummer Night's Sex Comedy* was a terrible warning to me, not least because the actor, José Ferrer, actually dared to sing *Wohin?* from Schubert's *Die schöne Müllerin* and *Ich grolle nicht* from *Dichterliebe* – terribly badly. I swore at the time: if I'm going to sing, it has to be good; desire alone isn't enough. And that was how I spent the next ten years.

It was also ten years of waiting for a bit of success. That hoved into view only when Gerold Huber and I – in my first year as a professional singer – received an invitation to the Schubertiade, the festival held in the Vorarlberg region of Austria. I wanted to sing *Dichterliebe* there, because at the time my repertoire still wasn't very large. But they insisted on me singing something else, something bigger. And that something else turned out to be *Schwanengesang*. I was extremely nervous (today I wouldn't even survive it) – not only because it was the first time I was on an international stage, but above all because while that last cycle of Schubert's had fascinated me for a long time, I hadn't dared to sing it, for a mundane reason: I simply couldn't master it from a technical point of view, right up to the time of the concert.

In those days the Schubertiade took place in different towns around Hohenems and Feldkirch, where it was founded. The recital was in Lindau, in the small auditorium of the Stadttheater, a former church, and therefore it had its own inbuilt 'memento mori'. I remember stepping onto the stage as if mounting the scaffold, not knowing if I would still be alive at the end of this concert. My performance must have come across as a bit unorthodox. The festival director told me off (perhaps rightly) for waving my arms about when singing the difficult high notes, and generally gesticulating wildly. However, the audience was swept along by my youthfully abandoned performance. Gerold Huber remained a secure anchor throughout the concert. A kindly elderly gentleman gave us 100 marks at the end so that we could afford enough champagne to celebrate the evening. Movingly, and probably moved as well, he stood there in front of us with his wallet open. At the sight of his moist eyes behind his glasses we simply couldn't refuse his gift. And we were allowed to return to the Schubertiade! After those years of studying *Dichterliebe*, *Schwanengesang* became our trademark for our initial years as professional musician (Gerold Huber) and singer (me).[1]

Schwanengesang, number 957 in the more or less chronologically arranged Deutsch catalogue (which ends at 993), is hard to categorise. Shortly after Schubert's death, and on the initiative of the composer's brother Ferdinand, Tobias Haslinger published thirteen lieder to texts by Ludwig Rellstab and Heinrich Heine, along with Schubert's last solo song, *Die Taubenpost* ('Pigeon Post'), D. 965A.[2] He declared this slightly artificial and distinctly non-homogeneous collection to be Schubert's 'last work' and also gave it its title. For this he used an image current since classical antiquity: Apollo bestowing on the whooper swan the gift of prophecy. That is why, as it recognises its own approaching death, the swan sings a song that is as moving as it is beautiful. In the *Phaido* Plato explains this (as Cicero will later do) as the swan's anticipation of the joys of the next world. There are many musical reflections of the myth in the early modern period, ranging from Jakob Arcadelt's *Bianco e dolce cigno* to Heinrich Schütz. The publisher Haslinger used the same topos.

It is indisputable that Schubert cannot have wanted the cycle in this form, not least because of its sentimental and conciliatory conclusion with *Die Taubenpost*. This is not changed by the fact that Schubert obviously offered the thirteen Rellstab and Heine songs for publication before his death.[3] Nevertheless, we have never had the heart to break up the *Schwanengesang* or perform the lieder in any other way.

The more important question facing Gerold Huber and me is what to combine these fourteen songs with. (At around 50 minutes they are too short for a programme on their own.) There are no other Heine settings by Schubert that one could put next to them or interweave with them. There are some Rellstab settings, but they too are out of the question: one of them (*Auf dem Strom*, D. 943) eludes simple performability because of the horn accompaniment, while the other (*Herbst*, D. 945) is unique, and because of its stylistic idiosyncrasy I have no idea where in the cycle to place it.

Another possibility, and one that is often resorted to, is to use other lieder to poems by Johann Gabriel Seidl (the *Taubenpost* poet). For me, however, this is not an entirely unproblematic solution, as I find his poems so Biedermeier-ishly absurd and illogical. (Admittedly that might not be the best criterion for assessing poems as good or bad.) Consider the lines 'Ich sende sie viel tausendmal / Auf Kundschaft täglich hinaus' ('I send [the carrier pigeon] out a thousand times / A day on reconnaissance'). I can't imagine how terribly exhausted the pigeon must be, let alone its owner. But then, for example, the songs *Am Fenster* ('At the Window') or *Im Freien* ('In the Open') are so curious, so lyrical and mysterious, that I think Seidl can't have been quite such a ninny if Schubert could make songs like that from his poems.

Yes, one could, as with Rückert (more of him later) even speak of a Seidl style in Schubert's songs. And that's not the only reason that I would prefer not to exclude *Die Taubenpost*. (In a programme I once found the intriguing typo 'Taubenpest', which translates pretty much as 'avian flu'.)

So putting Seidl's poetry next to the great poems of Heine and Rellstab is one option, although this does break up the 'cycle', as the only sensible place I can think of for the Seidl songs to go is between *Der Doppelgänger* and *Die Taubenpost*. And yet we tried this sequence in Stockholm and Helsinki, in a temperature of minus 20 degrees, where the windows actually did freeze, as they do at the beginning of the Seidl setting *Sehnsucht* ('Longing'). Our programme was looking like this: 7 × Rellstab – *Liebesbotschaft* ('Message of Love'), *Kriegers Ahnung* ('Warrior's Premonition'), *Frühlingssehnsucht* ('Spring Longing'), *Ständchen* ('Serenade'), *Aufenthalt* ('Sojourn'), *In der Ferne* ('In the Distance') and *Abschied* ('Farewell'); 6 × Heine – *Der Atlas* ('Atlas'), *Ihr Bild* ('Her Picture'), *Das Fischermädchen* ('The Fisher Maiden'), *Die Stadt* ('The City'), *Am Meer* ('By the Sea') and *Der Doppelgänger* ('The Doppelgänger'); 5 × Seidl – *Sehnsucht* ('Longing'), *Der Wanderer an den Mond* ('The Wanderer to the Moon'), *Am Fenster* ('By the Window'), *Im Freien* ('In the Open') and *Die Taubenpost* ('Pigeon Post'). And that worked well.

Dietrich Fischer-Dieskau suggested that *Schwanengesang* should be filled out with Schubert's late songs to words by Karl Gottfried von Leitner, and as his faithful admirer and emulator I followed his example for a long time. But then I found an even more convincing solution: now we like to begin a recital of *Schwanengesang* with five of Schubert's six *Rückert-Lieder*.[4] With their formal linguistic perfection, which can often seem rather artificial or stiff, Rückert's poems prompt a very particular, 'impressionist' tone in Schubert (a prime example being *Daß sie hier gewesen* ('That They Were Here'). After these songs the cycle follows in its original form – with the Heine songs separated by a concert interval. This means the very fine Rellstab poems, with their stirring content, stand in the middle of the concert as if mediating between Rückert and the very different Heine.

For many listeners – audience and critics – the Heine settings are the highlight of a performance of the cycle. I can understand that on the one hand lovers and admirers of *Winterreise* find a similar world-weary melancholia and emotional radicalism in these songs. Heinrich Heine was close to Wilhelm Müller, the poet of *Winterreise* – in his obituary for Müller he explicitly expressed his admiration, even his almost coquettish reliance on Müller's 'new' style. So, on the basis of the lyrics of the Heine poems in *Schwanengesang* alone, we might view them as a continuation of *Winterreise*.[5]

On the other hand, particularly in *Der Atlas*, *Die Stadt* and *Der Doppelgänger*, with their harshness, their harmonic openness and pallor, and, for lieder, extremely varied dynamics, Schubert develops a hitherto unknown and freely experimental expressive power. How these songs are supposed to relate to the two rhetorically and expressively quieter songs within the cycle, *Ihr Bild* and *Am Meer*, however, is not something I can explain. Are the latter two songs supposed to be a response to *Der Atlas* and *Die Stadt*? And in that case what would be the answer to *Der Doppelgänger* and what is the significance of the apparently conventional varied strophic song *Das Fischermädchen*? It does not really fit within this heroic-mysterious-dramatic construct.

It is reasonable to maintain that the order of the six Heine songs is almost irrelevant in dramatic terms. For a long time I was unable to find any structural or narrative dramatic arc in it, even though *Der Doppelgänger*, with its martial conclusion, represents an impressive emotional nadir and at the same time a dramatic highlight at the end of the songs – like a high cliff tempting us to hurl ourselves over the edge. For Gerold Huber, among others, this becomes a starting point: he sees the six Heine songs as harbingers of Schumann's conceptual song-cycles, which were to follow shortly after. In his opinion, it is the approach, the small emotional climb to *Das Fischermädchen* that creates the potential for the disastrous fall that arrives with *Der Doppelgänger*. He sees some similarity with, for example, Schumann's *Andersen-* and *Lenau-Lieder*, opp. 40 and 90.[6]

We might accuse Schubert of having developed no interest in and no real sense of the translation of literary irony into music, even though I do not consider his lieder to be free of humour.[7] Thus, for example, we do not have to hear his song *Der Einsame* ('The Lonely One'), D. 800, as a parody of the poem by Carl Lappe, which could hardly be more Biedermeier, but I do sense a humorous, perhaps even a detached wry assessment on the composer's part of the almost childlike poetic idyll. In the Heine songs, on the other hand, I can find no musical depiction of Heine's quintessential irony, the final destruction of a previously constructed expression of longing or genuine emotion. Neither, however, are the poems selected by Schubert characterised by the typical undercutting punchlines familiar from many of Heine's poems, set, for example, by Johann Vesque von Püttlingen (who sought most impressively to find a musical correlative for the phenomenon of literary irony).

In Schubert's Heine settings we are thus confronted with a loud, massive, heroic style, an unusually impressive sense of drama (*Der Atlas, Die Stadt, Der Doppelgänger*). If I do, however, recognise any aesthetic and reflexive twist (that we could still expect in a setting of Heine), then this might occur rather in the abrupt confrontations with lyrical images, as embodied in the songs *Ihr Bild, Das Fischermädchen* and *Am Meer*. At best as an equivalent for Heine's irony one could see Schubert's contrasting arrangement of the selected poems bringing together clashing moods.

Heine's poems also reflect a variety of literary allusions: *Der Atlas* is a Romantic response to Goethe's *Prometheus*; *Ihr Bild* makes reference to Pygmalion, or to Eichendorf's *Marmorbild* ('Marble Statue'), while the veiled atmosphere of the three 'sea songs' that follow (*Das Fischermädchen, Die Stadt* and *Am Meer*) sets an eerie Venetian mood like that of Schiller's *Der Geisterseher* ('The Ghost-Seer') over the whole cycle, and finally, in *Der Doppelgänger*, we find a revenant of Nathanael from Hoffmann's *Der Sandmann* ('The Sand Man'). In spite of all the contrasts, and in spite of the whole massiveness, the sketchy assemblage of these literary contents stands for something ungraspable, something that is unsettling and as such grabs hold of us immediately. As a result, the huge effect that these six allusive songs have on the audience is a constant in my experience of performance.

Something that preoccupied me for a long time was the pronounced rhythm of the five novel Heine songs (leaving to one side the more traditionally structured *Das Fischermädchen*): Gerold Huber always had trouble keeping me on track for these songs. Given the often intense dynamic volatility, in the double-dotting and the duplet-against-triplet tension that runs through them like a leitmotif, I often allowed myself to lapse into a rhapsodically free declamatory style. Gerold Huber repeatedly pointed out to me that the extreme expressive variety of the songs did not mean that I was right to believe that the still post-Classical rhythmical conventions of Schubert's music had happily become a thing of the past. So I had to defer to him, entirely conscious that with my inferior rhythmical gifts I here simply had to follow.

Out of this came something that made an unexpected but lasting change to my singing aesthetic, and has continued to shape it up to the present day. I certainly still did want to create the strongly felt expressive depth of the lieder, and at first there was not much that could be achieved in that respect with only a variation in volume. (I consider the relative weighting of consonant articulation to be quite a weak device, veering towards the superficial.) I would of course have been able somehow to illustrate the pallor of the first expository verse of *Die Stadt* ('Am fernen Horizonte / Erscheint wie ein Nebelbild / Die Stadt mit ihren Türmen / In Abenddämmrung gehüllt' – 'On the far horizon / Like an image in the mist / The city with its towers / Stands swathed in evening light'), for example with a degree of rhythmical modification, but the alternative, derived from the rhythmical Procrustian bed, was much better: Gerold Huber's disciplinary measures led me to what is perhaps my favourite interpretative instrument, indispensable to me still today – the coloration of the voice (not affecting the colour identity of the sung vowels), of the singing, as a systematic expressive necessity that I became aware of for the first time only while working on the Heine songs.

The previous seven songs, to poems by Ludwig Rellstab, almost provide a contrast to the aesthetic of the Heine songs. The poems alone are of course anything but the Promethean accomplishments of an era-defining poet and satirist, which does not to call their great quality into question at all.

Frühlingssehnsucht
Franz Schubert, *Schwanengesang* (3)

Säuselnde Lüfte wehend so mild,
Blumiger Düfte atmend erfüllt!
Wie haucht ihr mich wonnig begrüßend an!
Wie habt ihr dem pochenden Herzen getan?
Es möchte euch folgen auf luftiger Bahn!
Wohin?

Bächlein so munter, rauschend zumal,
Wollen hinunter silbern ins Tal.
Die schwebende Welle, dort eilt sie dahin!
Tief spiegeln sich Fluren und Himmel darin.

Was ziehst du mich, sehnend verlangender Sinn,
Hinab?

Grüßender Sonne spielendes Gold,
Hoffende Wonne bringest du hold.
Wie labt mich dein selig begrüßendes Bild!
Es lächelt am tiefblauen Himmel so mild
Und hat mir das Auge mit Tränen gefüllt.
Warum?

Grünend umkränzet Wälder und Höh',
Schimmernd erglänzet Blütenschnee.
So dränget sich alles zum bräutlichen Licht;
Es schwellen die Keime, die Knospe bricht,
Sie haben gefunden, was ihnen gebricht,
Und du?

Rastloses Sehnen, Wünschendes Herz,
Immer nur Tränen, Klage und Schmerz?
Auch ich bin mir schwellender Triebe bewußt!
Wer stillet mir endlich die drängende Lust?
Nur du befreist den Lenz in der Brust,
Nur du!

LUDWIG RELLSTAB

Whispering breezes softly blow,
Flowery fragrances' breathing pervade!
How blissfully wafting a welcome to me.
How have you affected the throbbing heart?
It's yearning to follow your ethereal path!
Where to?

Streamlets, so lively, rushing as well,
Silvery, race to the valley downwards,
There bubbling waters are rushing along,

Meadows and sky in them deeply reflected.
Why draw me, you yearningly questing mind,
Down below?

Sparkling gold of the welcoming sun,
You sweetly bring some hopeful bliss.
Your welcoming sight, how it lifts me up!
It is smiling so gently in the deep blue sky
And has filled my eye with streaming tears.
Wherefore?

In verdure wreathed are woods and hills,
Shimm'ringly gleams the blossoms' snow.
So everything throngs to the bridal light;
The seeds do swell and the buds do burst,
They all have found whatever they lack:
And you?

Tireless yearning, heart full of want,
Nothing but teardrops, plaint and pain?
I too am aware of a swelling urge!
Who satisfies my pressing desire?
Just you free the springtime in the breast,
Just you!

Formally these lines are unassailable, but they impress me time and again with the power of their content, their beauty and precision. I find the variety in shape – allowed, even required by the poem's argumentative clarity and development – to be an inspirational challenge in Schubert's strictly strophic song, released only to some degree by the minor darkening of the final verse. However, the fermatas on the final syllable in the fourth line of each verse, which seems only faintly defined in a rhythmical sense, because they simply extend to the first part of the bar, give the performer a variable instrument with which to define the progress of the emotional development. In the first verse what follows after the pause can be shaped as a separate thought before the concluding question, once again separated, can be posed. Then, in the second verse, the pause can be followed once again by an unhurried transition that also contains an explanatory parenthesis ('sehnend verlangender Sinn' – 'yearningly questing mind'), although with the repetition of the line arises the possibility of granting less importance to this parenthesis in order to continue directly to the last word, 'Hinab' ('Down below'). In the third verse the pause can be kept shorter so that the question 'Und hat mir das Auge mit Tränen gefüllt. / Warum?' ('And has filled my eye with streaming tears. / Wherefore?'), which is separated from the foregoing emphasis only dynamically, with a *subito piano*, can be posed. This *piano* can then be continued at the start of the fourth verse into the ravishing passage 'Grünend umkränzet Wälder und Höh', / Schimmernd erglänzet Blütenschnee' ('In verdure wreathed are woods and hills, / Shimmeringly gleams the blossoms' snow'), which while ending in a masculine rhyme could not be more feminine in expression. This is one of the most fulfilling phrases for me as a singer in my entire repertoire – dynamically falling silent it can be contrasted with an increasing *legato*. It is followed at the end of the fourth verse by the question addressed in internal dialogue to the lyrical 'I': amid all of nature's busy activity – the wind, the brooks, the sun, the wooded heights, all in themselves capable of inspiring enthusiasm, awakening longings in order to be satisfied by themselves – what is the speaker or the 'singer' doing here: blowing, flowing swiftly, shining, urging, swelling? No, he is frozen in longing for the real 'you', the beloved.

Here the meaning of this stormy poem appears retroactively: it is a love message in reverse.[8] The most important type of the art song as such is called into question: all communication via animate and inanimate nature – otherwise often gladly invoked – is cast into doubt, because the conveyance of oaths of love through water, wind, etc., at some point doesn't really lead to anything any more, because only one thing matters: 'Just you!' Only if that 'you' is really and entirely there, in the flesh, it becomes clear, through the trio of 'tears, laments and pain', that the long-distance relationship is no longer enough. The setting even makes it possible not to accentuate this list, this weariness, on the beats of the rhythm, without destroying the musical flow and context.

How could Schubert better have prepared for the *Ständchen* ('Serenade') that follows, and made it necessary as the reciprocal topos of vocal chamber music? Here, as in every serenade, topographical proximity is taken as an opportunity to convince the beloved to allow the small step towards physical closeness, or even to take that step herself. It is the contrary but corresponding theme of the 'message of love'. In the latter, the distance makes the actual consensual aspect – the declared love relationship – impossible for the moment; at the same time distance allows the lovers to yield to their longing for one another simultaneously, while in the serenade, there is no emotional synchronicity. If a relationship is sought at all, then it is primarily and above all physical, and perhaps only on a single occasion, while in the former instance the absence of physicality, in spite of the suffering caused by distance, is downright celebrated.

Ständchen
Franz Schubert, *Schwanengesang* (4)

Leise flehen meine Lieder
Durch die Nacht zu dir;
In den stillen Hain hernieder,
Liebchen, komm zu mir.

Flüsternd schlanke Wipfel rauschen
In des Mondes Licht,
Des Verräters feindlich Lauschen
Fürchte, Holde, nicht.

Hörst die Nachtigallen schlagen?
Ach, sie flehen dich,
Mit der Töne süßen Klagen
Flehen sie für mich.

Sie versteh'n des Busens Sehnen,
Kennen Liebesschmerz,
Rühren mit den Silbertönen
Jedes weiche Herz.

Laß auch dir die Brust bewegen,
Liebchen, höre mich!
Bebend harr' ich dir entgegen,
Komm', beglücke mich.

LUDWIG RELLSTAB

Quietly pleading go my songs
Through the night to you;
To the silent grove down here,
Darling, come to me.

Slender, whispering tree-tops rustle
In the light of the moon,
Of the traitor's hostile ear
Know no fear, my dear.

Do you hear the nightingales chant?
Ah, they are pleading with you,
With the singing's sweet laments
They are pleading for me.

They do grasp the bosom's longing,
Know the pain of love.
They do move with tones of silver
Every mellow heart.

> Let your breast as well be moved,
> Darling, hear me out!
> Trembling for you I'm waiting,
> Come and make me glad.

The famous *Ständchen* contains several references within the cycle, not only to the *Frühlingssehnsucht* that precedes it and the *Liebesbotschaft*, the first song of *Schwanengesang*. It stands in the middle between two groups of three, with the overall architecture of the seven songs becoming apparent in two ways. On the one hand, in the framing lieder (songs 1, 3, 5 and 7), there is a strikingly unified rhythmical structure – one **long** note, followed by two notes half as long: no. 1: 'Rau<u>schen</u>-<u>des</u> **Bäch**<u>lein</u>, <u>so</u> **sil**<u>bern</u> <u>und</u> hell', no. 3: 'Säu-<u>seln</u>-<u>de</u> Lüfte, **weh**<u>end</u> <u>so</u> mild', no. 5: '**Rau**<u>schen</u>-<u>der</u> Strom, **brau**-<u>sen</u>-<u>der</u> Wald', no. 7: 'Ade, du **mun**<u>tre</u>, <u>du</u> **fröh**<u>li</u>-<u>che</u> Stadt'. This also matches the underlying rhythm, in every case (in three songs a 2/4 beat and once a 4/4 beat). This may be something like Schubert's 'wandering rhythm', which also defines the introduction of the opening movement of the 'Great' C major Symphony, D. 944, or the whole of the *Wandererfantasie*, D. 760. The two songs framed in the outer groups of three, songs 2 and 6, on the other hand, both in 3/4, differ in a variation of that rhythmical pattern: a **dotted crotchet**, followed by a quaver and a crotchet. (In song 2, the whole of the prelude as well as, for example '**Waf**-<u>fen</u>-<u>brüder</u>'; in song 6, 'Wehe dem **Flie**<u>hen</u>-<u>den</u>, **Welt** <u>hin</u>-<u>aus</u> **Ziehen**-<u>den</u>.') This is in fact unspectacular, but if we shorten the last crotchet throughout its fading length to a quaver, which does not noticeably change the articulation, but in practical singing terms is often done in the interests of breathing economy, one comes to the following rather striking underlying pattern (the vertical lines separate the notes, the horizontal line characterise their length – in song 4 the horizontal lines symbolise triplets in three notes followed by the same length in two duplet crotchets):

1 (2/4) |--|-|-| 2 (3/4) |---|-|-| 3 (2/4) |--|-|-|
                   4 (3/4) |-|-|-|—|—|
5 (2/4) |--|-|-| 6 (3/4) |---|-|-| 7 (4/4) |--|-|-|

The leading rhythm in the basic 2/4 (4/4) songs (1, 3, 5, 7, with the lengths 2-1-1) is proportionally extended in the interposed 3/4 songs (2, 6) to the lengths 3-1-1. *Ständchen* is also based on a 3/4 rhythm, although it is fundamentally different from the other six songs because the vocal line, run through with triplets and grace notes, is unique in the cycle. Is this really significant (could the rhythmic motifs described above actually be thought trivial)? I think so – from my experience of performance. I didn't read that from the notes; it's more that I have become aware of it sensually, physically, while singing. It has become impossible to ignore the rather simple patterns by virtue of their frequent repetition. Perhaps Schubert found the performance of his songs in his circle of friends, with singing partners including Johann Michael Vogl, an indispensable aspect of his attempt to experience his own music – to experience it not only intellectually, not only empathetically and through its reverberation, but more particularly to explore and probe it through the senses. To this extent, then, these Schubertiades had an enormous historical significance: it was virtually only here that he was able to use the actual physical presence and reality of his songs as a yardstick and guideline for his vocal compositions.

Running parallel with the rhythmic structure, however, in the Rellstab settings there is also a structure in terms of material: song 1 is the 'classic' *Liebesbotschaft*, which is rendered problematic in song 3, *Frühlingssehnsucht*, in the way that I have described above, although in a thematically committed way. In between is the first radically gloomy song, the second, *Kriegers Ahnung* ('Warrior's Premonition'):

Kriegers Ahnung
Franz Schubert, *Schwanengesang* (2)

In tiefer Ruh' liegt um mich her
Der Waffenbrüder Kreis.
Mir ist das Herz so bang, so schwer,
Von Sehnsucht mir so heiß.

Wie hab' ich oft so süß geträumt
An ihrem Busen warm,
Wie freundlich schien des Herdes Glut,
Lag sie in meinem Arm!

Hier, wo der Flammen düst'rer Schein
Ach, nur auf Waffen spielt,
Hier fühlt die Brust sich ganz allein,
Der Wehmut Träne quillt.

Herz, daß der Trost dich nicht verläßt!
Es ruft noch manche Schlacht. –
Bald ruh' ich wohl und schlafe fest,
Herzliebste – gute Nacht!

LUDWIG RELLSTAB

In silence deep about me lies
The comrades' armed troop.
My heart is fearful and so down
With longing so aflame.

How did I often sweetly dream
Right at her ardent breast,
How kindly shone the stove's embers,
When she lay in my arms.

Here, where the sombre fire-glare
Ah, shines on guns alone,

> The heart is feeling all forlorn,
> The tear of yearning grief wells up.
>
> Heart, may your solace not go away!
> Still calls you many a fight –
> I soon rest well and soundly sleep.
> My dearest – sweet good night!

Here too the message of love is varied, with suffering and hopelessness foregrounded – the warrior will not survive. For that reason little appeal is made to nature's messengers. The communication of the farewell message, 'My dearest – sweet good night!', is entrusted only to the all-consuming flames in whose light the warrior once lay on his lover's breast, and to their smoke and ashes.

A similar, even gloomier song is also at the centre of the group consisting of songs 5–7.

In der Ferne
Franz Schubert: *Schwanengesang* (6)

> Wehe, den Fliehenden
> Welt hinaus ziehenden! –
> Fremde durchmessenden,
> Heimat vergessenden,
> Mutterhaus hassenden,
> Freunde verlassenden
> Folget kein Segen, ach,
> Auf ihren Wegen nach!
>
> Herze! Das sehnende,
> Auge, das tränende,
> Sehnsucht nie endende,
> Heimwärts sich wendende!
> Busen, der wallende,
> Klage, verhallende,

Abendstern, blinkender,
Hoffnungslos sinkender.

Lüfte, ihr säuselnden,
Wellen sanft kräuselnden,
Sonnenstrahl, eilender,
Nirgends verweilender:
Die mir mit Schmerze, ach!
Dies treue Herze brach,
Grüßt von dem Fliehenden,
Welt hinaus ziehenden.

LUDWIG RELLSTAB

Woe to the fleeing ones
Into the world going! –
Foreign lands traversing
Their own home forgetting
Their mother's house hating
Their friends forsaking
No boon will follow them
On their wandering.

Heart filled with longing
Eye sadly weeping
Endlessly longing
Homewardly turning
Breast deeply heaving
Woe away fading
Evening star twinkling
Hopelessly sinking.

You breezes, whispering,
Waves gently curling,
Sunbeam so hastening,
Nowhere then lingering,

> Who full of pain, alas,
> My faithful heart did break,
> Hail from the fleeing,
> Into the world going.

In this long poem there are only three verbs, and in the whole of the second verse not even a single one. The overall mood is negative, contemptuous of the world, despairing. Only in the first half of the third verse does a positive idea make a brief appearance, one that is appropriately set by Schubert in a passing major key before the song ends just as radically and disturbingly. Even now it strikes me as technically impossible to sing (for me). And perhaps the aforementioned negative effect is due to this very song – cruel and unpleasant, leaving a bitter aftertaste for many listeners, which cannot entirely be compensated for by the seventh song, *Abschied*.[9] But to me this particular song, in its remorseless unwieldiness, its unrestrained hopelessness, its cruel harshness, in its near insurmountable technical difficulties for a singer and the resulting ugliness, is the most radical Schubert song that I know of. In comparison, *Winterreise* seems to me rather more optimistic in presenting a figure who might be in the midst of a difficult and complex crisis, but who has not yet given up, and who would therefore like to return because he can still level accusations and wishes to do so. But what we have here is absolute helplessness, not an accusation but complete despair, a subject that still utters a friendly and polite final greeting, free from all pretentiousness. It is indeed a disturbing, alienating song, against which the subsequent Heine songs and *Winterreise* have the effect on me of an arranged feast of 'expressive existentialism'.

In der Ferne also bears out that the second group of three Rellstab settings has a different meaning from the first: the element of contact has vanished from the motif of the message of love, which, in different ways, characterises the first three songs. All that remains is distance, and the greeting has been replaced by a farewell, as in the first part's dip in mood, *Kriegers Ahnung*. In the fifth song, *Aufenthalt* ('Resting Place'), the impossible return from exile, from the 'resting place', appears only in the tears prompted by ultimate separation. And the cheerful closing song? Here too a farewell to love and connection as an idea, but a relaxed one. Of course I can only speculate: perhaps the cycle needed an uplifting conclusion. And perhaps that was also in Haslinger's mind when he added a conciliatory ending to the six Heine songs, a further and seventh song, *Die Taubenpost*.

To be honest, I must admit that in the sequence of songs 5–7 some structural inconsistencies are impossible to overlook, if one is expecting a continuation of an architecture similar to the one I have outlined for the first part. These discrepancies do cause a number of problems but, as far as I am concerned, they do not call into question the overall desire to achieve form. So, for example, I should grant that in the fifth song, *Aufenthalt*, the predominant basic rhythm |--|-|-| often adapts to that of the second and sixth songs, |---|-|-|, by the dotting of several notes, and that as a result the song almost assumes a hermaphroditic position between the two. If we place this kinship with the second and sixth songs at the centre of the second half, we might conclude that the sequence of the second group of three (5–7), as a reversal of the first (1–3), might originally have been conceived in the following order: *Aufenthalt* (5) – *Abschied* (7) – *In der Ferne* (6). *Abschied* would then be the mirror image of *Kriegers Ahnung* and the reversed fifth and sixth songs crushing correlatives of the essentially cheerful, at least lifeaffirming first and third – not only in terms of their content but also rhythmically. This order, which is also based on the explicit farewell in *Kriegers Ahnung* and *Abschied*, would, however, be impossible, because that same farewell is also expressed in *In der Ferne*.

But how could such a completely conceptual correspondence of lyrical forms even be imagined? Compromises are unavoidable in such a formally conceived collection, and Schubert seems to have opted for a compromise with which we are familiar, so as not to leave the audience with the devastating sixth song from the Rellstab settings. If everything was indeed conceived along these lines . . .

At any rate the sequence of one long note and two notes half as long (--|-|-) might fall among the cheerful, positive moods (songs 1, 3 and 7), while the sequence of a dotted note followed by two short notes (---|-|-) characterises the negative content (songs 2 and 6). The fifth song, in which an alternation between dotted and non-dotted opening notes makes them more difficult to categorise, would also do justice to its not entirely unambiguous position with regard to its content, given the central third verse with its happier thought.

Anyway, all six songs surrounding *Ständchen* speak of the remoteness of the beloved, and the five framing songs that follow the opening *Liebesbotschaft* diminish and qualify its love-filled greeting in one way or another. While in the first part (songs 1–3), possible, past or desirable proximity occupy the foreground, the second part (songs 5–7) places greater emphasis on farewell and alienation. If one sees this as the expression of a development unfolding over the course of the songs, that does not cast a very optimistic light on Schubert's basic message. With *Ständchen* in the fourth place, however, the Rellstab settings seem like a seven-pointed crown with a solitary gem set at its central, highest and brightest point – a precious stone, the expression and embodiment of the floating, melancholic idiom of the Schubert lied as such. Here the song would earn its place not so much as a statement of content but perhaps rather as a formally aesthetic confession.

This is how *Schwanengesang* strikes me as Schubert's art-song legacy, the expression of a truly bipolar poetic, a conceit manifested in two diametrically opposing ways. Both possible views of the song as an artwork are clearly discernible; they stand side by side with equal importance – and it remains impossible to say today which would have been Schubert's favourite. On the one hand there is the almost rhapsodic style, tending towards the declamatory, as developed in *Winterreise* and the Heine settings, and on the other an approach that inclines towards form and structure, with a tendency to create an overarching concept across the whole of the cycle. This appears in paradigmatic form in the Rellstab settings with the juxtaposition of the two central song themes of 'love message' and 'serenade'. These two aesthetics, chronologically so close in this context and yet almost antithetical within the genre of the art song, have undoubtedly shaped the evolution of the German-language lied over a long period. To extend this thinking, however, to stylistic schools such as Schumann–Brahms or Wolf–Strauss would not in my view do justice to the genre, which in the end escapes rigid categorisation because of its sheer quality.

Juxtaposing Schubert's five songs to poems by Friedrich Rückert with *Schwanengesang* is certainly one interpretative statement. In these texts the idea of form appears to be even more pronounced than it is in the Rellstab settings. In the compilation that we devised, if we put the plain and concise song *Lachen und Weinen* ('Laughing and Weeping'), D. 777, at the centre of this group of five, there is also a certain echo, however faint, of the seven-pointed structure of the first part of *Schwanengesang*. We group the other four lieder, very significant in their stylistic uniqueness, around it. The two lieder that are in my view particularly gripping, astonishing and structurally compact, *Daß sie hier gewesen* ('That They Have Been Here'), D. 775, and *Du bist die Ruh* ('You are the Calm'), D. 776, form an internal frame as the second and fourth songs. *Sei mir gegrüßt* ('Feel My Greetings'), D. 741 – rhythmically very closely related to these two, but less concise in its content, in fact overflowing its strophic form – we place at the beginning, and *Greisengesang* ('Old Man's Song'), D. 778, also of greater weight and the longest

30 Franz Schubert: *Daß sie hier gewesen*, bars 13–16

31 Franz Schubert: *Sei mir gegrüßt*, bars 36–40

32 Franz Schubert: *Du bist die Ruh*, bars 16–25

of the five songs, stands at the end in stylistic isolation. The two are thus able to form a more substantial external frame: one with its titular line, repeated mantra-like, a complementary beginning to the later conclusion of the Rellstab settings (song 7, *Abschied*), and the other a retrospective look at life in strophic rigidity (as a symbol of physical reality) and inner flexibility (as a symbol of preserved mental and spiritual freshness) – this leads into Schubert's last work, *Die Taubenpost*, and in a sense pays its respects to it.[10]

Three of these five songs now form, as has just been suggested, a kind of triad. These three are also linked by a tiny rhythmical motif, which, as in the Rellstab settings, contributes to the style of the work in spite of its faint characteristic – precisely because of its sheer frequency. In fact this is only an instance of **dotting**, albeit one that is followed by a <u>long note</u>. In *Daß sie hier gewesen* I am concerned with the broader dotted notes: 'daß du hier ge**we**sen, daß du hier gewesen'; and in *Sei mir gegrüßt*, for example, the passage 'mit diesem Träne**gus**-se' ('with this flow of tears'). In *Du bist die Ruh*, the motif originally appears in an even less rigid form ('Du **bist die** <u>Ruh</u>'); then later, at the end of the second, fourth and fifth verses, in its idealised form: '. . . **und** Schmerz', '. . . **und** <u>Herz</u>', '**dieser** <u>Brust</u>', 'deiner <u>Lust</u>', 'füll es ga<u>nz</u>' (see music examples 30–32).

For me, however, the crucial thing about this rhythmical figure is its vocal articulation: a quick *vibrato* beginning immediately on the long, dotted note (*vibrato* on longer notes generally begins rather slowly, before picking up speed and leading to the next note), followed by a short note without *vibrato* leading to a slower oscillation of the following long note. This might sound random but it is not. It also sounds almost innocuous, but it is not that either. Without my voice at its best I have no chance here – if the voice is not rested and elastic, I can't do it. The goal, then, is to stick with the ideal example of *Du bist die Ruh* and, in view of its great personal significance, bring the considerable agitation of the 'singer' into a state of peace. Excitement towards the fellow being should transform into peaceful togetherness – the common theme of these three songs. The first three occurrences of 'O, füll es ganz!' ('O, fill it entirely') in *Du bist die Ruh* could be seen as the ideal formulation of this emotional state. And in an interpretative sense this is bound up for me with the brief but precise vocal development in the *vibrato*. (I will shortly turn to the setting of the final repetition of 'O, füll es ganz!')

Daß sie hier gewesen
Franz Schubert; D. 775

Daß der Ostwind Düfte
Hauchet in die Lüfte,
Dadurch thut er kund,
Daß du hier gewesen.

Daß hier Thränen rinnen,
Dadurch wirst du innen,
Wär's dir sonst nicht kund,
Daß ich hier gewesen.

Schönheit oder Liebe,
Ob versteckt sie bliebe?
Düfte thun es und Thränen kund,
Daß sie hier gewesen.

FRIEDRICH RÜCKERT

Blows the east wind softly
Scents into the air
Then it makes us know,
That you have been here.

When the tears are flowing
You become aware,
Else you would not know,
That I have been here.

Beauty, even passion,
Can they hidden stay?
Scents and tears they make us know
That they have been here.

HELSINKI, JANUARY 2021

Daß sie hier gewesen is not only particularly charming as a song, with dissonant, diminished opening chords and resolving grace notes that conceal the key for twelve bars – all of this creating the sense that an impressionist is at work here, rather than an early Romantic. I am also fascinated by the poem itself: the first two verses are the words of a man who is plainly unable to win a woman – she is associated with scents; he identifies himself through tears. In the third verse, however, this 'I' has disappeared, and a complacent observer provides a lightly ironic summary. Retrospectively, a 'speaker' was introduced in the first two verses, to be unmasked as pretentious in the final verse. The fact that the man speaks and not the woman shows that she probably knew nothing, could have known nothing, about her good fortune. She is registered and described only from a distance, in as materially intangible a sense as possible – by scents. And he . . . by tears. And the narrator says nothing further. They have just been here, that's all.

Schubert's setting leaves room (even though the first two verses are musically identical) to pursue this characterisation. I have already described the *vibrato*. The first two verses can also be differentiated in terms of vocal colour: for example, the self-confidence of the adored woman can be marked by a bright, concise tone; the man's suffering, by contrast, through a colour distinguished by a lesser degree of tension. If the two elements, not physically comparable in themselves – the tension of the glottis's closure (bringing the two vocal folds closer together) and the power of the breath's flow – are almost equally balanced, a brighter, tenser sound results, one that may tend to be a little sharp, somewhat similar to the effect of singing 'into the mask' (with the sound resonating forward).[11] If, however, the glottal tension is weaker and the respiratory flow greater, the tone softens, and produces a characteristic quality of timbre. I believe this allows the voice to introduce a brightness of its own, promoting the individual aspects of the resulting sound. However, this should not be confused with breathiness, which is not a sign of vocal health: here the flow of air sounds far more dominant, even though the glottal tension might be marked. At the same time, an even tightening of the glottis along the entire length of the vocal folds is no longer possible, so that air 'escapes', causing the breathy soughing sound.

If one wishes to suggest that the object of desire (verse 1) stands more stably on her feet than her admirer (verse 2), an agogic differentiation (on a small scale) can also contribute to this effect. It seems to me to be very much a characteristic of the fundamental 'impressionistic' quality of this song that Schubert's post-Classical rhythmic severity can here be considered to have softened to a degree. It is therefore imaginable to end the second verse a little more calmly in terms of tempo, before the pretension of the 'I' ends with the summarising contribution of the objective observer.

In the third verse, however, 'scents' and 'tears' are contemplated and compared in two different ways: the first time a development over three bars is devoted to them, characterising the indefinable perception of an iridescent scent;[12] the tears of the admirer thus seem to be trapped in the irritation provoked by it (the turn on the sound of the word can be seen as an embodiment of this impression). The second time, the scent is dealt with more briefly and in a more neutral way, while the tears and their hesitancy are given an appoggiatura lasting twice as long. Also interesting is the closing 'Daß sie hier gewesen'. While in the first iteration of the last verse it leads to the second iteration via an upwardly inflected melody, in the end it corresponds precisely to the endings of the first two verses – once more a reference to the impressionistic aura of the song: 'Daß du [. . .] ich [. . .] sie hier gewesen' ('That you [. . .] I [. . .] they have been here'). Only the impression of the situation is indicated, with delicate differences in shading (clear – soft – ironically detached), but without bestowing greater significance or even expressiveness on events.

Du bist die Ruh
Franz Schubert; D. 776

Du bist die Ruh,
Der Friede mild.
Die Sehnsucht du,
Und was sie stillt.

Ich weihe dir
Voll Lust und Schmerz
Zur Wohnung hier
Mein Aug und Herz.

Kehr ein bei mir,
Und schließe du
Still hinter dir
Die Pforten zu.

Treib andern Schmerz
Aus dieser Brust,
Voll sei dies Herz
Von deiner Lust

Dies Augenzelt
Von deinem Glanz
Allein erhellt,
O füll es ganz!

FRIEDRICH RÜCKERT

You are the calm,
The gentle peace,
The longing, you,
And what it sates.

I give to you
In lust and pain

As dwelling here
My eye and heart.

Come to my home
And fasten then
Soft behind you
The gate tight shut.

Drive other pain
From this my breast
Filled be this heart
With all your lust.

This shrine of the eyes,
With all your gleam
Only lit up,
Do wholly fill!

I heard this story about one of my most distinguished colleagues second hand. He was enjoying a leisurely bike ride when he got a call from his wife: she couldn't make it to a funeral where she was due to sing and could he take her place? He was aware of the service and had sung all the music before, so it was bound to be fine. He said he would try and just made it on time. The organ was already playing an introit, so he went straight to the organist and they checked the order of service before he was due to sing . . . *Du bist die Ruh*. I assume he doesn't have perfect pitch, so only as the piece began must it have dawned on him that this really wasn't his key. The first four verses of the text (combined into two musical verses) are difficult enough, but the last verse, repeated twice, which in my C major transposition rises to a top F that is always highly risky for me, ended here, if I remember correctly, at least with a top G or even, in the original key of E flat major, with an *A flat*, fading away from a *mezzoforte* or *forte* at least to a *mezzopiano* if not a *piano*. This colleague has a really big voice, very good in the upper register, but he doubtlessly hadn't planned or ever rehearsed the song at such a pitch. The inevitable happened – a serious musical car crash with the grieving congregation having no idea how to respond. Admittedly, there have been many occasions on which I have not managed to sing the comparatively relaxing top F in recital as I would have wished to do, but I have recorded it once on CD as I imagined it – open, bright, inconclusive.[13]

How does this happen? It's a song full of surprises: contrary to expectations everything calm is changed and broken down. The start of the introduction, for example, is a paradigm of calm with repeating undulations of thirds and then fourths from the bass upwards. Suddenly, however, this changes at the end of the second bar, when the leaps, introduced with an upbeat to the third bar, oscillate from the top downwards. Then the first two musical verses are almost identical, except at the end of the second a small change follows, one that is probably not consciously noticed by the listener: a whole-tone step upwards at 'Voll sei dies Herz' quickly produces a different kind of tension. Then, in the last verse, which contains only one verse of text, albeit one that is repeated, this tool is developed exponentially: in place of the A minor, the relative minor to C major, which was heard in the first two verses on 'die Ruh' and 'bei mir', the analogous 'Augenzelt' rises only a semitone to A flat major. Connected to this is a whole-tone scale with some resulting dissonances, which finally resolve in the last semitone step in F major (see music example 33). Then the same again – but while the second A flat no longer comes as a surprise, there is another one: the previous whole-tone step to 'Von deinem' is followed by a leap of a fourth as an appoggiatura to the word 'Glanz' (see music example 34).

During this rise the difficult thing about the final high F for me is keeping the vocal colour constant, so that the crescendo and, the second time, the final decrescendo (which is marked only in the Friedländer edition) sound ecstatic but not extreme. In the

33 Franz Schubert: *Du bist die Ruh*, bars 54–60

34 Franz Schubert: *Du bist die Ruh*, bars 68–74

Urtext edition there is only a crescendo in both passages, albeit with the second beginning a bar earlier with the textual repetition, and bringing with it the risk of attaining a violent *forte*. This makes the idea of a final, concluding decrescendo seem entirely sensible.

Another colleague, also one of the great masters of his craft, asked me, after listening to my recording of the song, how it was that I didn't 'cover' that F. In fact I couldn't bring myself to. Even as a student I wouldn't, because I didn't want to sacrifice vocal colour – and often enough vowel colour as well – to a technical necessity. For me an open or 'white' note, taboo though it might have been to some colleagues and hated by some conductors, was better than 'covering'. The related but rather different Italian *coperto*, however, I would still need to acquire later – at least to some extent. I found a way that suited me of avoiding putting a dark woolly cap on the end of a homogenous scale. Even today I am more comfortable starting a *passaggio* note with a rather flat tone before opening a broadening dome over it. Perhaps though that's what my colleague meant.[14]

The last surprise in *Du bist die Ruh* comes in the final line 'O, füll es ganz!', which is sung four times: the leap of a fifth downwards to C, which occurs three times, is omitted on the final occasion. The vocal line ends with the fifth extended by two quavers. I see that as a drawn-out pause of the impressively building ecstasy that reaches its climax on the top notes of the song, but is not completely extinguished at the end. Rather, it glows faintly once more, as the final leitmotif-esque dotted note indicates, when it does not lead comfortably downwards but instead holds the experience aloft.

CODA WITH STIFTER

MADRID, FEBRUARY 2021

So. And then write diligently in the leather book [. . .] and do not read it until three years have passed [. . .] to see whether you can also find yourself moving forward[1] [. . .] I was able to open my first package not in three or four but only in five years [. . .] Everything had become different from what I had once thought, I recognised that only now I had the right views, and burned with desire to write them down straight away[2] [. . .] I wrote very diligently on my packages, they grew increasingly similar, until the ones that I am now opening in my old age are all alike.[3]

ADALBERT STIFTER

Lyrical Diary is a collection of thoughts and ideas that I have been developing and collecting, mostly on the evidence of my own senses, about performance practice and the meaning of the songs that I have sung over the course of my professional career during the last twenty or so years. My collaboration with the pianist Gerold Huber has lasted a decade longer than that. It has, however, become clear to me only in recent years that above all else I am forever seeking improvement and – yes – progress in my work as a singer, even though progress may be a human quality that partially goes against its own nature and generally against the whole environment. So, for a long time, I resisted accepting it as a determining impulse.

I came to terms with this phenomenon on finally making the acquaintance of the Austrian-Bohemian novelist Adalbert Stifter, currently my favourite German prose writer, whose works are fine enough to stand alongside those of Joseph Roth. This was not so much because of the perfection of one's living conditions and their idealistic systemisation, not unlike that of the aristocrat Gustav von Risach in Stifter's novel *Der Nachsommer* ('Indian Summer'). In fact it was Stifter's 'favourite child' that impressed me most: his story *Die Mappe meines Urgroßvaters* ('My Great Grandfather's

Portfolio'). Much of Stifter's life was taken up with working on this book. He produced four versions, the last of which he left unfinished. These were all attempts at improvement, as also set out in the principle of the 'portfolio' itself: a collection of diary-like texts is sealed shut in a folder and can be reopened only after a long time of forgetting and ignoring them. And what fascinates me here is not the truly concrete and varied progress that is described, particularly in the 'last portfolio': not the building of roads (the narrating great-grandfather, Augustinus, one of the first doctors in rural Bohemia in the early eighteenth century, has had enough of being delayed on visits to his patients by encounters with farmers' carts on single-track roads); nor the improvements in agriculture, or construction, or land reclamation, nor even the princely park with its designed and discreetly managed landscape, which both impresses and surprises him, and which aroused an aesthetic response in him and in his time in general.

What interests me, rather, is the method of self-knowledge and self-improvement introduced with the 'portfolio'. It does not proceed in steadily developing striving, but rather in intermittent moments of revolutionary self-affirmation, in stages. It was the result that struck me: the long-interrupted recognition of the writer's own nature and its evolution is also prospectively corroborated. In other words: the goal of personal and artistic development is not the forced, Faustian crossing of the horizon of one's own possibilities through constant comparison with oneself and others, but rather an asymptotic approach to the genuine potential of one's own individual talent over the course of one's life. This is made possible by a gradual affirmation of one's own actions and expressions. And entirely in line with the passage from Stifter quoted above, after an initial reflexive shock, an increasing familiarity with the self will happen, in the sense of the fulfilment of one's own talent.

This method is also, for me, the most plausible kind of artistic progress. In my work as a singer I do not try – or at least I no longer try – to force an imagined development through constant re-examination and strict control, which would have to realise itself by permanent observation as if from outside. I do rather commit to an inner process of further development, which sometimes allows itself less and less astonishing retrospectives to the early achievements and what has happened in the past. That also means that the constant work of criticism and affirmation looks 'inward', less to oneself than to the meaning of the works under examination. The essence of my job and theme of this 'diary' is therefore not self-reference and self-optimisation, but rather this 'daily' work in the search for meaning. This diary is entitled 'lyrical' because it deals chiefly with the lyrical, that is poems and their settings. And although in Italian an opera singer is called a *cantante lirico*, meaning that the concept of the lyrical can also be extended to the theatrical, the experiences that I am recording here are more specifically the ones that I owe to the lied podium.

Of course this is not an academic contribution. I do use ideas and conclusions developed by others, and I make every effort to document them as being not my own. But – as one can probably imagine – given the rather synthetical nature of work in the arts, it is not my intention, and not my role, to allow the demands of utmost academic caution to prevail, out of a sense of informed completeness. Indeed I do not want to, in fact I cannot, offer anything that might be called analytic consequence. If one is willing to call the work of a performer – a musician, a singer or an actor – artistic, then it will doubtless be on the basis of an inspired and inventive richness, one that allows them to use the impressions, associations and arguments that touch and affect their own field of work – if not eclectically, then with an artistic freedom and incompleteness, to allow a fresh understanding of existing art in a contemporary and truthful way.

Lest I go awry with my own thoughts, I have entrusted myself to people who have allowed me to share in their scientific precision and method, their stylistic confidence and comprehensive knowledge, and who have thus won my undying gratitude. Frank Zipfel, Dieter Borchmeyer, James Cheung, Ingrid Bodsch, Hans Joachim Köhler, John Carewe and Stefanie Hölscher, but above all and very particularly Laurenz Lütteken, have been an indispensable, greatly admired and extremely welcome help to me in shaping this collection of essays, which I call a diary of my work with and on the lyrical. While editing Shaun Whiteside's superb English translation, I had the opportunity to correct some discrepancies and add new insights. This required great patience on the part of Belinda Matthews, and in particular the highly detailed and supportive work of Jill Burrows – for which I would like to express my deepest gratitude.

NOTES

Prelude with Low-flying Fighter Jet

1 As early as 1834, six years before he began to compose lieder, Robert Schumann wrote to Clara Wieck, 'At first I had various plans for our correspondence. I wanted to fill my balloon (you know that I have one) with ideas for letters, and let it rise in a favourable wind to the appropriate address. I wanted to catch butterflies as postmen to you (. . .) In short, I had many witty dreams in my head, from which I was awakened only today by a trumpet-blowing postillion.' (Robert Schumann, *'Schlage nur eine Weltsaite an'. Briefe 1828–1855*, selected and annotated by Karin Sousa, with an afterword by Rüdiger Görner (Frankfurt am Main and Leipzig, 2006), p. 140.)
2 'It would be churlish to resist this song (. . .). The opening strain is perhaps oversweet (. . .). It must be confessed however that the contrived peroration, which is the last if not the lasting impression, mars the total effect.' (Eric Sams, *The Songs of Robert Schumann* (London, 1969), p. 154.)
3 See 'Schumann's Abstract Opera', pp. 59–80.

Lyrical Dramaturgy

1 Friedrich Nietzsche, *Über Wahrheit und Lüge im außermoralischen Sinne* [1873], in Nietzsche, *Die Geburt der Tragödie* [. . .] Kritische Studienausgabe, edited by Giorgio Colli and Mazzino Montinari, vol. 1 (Munich, 1988), pp. 873–90; p. 882.
2 Cf. Silke Schwarz, '"Darfst mich niedre Magd nicht kennen". Eine geistliche Metaebene in Schumann's Opus 42 *Frauenliebe und Leben*', in Dieter Borchmeyer *et al.* (eds), *Musik verstehen – Musik interpretieren. Festschrift für Siegfried Mauser zum 65. Geburtstag* (Würzburg, 2019), pp. 201–18.
3 As a general rule I find psychological reconstruction to be a second-order phenomenon in Schumann's song-writing – cf. Matthias Walz, '*Frauenliebe und -leben* op. 42. Biedermeierdichtung, Zykluskonstruktion und musikalische Lyrik', in Gerd Neuhaus (ed.), *15. Wissenschaftliche Arbeitstagung zu Fragen der Schumann-Forschung* (Cologne, 1996), pp. 97–118.
4 It's important to point out that these are not superficial and sentimental references to Schumann's own life, but demanding, self-supporting concepts.
5 Cf. John W. Finson, 'Schumann, Antisemitism and the *Drei Gesänge aus Lord Byron's Hebräischen Gesängen* op. 95', in Helmut Loos (ed.), *Robert Schumann. Persönlichkeit, Werk, Wirkung. Bericht über die Internationale Musikwissenschaftliche Konferenz vom 22. bis 24. April 2010 in Leipzig* (Leipzig, 2011), pp. 126–35.

6 See the booklet for the CD recording of the complete Schumann lieder: *Robert Schumann: Alle Lieder*, with Christian Gerhaher, Gerold Huber, *et al.* (Sony Classical, 2021).

7 The exceptions to this are a few remaining lieder grouped together in opp. 127 and 142, and the two ballads, *Belsatzar* ('Belshazzar') and *Der Handschuh* ('The Glove') published as opp. 57 and 87 respectively.

8 Richard Strauss, 'Aus meinen Jugend- und Lehrjahren', in Strauss, *Betrachtungen und Erinnerungen*, edited by Willi Schuh, 2nd enlarged edn (Zurich and Freiburg im Breisgau, 1957), pp. 203–18; p. 210.

9 Cf. Nietzsche's regrettable observation, which had a greater effect than the fact that he solemnly laid a wreath on Schumann's grave in 1864: 'The "youth", as the Romantic lieder poets of Germany and France imagined him around the first third of this century – this youth has been completely translated into song and music – by Robert Schumann, the eternal youth, for as long as he felt himself to be fully in charge of his own powers: of course there are moments when his music reminds one of an "old maid".' (Friedrich Nietzsche, *Menschliches Allzumenschliches. Kritische Studienausgabe*. vol. 2 (Munich, 1988), p. 619.) And, worse still: 'But with regard to Robert Schumann, who took things hard and from the beginning was also taken hard – he is the last one who founded a school. Do we not today, among ourselves, consider it a blessing, a breath of relief, a liberation, that Schumann's romanticism has been overcome? Schumann, fleeing into the "Saxon Switzerland" of his soul, half Werther, half Jean Paul in style, certainly not taking after Beethoven! Certainly not Byronic! His *Manfred* music is a mistake and a misunderstanding to the point of wrongness – Schumann with his taste, which was essentially a *small* taste (a dangerous tendency, doubly dangerous among Germans, to quiet lyricism and an emotional drunkenness), constantly going aside, shyly apologising and withdrawing, a noble epicene figure who wallowed in anonymous joy and woe, a kind of girl and *noli me tangere* from the beginning: this Schumann was already only a *German* event in music, not a European one as Beethoven was, as, to an even greater degree, Mozart was – with him German music was threatened by its greatest danger of losing *its voice for the soul of Europe* and degenerating into mere fatherland-worship.' (Friedrich Nietzsche: *Jenseits von Gut und Böse. Kritische Studienausgabe*, vol. 5 (Munich, 1988), p. 188.)

10 Nietzsche, *Über Wahrheit und Lüge im außermoralischen Sinne*, p. 889.

11 Not, of course, in the sense of Nietzsche's 'Abstractions'.

12 Schumann writes the same thing himself: 'In order to speed up the development [after Schubert], a new school of German poets also came into being: Rückert and Eichendorff, although they blossomed earlier, became more familiar to musicians, while Uhland and Heine were most frequently set to music. This led to that more artistic and profound style of song in which the earlier writers of course took no interest, because it was only the new spirit of poetry that was reflected in music.' (R[obert] S[chumann]: 'Lieder', in *Neue Zeitschrift für Musik*, vol. 19 (1843), pp. 33–5; p. 35.

13 Eric Sams, *The Songs of Robert Schumann* (London, 1969), p. 65.
14 Ian Bostridge, *Winter Journey, Anatomy of an Obsession* (London, 2015).
15 See 'Prelude with Low-flying Fighter Jet', pp. 1–36.

Schumann's Abstract Opera

1 The depiction of Goethe's *Faust* cinematographically is maybe most meaningfully suggested by the subtitle of the third act, the *Helen Act* from *Part II* of the play – 'Classical-Romantic phantasmagoria'. In his afterword to *Faust*, Dieter Borchmeyer says of the phantasmagoria that 'in the eighteenth century it referred to the representation of spirits by means of an optical apparatus developed from the magic lantern, which is also used in "magic theatre" for the conjuring of Helen at the imperial court' (Dieter Borchmeyer, 'Afterword', in *Johann Wolfgang von Goethe: Faust. Sämtliche Dichtungen. Mit einem Nachwort von Dieter Borchmeyer. Anmerkungen von Peter Huber* (Dusseldorf and Zurich, 2003), pp. 761–815; p. 779).
2 Goethe's 'pageant' *Pandora* contains a sentence that constitutes the ideal paraphrase for the central phrase in Schumann's *Scenes from Goethe's 'Faust'*: 'Am farb'gen Abglanz haben wir das Leben' ('Our life lives in the colourful refraction'): man is determined 'to see that which is illuminated, not the light' (*Goethes Werke (Hamburger Ausgabe)*, edited by Erich Trunz, vol. v, 11th edn (Munich, 1993), p. 362.
3 'Entelechy' refers to the will within a body that is equipped with a goal of knowledge and meaning (*telos*) – or simply something like the 'soul'.
4 A resurrection in the sense of life after death is not the explicit goal of the Na'vis' natural religion, which is symbolised in two trees – a huge 'tree of life', and a 'tree of principles' fundamental to the life force.
5 The two perhaps most expansive and most usurping characters of theatre meet here: while Faust attempts to grasp and understand infinity by extrapolating the wealth of knowledge and sensuality, Don Juan understands infinity by negating all reflection (he is his own Mephisto), and they meet in this singular moment that cannot be captured – one, Don Juan, bases his whole life on the moment; the other, Faust, only his departure from it – see 'Drama of the Moment', pp. 147–60.
6 Here I am citing the version in Alban Berg's libretto, which impresses me even more than the passage in Georg Büchner's drama. Cf. Alban Berg: *Georg Büchners Wozzeck. Oper in 3 Akten (15 Szenen)*, op. 8. Piano transcription by Fritz Heinrich Klein (Vienna, Universal Edition (UE 7382)), pp. 11ff.
7 Recent editorial findings (in the draft score, the working manuscript of the score and the engraver's template for the piano reduction) prove Schumann's intention that Goethe's original text ('It's over!') should be the final words in this scene. However, to conclude that this philological discovery rejects the heroic interpretation of the error previously assumed to be intentional is just as wrong.

In my opinion, that is out of the question: the solemn, devout, even reverent tone in honour of Faust's memory remains the same. There is absolutely no sign of the agitated, corrective, even angry tone suggested by the exclamation mark. The choir closes with the same sound that supports the established interpretation and may even have largely caused the latter.

8 I owe this explanation to Dieter Borchmeyer and Anne Bohnenkamp. From the latter I also borrowed the reference to the following passage from a letter (Schiller to Goethe, 26 June 1797): 'With regard to the treatment, I think the great difficulty lies in making one's way happily through the fun and seriousness. In this matter, intelligence and reason seem to be battling for life and death. One feels this very much in the current fragmentary figure of Faust, but one defers expectation to the fully developed whole. With his realism, the Devil stands for understanding, Faust for the heart. Sometimes, however, they seem to swap roles, and the Devil takes Reason under his protection against Faust.' (*Der Briefwechsel zwischen Schiller und Goethe*, edited by Paul Stapf (Berlin and Darmstadt, 1960), p. 311.)

9 Goethe introduces the pair of concepts 'to self' (*verselbsten*) and 'to de-self' (*entselbstigen*) in *Dichtung und Wahrheit* (*Goethes Werke, Hamburger Ausgabe*), vol. IX, 14th edn (Munich, 2002), p. 353.

10 Schumann suggested the title to Franz Liszt in a letter of 10 August 1849. Liszt conducted one of the three simultaneous premieres for the Goethe-Fest in Weimar on 29 August 1849; Schumann held the baton in Dresden, Julius Rietz in Leipzig (Wolfgang Seibold, *Briefwechsel zwischen Franz Liszt und Robert und Clara Schumann*, accessed at https://www.schumann-portal.de/korrespondenz-franz-liszt-mit-clara-schumann.html, p. 83).

11 Once, just once, I would like to hear the many loud passages of this overture performed as loudly as possible, so violently, and tugging so hard on the chandeliers and on the walls, that the auditorium is reduced to rubble.

12 Cf. Erich Trunz: 'The consecutive in drama is (in *Faust Part II*) is almost only a juxtaposition in being, the structure of individual scenes *juxtaposed and effectively reflecting one another* ([Goethe] an Iken, 27 September 1827)', in *Goethes Werke, Hamburger Ausgabe*, vol. III, 11th edn (Munich, 1993), p. 582.

13 Cf. 'The one who acts is always without a conscience; the only one with a conscience is the contemplative person.' (*Goethes Werke, Hamburger Ausgabe*), vol. XII, 11th edn (Munich, 1993), p. 399.)

14 Cf. Borchmeyer, 'Afterword', pp. 769ff.

15 I should like to mention in passing what Schumann wrote on this subject to Eduard Krüger, probably in December 1844: 'What do you think of the idea of treating the whole material [i.e. the whole of *Faust*] as an oratorio? Isn't it bold and beautiful? Except I can't think about it now.' (*Robert Schumann: "Schlage nur eine Weltsaite an". Briefe 1828–1855. Ausgewählt und kommentiert von Karin Sousa. Mit einem Nachwort von Rüdiger Görner* (Frankfurt am Main and Leipzig, 2006), p. 93.

16 The similarity between the term and Boris Blacher's *Abstrakte Oper Nr. 1* is pure coincidence.

17 As an example of extremely volatile dynamics and agogics in the opera *Genoveva* I would like to mention the 10-minute passage featuring recitative, scene and duet from the third act, in which Siegfried, Genoveva's husband, is dealt an emotional blow by his treacherous friend Golo. I have perhaps never seen a conductor working in such detail as Daniel Harding when rehearsing this scene with the Bavarian Radio Symphony Orchestra. If such care were taken more often with Schumann's works, the attractiveness of his orchestral works for the audience and also for some musicians might be greatly enhanced.

18 Perhaps, apart from the third act, the one devoted to Helen, this may be the scene in *Faust II* that is true drama and therefore especially far from any association with an epic in verse.

19 Of course, for Goethe the consequence of the recognition of fundamentally limited human perception is not that man needs to step out of the cave of his limitations in order to understand the idea as a whole; unlike in Plato, given the earthly refraction as a rainbow in its colourful abundance, there is no cause – in Goethe, man has already stepped astonished from the cave. Cf. Wilhelm Emrich, *Die Symbolik von Faust II. Sinn und Vorformen* (Bonn, 1957), p. 89.

20 Cf. 'The Souls of the Crags', pp. 99–122.

21 *Goethes Werke, Hamburger Ausgabe*, vol. XII, 11th edn (Munich, 1993), p. 248.

22 Richard Wagner, 'Über Sänger und Schauspieler [1872]', in Wagner, *Gesammelte Schriften und Dichtungen*, vol. 9. 2nd edn (Leipzig, 1888), pp. 157–230, pp. 183ff.

Tradition and Role-Playing

1 Chris Walton, *Othmar Schoeck. Eine Biographie*, translated into German by Ken W. Bartlett (Zurich, 1994), p. 159.

2 I can't help it, but I think all falsetto notation (especially in contemporary vocal music) is wrong and unlovely. I accept that it is probably done out of a desire to makes life easier, or a belief that falsetto corresponds vocally to the flageolet, which is much more interesting in terms of sound. But unlike the flageolet, I cannot find any positive extension of the vocal potential of the singer (at least the one who is not actually a counter-tenor). Inside a phrase sung in a mixed voice, the falsetto sounds to me like a sudden collapse in musical activity, continuity and expressiveness (and that is how a voice unpractised in falsetto almost always comes across).

3 See also Susan Youens, 'Schubert, Mahler and the Weight of the Past: *Lieder eines fahrenden Gesellen* and *Winterreise*', in *Music and Letters* 67 (1986), pp. 257–68.

4 For example, with the rushing stream, the flowers, the alder trees.

5 Especially in songs 1, 2 and 4: 'Blümlein blau', Vöglein süß', 'Ach! Wie ist die Welt so schön', 'Ziküth', 'Tau noch auf den Gräsern hing', 'der lust'ge Fink',

'Zink', 'Und da fing im Sonnenschein / Gleich die Welt zu funkeln an', 'Ist's nicht eine schöne Welt?', 'Unter dem Lindenbaum! / Der hat seine Blüthen über mich geschneit'.

6   This also occurs in Schubert's *Winterreise*, with the frozen river, the linden tree as a promise of death's consolation, with ice flowers, death crows, mock suns – but also in his *Müllerin*, for example in the green colour that appears everywhere in nature, and the stream in which the journeyman miller drowns.

7   Federeco Celestini lists an amazing abundance of auratic and associative references to Schubert in the *Lieder eines fahrenden Gesellen*, which he terms 'mémoire involuntaire' (Federico Celestini, 'Die tönende Nähe einer zeitlichen Ferne. Der auratische Klang in Mahlers "Lieder eines fahrenden Gesellen"', in Celestini and Andreas Dorschel (eds), *Arbeit am Kanon. Ästhetische Studien zur Musik von Haydn bis Webern* (*Studien zur Wertungsforschung 51*) (Vienna, 2010), pp. 156–8.

8   The middle part of the third and the beginning of the last song ('Die zwei blauen Augen / Von meinem Schatz') are echoes of the blue eyes of *Die schöne Müllerin*, which first appear as forget-me-nots, and the sky, reflected in the stream in this cycle as a messenger of death and eternity. Contrasting with this is the image of the blond hair that tends to merge with the background ('im gelben Felde [. . .] das blonde Haar'): here the colour yellow, rarely used in lyrics, certainly symbolises betrayal and deceit of which the blond beloved stands accused.

9   Here again I would like to express my conviction that the frequently cited parallels with Mahler's life (particularly an unhappy infatuation with a singer in Kassel) are without interest or significance for the understanding and interpretation of the *Lieder eines fahrenden Gesellen*. (That infatuation was in my view a trigger at most.) In terms of their content, the songs are universal and do not need a biographical foundation in order to understand them.

10   This also occurs in the postlude to the *Kindertotenlieder*, the *Rückert-Lieder* (if we put *Ich bin der Welt abhanden gekommen* at the end of the cycle) and *Das Lied von der Erde*.

11   See 'Steles in an Ice Field', pp. 255–84.

12   See 'Farewell to the Familiar', pp. 123–46. Perhaps Mahler also took this step deliberately, although of course without knowing how modern music would develop. That might be evident, in fact, in the way that he always showed solidarity with Schoenberg and his school, not least by attending concerts, although at the same time he could not conceal his personal lack of understanding of Schoenberg's aesthetic development.

13   So not a journeyman or, say, a miller (as in *Die schöne Müllerin*). What is probably envisaged is something like a wandering contemporary or colleague – see 'Meaning or Being', pp. 303–22.

14   For example, the motif of an upward leap of a minor sixth that occurs (several times), with a subsequent fall in the melody: see 1: 'hab ich meinen traurigen Tag'; 2: 'mir nimmer (here only a fifth) 'blühen kann'; 3: 'ich wollt' ich läg auf der schwarzen Bahr' and 'vom allerliebsten Platz'l'. And also the apparently central role of the fifth in every song's quite traditional lyrical main

theme as a melodic starting and end point: see 1: 'wenn mein Schatz Hochzeit macht' and 'Blümlein blau'; 2: 'Ging heut' morgen übers Feld'; 3: 'seh' ich von fern das blonde Haar'; 4: 'Auf der Straße seht ein Lindenbaum'.

15 See, on the concept of distance: '[. . .] the distinction between aesthetic interest and mere effect: the first creating a distance that the second destroys. The purpose of this distance is not to prevent emotion, but to focus it, by directing attention towards the imaginary other, rather than the present self. [. . .] Imagined scenes, by contrast, are not realised but represented; they come to us soaked in thought, and in no sense are they surrogates, standing in place of the unobtainable. On the contrary, they are deliberately placed at a distance, in a world of their own.' (Roger Scruton, *Beauty. A Very Short Introduction* (Oxford, 2009), pp. 104ff.)

16 One of my most intelligent and cultured colleagues once said to me, on this subject, that he saw singers of lieder as character actors because of their shameless efforts to achieve colouristic variety, and hence singers like myself reshaped operatic roles such as Wolfram in Wagner's *Tannhäuser* into character parts.

17 See Peter Revers, *Mahlers Lieder. Ein musikalischer Werkführer* (Munich, 2000), p. 27.

The Souls of the Crags

1 At first Schumann clearly thought of giving the work the title *Sechs Gedichte von N. Lenau und Requiem altkatholisches Gedicht*; see Kilian Sprau, *Liederzyklus als Künstlerdenkmal* (Munich, 2016), p. 34.

2 See Lebrecht Dreves, *Gedichte*, edited by Joseph Freiherrn von Eichendorff (Berlin, 1849), p. 548.

3 See Sprau, *Liederzyklus*, pp. 230ff.

4 See Dreves, *Gedichte*, p. 548.

5 Eichendorff's sarcasm with regard to the revolutionaries of poetry continues in this vein for a long time, and in this preface his Catholicism also assumes an almost reactionary note. From Dreves, *Gedichte*, pp. v ff.

6 '[. . .] otherwise I would probably also have to take the following further sentences from Eichendorff's preface seriously: "They had of course thought differently and believed that the enraptured humanity for whom they had made the new kingdom of heaven so appealing and comfortable would obligingly give them gold laurel wreaths on silk cushions in return. But the vast proletariat of poets, long sensitive under the pressure of the aristocracy of genius, understood what those elegant poets wanted in practical terms and took it literally, point for point, with dreadful consistency; the bare bulbous fruit had finally emerged from the long-nurtured blossom, and the blossoms scattered to the four winds, no one asks about them any more; the Muses run about in loose blouses, fraternise with liberalism, drunk on victory, and have it would seem reached the final stage of the Revolution, literary terrorism.'" (Dreves, *Gedichte*, pp. vi ff.)

7 Faust's disgust is apparent in his direct response to the blacksmith's song: 'Mein guter Schmied, wenn euer Eisen / Nicht fester haftet an der Mähre / Als eure weise Sittenlehre, / So wird's nicht lang emit mir reisen.' ('My good blacksmith, if your iron / Does not adhere more firmly to the mare / Than your wise moral teaching, / It won't be travelling with me for long.' Nikolaus Lenau, *Sämmtliche Werke in einem Bande*, edited by G. Emil Barthel (Leipzig, [1883]), p. 403.

8 A small anecdote: on a small tour, it must be nearly twenty years ago, Gerold Huber and I performed a Mahler recital in Kaiserslautern. On the day of the concert, a sudden cold: it was too late to cancel, so we somehow had to make the best of it. I had them make an announcement, as the recital included many (highly expressive) *Wunderhorn* songs, and without making economies, without sparing myself to some degree, I certainly wouldn't have stayed the course. A lady who said she was an expert and who worked in radio in Berlin – which impressed me greatly – said afterwards (I survived, and so, relatively speaking, did Mahler's songs) that she had liked things better this way in any case, because she had had enough of all that excessive expressiveness. I have thought time and again about those words because I actually believe that expressiveness cannot be fake expression unless it becomes caricature.

9 For the considerable practical difficulties that *Wasserflut* throws up for performers, see 'Steles in an Ice Field', pp. 255–84.

10 See Sprau, *Liederzyklus*, p. 220.

11 Nikolaus Lenau, *Sämmtliche Werke*, p. 424.

12 See the poem reprinted in 'Holliger's Lunar Landscape', pp. 171–202.

13 Lenau has Mephistopheles put it more extremely, almost as if subject to mortal emotions: 'But these once more are mere antics / And pitifully limping parables / Nature lives only for itself, enclosed / And concerns herself not at all with you / And if she lets you make an echo / She casts your word protesting back.' (Lenau, *Sämmtliche Werke*, p. 425.)

Farewell to the Familiar

1 Ludwig Börne, *Denkrede auf Jean Paul Friedr. Richter. Eine Neujahrsgabe für die Freunde und Verehrer des unsterblichen Jean Paul's* (Erlangen, 1826), p. 5.

2 I am indebted to my colleague Andreas Schmidt who pointed out its significance to me.

3 See also: 'The paradoxical ways in which Mahler's music proposes itself as authentic expression, called forth from a mysterious origin, and yet also draws attention to itself as something made – as artifice [. . .]' Julian Johnson, *Mahler's Voices: Expression and Irony in the Songs and Symphonies* (Oxford, 2009), p. 93.

4 See also 'Art Nouveau Rose', pp. 285–302.

5 See also the note in the Critical Report, in Gustav Mahler, *Sämtliche Werke. Kritische Gesamtausgabe. Leitung: Reinhold Kubik. Herausgegeben von der*

Internationalen Gustav Mahler Gesellschaft, Wien. Band. XI V, Teilbd. 2: Des Knaben Wunderhorn. Gesänge für Singstimme mit Orchesterbegleitung. Vorgelegt von Renate Hilmar-Voit (Vienna: Universal Edition, UE 19 951), p. 340.

6 See ibid.

7 Quoted in the copy that Mahler in all likelihood used, perhaps in a later but identical edition (thanks to Jens Malte Fischer for kindly pointing this out): Achim von Arnim und Clemens Brentano, *Des Knaben Wunderhorn.* vol. 3. (Heidelberg, 1808), pp. 81ff., 112.

8 Gradual reshaping (*Umsingen*) is one of the chief characteristics of the folk song – it refers to the constant change and further development of a traditional song in the 'mouth of the people' (*Volksmund*), in the sense of oral transmission.

9 Mahler himself contributed the lines: 'Willkommen, lieber Knabe mein! / So lang hast du gestanden! / [. . .] Von ferne sang die Nachtigall' ('Welcome, dearest lad of mine / You have been out there for so long! / [. . .] The nightingale sang in the distance.'

10 Similar movements in the second harp in the orchestral version are 'submerged' in the overall sound, and hence not comparably characteristic. (Gustav Mahler, *Das Lied von der Erde*, orchestral version (New York: Dover Publications, [1912]), 1 bar before fig. 67 – fig. 68, pp. 144ff.

Drama of the Moment

1 Friedrich Nietzsche, *Also sprach Zarathustra* [1871], *Kritische Studienausgabe*, vol. 4, edited by Giorgio Colli and Mazzino Montinari (Munich, 1988), p. 287.

2 In the first finale, shortly before the attempted rape of Zerlina, Don Giovanni opens the party: 'È aperto a tutti quanti, viva la libertà' ('It's open to all, long live freedom'). Compare Nietzsche in the *Götzen-Dämmerung*: 'For what is freedom! That one has the will to self-responsibility. [. . .] That one becomes more indifferent towards hardship, harshness, deprivation, even towards life itself. [. . .] Freedom means that masculine instincts, those which delight in war and victory, have the upper hand over other instincts, for example that of "happiness".' (Friedrich Nietzsche, *Götzen-Dämmerung. Oder wie man mit dem Hammer philosophirt* [1888], in Nietzsche, *Der Fall Wagner* [. . .], *Kritische Studienausgabe*, vol. 6 (Munich, 1988), p. 139.

3 See also: 'But all desire wants eternity, / Wants deep, deep eternity!' (Nietzsche, *Also sprach Zarathustra*, p. 404.) But desire (or pleasure) does not need to be deep for Giovanni. If he had a goal, he would expect the void. He wants only desire; he wants the moment, but no eternity, or not deep eternity, at least.

4 See also Giovanni's observation: 'Chi a una sola è fedele, verso l'altre è crudele' ('He who is true to one is cruel to all the others'). This sentence, often considered central for his nature, but which to my mind follows a simple moon– June rhyme aesthetic, is only a facade. Otherwise his nature, the irresponsibility of life in the moment, would not be understandable or only as deceitful.

5 Or almost all: 'Lo giuro sul mio onore, purchè non parli del Commendatore,' ('I swear on my honour, as long as you do not speak of the Commendatore') he says to Leporello, and in the conditional of the tormenting consciousness he seals himself within his transformation into a murderer.

6 James Joyce, *A Portrait of the Artist as a Young Man*, edited with an introduction and notes by Seamus Deane (London, 1992), pp. 116–46.

7 'You have often seen the sand on the seashore. [. . .] Now imagine a mountain of that sand, a million miles high, reaching from the earth to the farthest heavens, and a million miles broad, extending to remotest space, and a million miles in thickness: and imagine such an enormous mass of countless particles of sand multiplied as often as there are leaves in the forest, drops of water in the mighty ocean, feathers on birds, scales on fish, hairs on animals, atoms in the vast expanse of the air: and imagine that at the end of every million years a little bird came to that mountain and carried away in its beak a tiny grain of that sand. How many millions upon millions of centuries would pass before that bird had carried away even a square foot of that mountain, how many eons upon eons of ages before it had carried away all. Yet at the end of that immense stretch of time not even one instant of eternity could be said to have ended. [. . .] And if that mountain [. . .] rose and sank as many times as there are stars in the sky, atoms in the air, drops of water in the sea, leaves on the trees, feathers upon birds, scales upon fish, hairs upon animals [. . .] after that eon time the mere thought of which makes our brain reel dizzily, eternity would have scarcely begun.' Ibid., pp. 142–3.

8 In the second recitative, which finally leaves the D minor darkness of his first appearance behind, Giovanni swears on his honour, which he immediately calls into question half a sentence later by mentioning his murder, and which he can thus claim for himself only if he obscures the fact that he has become a murderer: 'Lo giuro sul mio onore, purchè non parli del Commendatore' (see note 5 above).

9 Hemiolic and internally syncopic, it feels paroxysmal.

10 'Ah credimi, o m'uccido, io m'uccido, ah m'uccido!' ('Oh believe me, or I will kill myself, I will kill myself, oh, I will kill myself!') This outburst is of course a piece of acting, but it too seems to me, with its rising intensity and variation ('o' – 'io' – 'ha') to be the expression of an inner, or at least a felt disposition.

11 I do not believe that it is fundamentally impossible, but the learning process involved in the making of sounds may not provide for such a trick. Such a thing is reserved for truly great art – just as Mozart is able to combine four very divergent attitudes into a harmonic whole in the quartet of the first act.

12 This idea was first developed by Alonso de Cóordova y Maldonado in his play *La venganza en el sepulcro* at the end of the seventeenth century. In terms of the history of Mozart's opera, however, it assumes importance only through E. T. A. Hoffmann's novella *Don Juan*.

13 After the list of all possible types of women, he concludes with the words 'Non si picca se sia ricca se sia brutta se sia bella [. . .] purché porti la gonnella'

('He cares not a jot whether she is rich or ugly or beautiful [. . .] as long as she wears a skirt'), before adding in a quiet duet with the bassoon, with an unexpected, but all the more shattering melancholy: 'Voi sapete quel che fa' ('You know what he does').

Intermezzo

1 Florian Mehltretter (ed.), *Wie semantisch ist die Musik? Beiträge zu Semiotik, Pragmatik und Ästhetik an der Schnittstelle von Musik und Text* (Freiburg im Breisgau, Berlin and Vienna, 2016), p. 7.
2 Eduard Hanslick, *Vom Musikalisch-Schönen. Ein Beitrag zur Revision der Ästhetik der Tonkunst* ([Leipzig, 1854], Darmstadt, 1991), p. 21.
3 See also: 'I never meant you shouldn't explain or understand something, but just don't say that the true meaning of x is y.' Jonathan Cott, *The Complete Susan Sontag Interview* (New Haven and London, 2013), p. 25.
4 Ludwig Wittgenstein, *Philosophical Investigations*, trans. G. E. M. Anscombe, P. M. S. Hacker and J. Schulte (London, 2010), p. lxvii.
5 Josef Freiherr von Eichendorff, *Erzählungen*, edited by Werner Bergengruen (Zurich, 1988), p. 168.

Holliger's Lunar Landscape

1 These fluctuations of intonation (I would call them the vertical element of the vibrato) oscillate synchronously with the dynamic oscillations (the horizontal element) – a particular quality of vibrato when used by singers and wind instruments, unlike the vibrato of string instruments. The combination of the two elements, in spite of their essential synchronicity, allows a wide range of variety and hence a significant diversity of interpretation with this singer's tool. However, to increase the lack of ambiguity of a deliberate quarter-tone, the extension of vibrato must be explicitly limited in breadth.
2 Holliger mentions that – in a similar way to the incorporation of the pitch of sung micro-intervals into an orchestral sound – the treatment of rhythmical complexity is much more easily resolved than mathematics might suggest. (I understand that – perhaps erroneously – as meaning that one does not need to be able to hear and play three against four against five against seven beats, but that one can learn to trust that what has been notated and experienced can and will come together; this can at least serve as an aid for the singer, because of course Holliger understands everything, even if he can simply set aside that ability, which might become an obstructive obsession to others, out of emotional necessity. For me that is where his genius lies.) 'I also think [. . .] that, after the abstract piano sound of the rehearsal, the colourful orchestral sound integrates micro-intervals much more naturally than one might have feared when initially

studying the piano reduction. It's the same with rhythm: why should one banish from music the infinitely sophisticated rhythms of speech, of heart-notes, of breathing, of natural sounds (dripping, waves, wind), the asymmetry of a crystal, a blossom, a butterfly?' (letter of 5 December 2018.) How aptly Holliger makes the point that he does not take the universally visibly perceived forms of crystal, blossom, butterfly as occasion to create a rigid artistic form, but constantly takes their individual appearance as occasion for new contemplation, thus characterising all phenomena as individuality.

3 Holliger and his librettist Händl Klaus interpreted the concept of the palindrome, meaning a word that sounds the same when read in either direction, quite freely: not least in the sense of an anagram, which also links the title *Lunea* with 'Lenau', along with the phenomenon of the 'crab', the retrograde inversion of a melody.

4 Nikolaus Lenau was closely connected with Justinus Kerner via the school of Swabian poets. His play with the 'psychognomic' significance of symmetrical images produced by folding sheets of paper with fresh inkblots made its way into the tests of the psychologist Hermann Rorschach: in these, personality traits are identified with reference to the associations found in the inkblot pictures. These days, Rorschach tests are used only as parts of large series of tests. They have never been considered as valid in evidence.

5 Reflection of a musical motif along a horizontal (mirror) or vertical ('crab') axis.

6 In Zurich Opera House's monthly bulletin for March 2018, p. 15, Holliger says, 'A normal person does not compose [or write] – or he composes like Czerny or Pleyel. [. . .] I'm not in search of what is abnormal in a person. I look for people whose imagination knows no bounds.'

7 Ibid.

8 EEG (electroencephalogram): brainwave recording. The concept of splitting is used here more in the sense of a callosotomy, a cut through the corpus callosum that synchronises the two hemispheres of the brain, even though it actually tends to refer to the partial functional disturbance of a hemisphere that is suffering a stroke. I see this as a classic example of artistic freedom on the part of a composer who is also very well versed in medical matters (Holliger's father was a physician).

9 For this reason the opera also begins as *Einklang* ('tuning in') with the epilogue-like song that closes the song-cycle (*Nachklang* – 'aftermath'). Incidentally, it is the only poem by Lenau in the collection of songs that otherwise consists entirely of prose fragments from the *Winnenthal* notes: 'Um Mitternacht entstand dies Lied, / Zwölfmal erklang das Glockenerz, / Und zwölfmal Antwort gab mein Herz / Im dumpfen Strophensang / Dem dumpfen Glockenklang.' ('This song appeared at midnight, / Twelve times the bell sounded / And twelve times my heart replied / In dull strophic song / To the dull bell's toll.')

10 Such constant changes also characterise Lenau's poetry, described in exemplary form in the last of his *Waldlieder* (Forest Songs). This is one of his most mature works, in which he concludes by comprehending the obsessive

experience of threat from earthly transience: 'In dieses Waldes leisem Rauschen / Ist mir, als hör ich Kunde wehen / Daß alles Sterben und Vergehen / Nur heimlichstill vergnügtes Tauschen.' (In this forest's quiet rustling / I feel as if I hear the approach of understanding: / That all dying and passing / Is only secretly and silently pleasurable change.')

11 For me, the live recording of a performance of *Utopie Chorklang* (2004) for three twelve-voice choral groups a third of a tone apart from each other by the SWR Vokalensemble was a fundamentally revelatory decoupling of hearing from the expectation of an educated hearing. The division of familiar intervals into third tones and – in combination with semitones – even sixth tones is a sound-space that can no longer be experienced in a 'macromolecules' way. Instead, I was granted an image of every corner, every crack, available to experience being filled with 'elementary particles' of sound, which would normally be bridged in form-awareness, transgressed on purpose.

12 So what should be sung is not 'he-e-i-ssen' but 'he-e-ei-ssen Strahl der Sonnen', which of course sounds like 'ha-a-ai-ssen'.

13 I remember a recurring nightmare that I had for decades, in which the perfect and ideal smoothness of my pillow signified the reduction of the meaning of the world to the number 1, which through a lack of alternatives became a universe-in-one and abolished everything individual and singular. How does one appropriately communicate to one's fellow beings the urgency and the huge, nothing-less-than-existential burden of such experience?

14 But if a work does not correspond to this formal foundation – for example, Mendelssohn's *Reformation Symphony* (one of my favourite works) – it often becomes its creator's problem child, and may sadly find itself rejected.

15 A completely nonsensical image opened my eyes to what exactly it is that fascinates me about big cities such as New York: a photograph of Manhattan taken diagonally from above had been projected over a photograph of the Grand Canyon. Contrary to what one might have imagined, it looked not spectacular, but banal and ridiculous. I think because the outsize, monumental human creation is already an (anthropomorphic) landscape, run through by many canyons, such as 6th Avenue, which divides Manhattan.

16 Only the last leaf, the twenty-third, is an exception. As if we are walking on the far side of the moon, Lenau's death-state is transformed by sound (exemplified particularly by the *Strohbass*, rasping subharmonic undertones of the chorus) into a concluding blackness that was embodied by the staging at Zurich. This is the eternal dark side of the moon – effectively a *notturno* by Holliger. This is how Lenau expresses it, before rising to a song of transubstantiation with his final sentence: 'Der Tod hat keine Stimme' ('Death has no voice'). The last word, 'Stimme' (voice), is breathed, not voiced; it loses all colour and thus itself relates to the eternally black, dead side of the moon.

17 The sequence B flat – G flat – D – E flat – (A) – B flat in the middle of the ninth page (bar 40) is a reminder of the first notes of the song *Einsamkeit*.

18 To the text 'Vivat, Guarnerius'. This absurdly hymns Lenau's violin as his rescuer (represented by the previous song 'Der Schwimmer, mit den Händen ausschlagend, schlägt den Tod beständig ab' ('The swimmer, striking out with his hands, constantly beats away death').

19 Lenau's last poem (25 September 1844).

20 I have sung the words 'Fata Morgana' only twice as a singer; the other time in the eleventh leaf or the twenty-second song of *Lunea*: 'Die Wüstenwanderer strecken ihren Becher der Phantasie hinauf nach den Quellen der Fata Morgana' ('The desert wanderers reach their cups of imagination up to the springs of Fata Morgana'). The Fata Morgana symbolises the reflection of the eternal inside the earthly, with the desert in the role of religion, and with the wanderer as the priest of the religion of pointlessness.

21 Schoeck's score has 'Spielgefährte' (meaning playmate, which seems a real possibility), but the poem has 'Spiegelfährte' (meaning mirror-trail, which fits the Fata Morgana better).

22 Holliger also wrote to me about the even more surprising resemblance to Schoeck's *Die Drei*, WoO, no. 39, which sets the text about the three riders, also included in *Lunea* (fourteenth leaf), for a similar cast: 'One more fascinating curiosity about the Schoeck elective affinity (unconscious! I only know a part of his work [Sure you do!]): Raphael Immoos came across the enclosed score *Die Drei*, which I had never seen or heard before. Quite something... same key, same metre, same vocal pitch!' (letter of 5 December 2018).

23 For readers who would like to check this against the score, here are some examples (Holliger's fundamental and frequently expressed dislike of bar lines is unfortunately so radical that it is impossible to give a precise indication as to where one is in the score: for that reason I have used the page numbers of the piano score): 1. 'Ist's gut in einen Strom' – Holliger, p. 180. End of the first system in the alto voice that begins the canon; Schoeck, first movement, second and third bar after fig. 59: not a precise tonal relation, but the same movement in the motif to the same words. 2. 'O, starre nur hinein, hinein' – Holliger, p. 181, first system; Schoeck, the three bars before fig. 61: the first four syllables and notes a mirror, not exact to the semitone, but unmistakable, the two 'hineins', however, not quite mirrored in total but only partially. 3. 'Was dir, und soll's dein Liebstes sein' – Holliger, p. 181, second system; Schoeck, second and third bar after 62: a very free 'crab'. 4. 'Die Flut hinunterwallen' – Holliger, p. 185; Schoeck, first and second bar of 64: a thematically similarly descending beginning, which ends in a mirror. 5. 'Hinträumend' ('Dreaming') – Holliger, end p. 185; Schoeck, second and third bar after 65: in terms of motif, an almost identical tune up to the syncopic use of the subsequent 'wird Vergessenheit' ('oblivion will'). 6. 'die Seele sieht mit ihrem Leid' – Holliger, p. 187; Schoeck, the two bars around 67: very similar melodic structure.

24 There are only very occasional slurs of a quaver and a subsequent crotchet that seem to me like a tribute to Schoeck's 6/8 beat or melismas, with a similar rhythm appearing in his third movement ('Wehmut' – extended at 13; 'Vögel' two bars before 14; 'fährt auf und will' in the two bars after 15).

25 At first these memories of anxiety are announced by trombones and xylophone, then at the end of the chorus percussion and brass assume a continuous role, or rather they no longer appear intermittently but become the symbol of a permanently shining, dazzling, painful spotlight.

Hope – Love – Faith

1 There is also *Der frohe Wandersmann* ('The Happy Wanderer'), op. 77 no. 1; *Der Schatzgräber* ('The Treasure-Digger'), op. 45 no. 1; and *Frühlingsfahrt* ('Spring Journey'), op. 45 no. 2.
2 The Eichendorff poem *Der frohe Wandersmann* – 'Wem Gott will rechte Gunst erweisen . . .' ('He to whom God wants to show true favour . . .' – has become a kind of (ersatz) folk song; not in Schumann's setting (op. 77 no. 1; 1840), however, but in that of Theodor Friedrich Fröhlich (1833).
3 *Der Lindenbaum* from Schubert's *Winterreise* does not count as a folk song either, primarily because of the problematic fifth verse. But it has become thought of as something akin to a folk song – albeit in a distorted and, to my mind, repellent way, even if one cannot describe Friedrich Silcher's tasteless interventions as the actual genesis of a folk song. See 'Steles in an Ice Field', pp. 255–84.
4 For that reason I do not consider duets, tercets and quartets to be lieder, even if they come close and have many points in common. The increasing appearance of monody in the sixteenth century was not revolutionary because three out of the four singing voices were moved to the instrumental section, but because the meaning of the sung words was entrusted to only one voice, one particular vocal sound, and that individualisation of expression made the operatic emphasis on the individual possible for the first time. As proof, we have as the first 'character', Orpheus, an exemplary musical individualist (even though Monteverdi's *L'Orfeo* was not the first opera – that honour goes to Peri's *La Dafne*).
5 The first verse, we might say, represents the father as an existential exposition; the second, the son coming into the world ('Da tratst du wunderbar zu mir' – 'You came to me most wonderfully'); the third the spirit as a synesthetic absorption of both principles.
6 Who, for example, could read the poem *Liebst du um Schönheit* ('If You Love for Beauty') and completely ignore a certain moralistic aftertaste? In my view it is the settings that make it so popular – for example, in Mahler's *Rückert-Lieder* and in the Schumanns' joint *Liebesfrühling*, op. 37 no. 4. See 'Art Nouveau Rose, pp. 285–302.
7 At the same time I should mention one overwhelming motif that appears in both songs. If I had to name one typical Schumann melody – this one would be it. I mean the sequence in the descant of the interlude for the fourth verse in op. 83 no. 2: D – C sharp – G sharp – (A–B–) – A – E – D – C sharp, and the melodies in some of the lyric parts in op. 90 no. 7: '. . . und heißem Liebesglühen', 'Sterne in des [. . .] als Stern der Nacht', as well as multiple variations.

The two song-cycles were composed very close together (opus 83 in the spring, opus 90 in the August of the second year of lieder, 1850).
8 Non-vibrato notes can sound different: inexpressive when unsupported, but not without beauty, a bit like concrete; supported, on the other hand, when the continuing vibration of the voice is balanced by counter-vibrations: effortful, strenuous, exhausted – and deliberate.
9 However, why Buddeus writes, 'Will Gegenwart nicht trüben' ('The present not to darken') does not seem entirely clear to me. If it is an affirmative main sentence (in the sense of the lyrical 'I'), why then in negation, because 'trüben' ('darken') is entirely pejorative, even though it describes the present? The solution is probably that this sentence is a conditional subclause and 'trüben' used only intransitively, in the sense of: 'If pain does not cease in the moment, then perhaps in the future?'

Rihm and Goethe: Building a Programme

1 In this context, please bear in mind Max Reger's charming way of ordering in the pub: 'Two hours of Weißwurst please, Fräulein!'
2 We are still hoping for settings of *Wanderers Sturmlied* ('Wanderer's Storm Song') and *Der Wanderer* ('The Wanderer'), and perhaps the completion of Schubert's gripping, compelling first fragment version of *Mahomets Gesang* ('Mohammed's Song'). Schubert made two attempts (D. 549, D. 721) that were not entirely successful because in both the flow of the great religious leader surged too soon, with the result that the estuary delta as a release into the ocean of the global religion of Islam could no longer be represented musically – in both of these works, which would remain as fragments, the expected mass exceeded the possibilities of the Schubertian piano song. So it is hardly surprising that most settings of this exponentially expanding poem do not use only solo voice and piano: August Bergt composed for vocal trio with piano; Ernst Paul Flügel, Robert Kahn and Lothar Kempter for choir with orchestra. Only Carl Loewe created a classical piano song, which evades the difficult depiction of a massive historic development with a simple, aria-like narrative attitude – and thus also fails.
3 The only setting of the *Harzreise* before Rihm, and then only of a section of Goethe's poem, begins at 'Aber abseits, wer ist's?' ('But who is that away from the path?') and drops out again three verses later: Johannes Brahms's *Alto Rhapsody*, op. 53.
4 See Albrecht Schöne, *Götterzeichen, Liebeszauber, Satanskult. Neue Ein-blicke in alte Goethetexte* (Munich, 1993), p. 40.
5 Johann Wolfgang von Goethe, *Maximen und Reflexionen über Kunst* [1823], quoted in Schöne, *Götterzeichen, Liebeszauber, Satanskult*, p. 48.
6 Albrecht Schöne stresses the multiple nature of the addressed 'Du': 'It refers to the mountain, and the divine nature revealed in it, and also the one who managed to climb that mountain. [. . .] There is a quote from the Gospel of

Matthew (4:8ff.), from the account of the temptation of Christ, whom the Devil leads 'up to a very high mountain', where he is shown 'all the kingdoms of the world and their splendour'. (Schöne, *Götterzeichen, Liebeszauber, Satanskult*, p. 50.)

7 I ask myself the question whether Tasso, after this ending, following Goethe's example, can develop into a classical artist, or whether he is more likely to perish along with Plessing and his kind.

8 Monologues like those in a drama by Schiller or Shakespeare do not tend to occur in Goethe's drama. Also, no figure is granted a long time alone on the stage – Rihm's selection of text for the *Tasso-Gedanken* leaves out the occasional words from other protagonists, and thus artificially creates longer passages of text for Tasso.

9 Quoted in Jochen Schmidt, *Die Geschichte des Genie-Gedankens in der deutschen Literatur, Philosophie und Politik 1745–1945*; vol. 1: *Von der Aufklärung bis zum Idealismus* (Darmstadt, 1985), p. 342.

10 Letter from Caroline Herder, 20 March 1789, to her husband Johann Gottfried Herder.

11 As his employer, the Duke is allowed access to Tasso's work, particularly since he has already solemnly handed the finished poem to him. Childishly, dissatisfied with the copy Tasso has offered him, the Duke demands the original.

12 See Dieter Borchmeyer, *Weimarer Klassik. Porträt einer Epoche* (Weinheim, 1994), pp. 177ff.

13 I find it interesting that Goethe, whose Weimar incarnation does not allow for an autobiographical interpretation of the figure of Tasso, could himself have drawn on this precise source of inspiration. On 10 January 1788, during his second stay in Rome, Goethe wrote to Charlotte von Stein, 'If my writing is to be completed under similar conditions, over the course of this year I must fall in love with a princess in order to be able to write Tasso.' (*Goethes Werke, Hamburger Ausgabe*, edited by Erich Trunz; vol. XI, 14th edn (Munich, 2005), p. 476.) This is of course a joke, and yet it may contain a certain reference to his own creative method (in the *Sturm-und-Drang* period, or even earlier). Dieter Borchmeyer even tells me about a flirtation with a 'princess' in Naples (so a short time before), even though he himself does not attach any great importance to this episode, this quotation. On the other hand, the self-quotation of lines 6–7 as a motto to the *Marienbader Elegie* (with the slight change 'was ich leide' – 'what I suffer') also suggests that poetry can be a very direct expression of the poet's own personal experience.

14 See Schmidt, *Die Geschichte des Genie-Gedankens*, vol. I, p. 344.

15 'In dieser Woge [. . .] Verschwunden ist der Glanz' ('In this wave [. . .] the brilliance is gone'). Tasso's life has lost its sheen. To me, that is what makes Rihm's startlingly clear transposition of Tasso's finally authentic confession possible: 'Und schäme mich nicht mehr, es zu bekennen' ('And am no longer ashamed to admit it').

16 See Schmidt, *Die Geschichte des Genie-Gedankens*. vol. I, p. 342.

17 In addition to the role of Goethe and Rihm, consider also the role of Duke Alfons, the performer and the audience: 'In this context the shipwreck is something like the "legitimate" consequence of seagoing, safe arrival in the harbour or serene calm at sea merely the deceptive aspect of such profound doubtfulness [. . .], that there must be another, pithy configuration as an intensification of ideas of stormy seas and shipwrecks, in which the unaffected observer on land is assigned to the shipwreck on sea.' Hans Blumenberg, *Schiffbruch mit Zuschauer*. (Frankfurt am Main, 1979), p. 13.

Steles in an Ice Field

1 I read this explanation in Fischer-Dieskau – and found it inadequate, even forced, until the Italianist Florian Mehltretter informed me (to my shame) that this was an obvious interpretation in the tradition of the reading of Petrarch, and hence absolutely deserved to be taken seriously. See Dietrich Fischer-Dieskau, *Schubert und seine Lieder* (Stuttgart 1996), p. 340.
2 Rigidly orthodox attitudes such as Richard Kramer's statements concerning the correct reception and performance of Schubert's cycles, even down to the preservation of the original keys, are no real help, as their categorical demands remain too remote from the reality of performance. See Richard Kramer, *Distant Cycles: Schubert and the Conceiving of Songs* (Chicago, 1994), pp. 3–21 and 151–87.
3 This controversy around irony in the art song, which arose especially in the context of the lieder of Schumann, who set many poems by Heine, is actually an unfortunate one, and in my view largely unnecessary. A substantial part of this argument was revealed to be more or less based on a misunderstanding, which actually found a correlative to the linguistic tool of irony in Schumann's settings, which is expressed not primarily musically, but especially extra-musically, for example in the cyclical combination and sequence of the songs (see 'Lyrical Dramaturgy', pp. 37–58; and the phenomenon of the 'Humoresque', which particularly in Mahler's later *Wunderhorn* lieder allows the possibility of shrill laughter as primarily non-musical content. See 'Art Nouveau Rose', pp. 285–302, and 'Farewell to the Familiar', pp. 123–46.)
4 For example, Schubert leaves out the exclamation mark that Müller added to the title 'Mut!'. I see the fact that in no. 20, *Der Wegweiser*, the first line of the third verse closes with 'Wegen' (ways, paths) rather than the original 'Straßen' (roads) as a simple error of transcription (probably caused by the 'Wege' in the first verse), as it makes little semantic difference; but it contradicts the rhyme scheme, and is also an unnecessary verbal repetition.
5 For example, Ian Bostridge refers to the title of the last song, *Der Leiermann* as ironic, because of the positive connotations of *Leier* (see, for example, the song *An die Leier* ('To my Lyre', D. 737). *Leier* would normally be translated into English as 'lyre'. Of course I have never had this association, as for me this title

always meant simply 'The Hurdy-Gurdy Man' or 'The Man with the Hurdy-Gurdy'. Note the words *Leierkasten* (lyre case) or *Drehleier* (turning lyre). (In German one would never combine 'Mann' with a serious instrument, just as one would not normally refer in English to a 'guitar man', 'violin man' or 'piano man'.) Particularly after Schubert installs the instrument's typical drone (an accompanying note that remains at a constant pitch), the hurdy-gurdy can no longer be the object of ironic connotation. Note also the definition in *Grimms' Dictionary* of *Leiermann* as 'singer', 'poet' or 'bad minstrel'. See Ian Bostridge, *Schubert's Winter Journey: Anatomy of an Obsession* (London, 2015), p. 375.

6 Further associations of real danger are: 'Es war zu kalt zum Stehen' (It was too cold to stand') in no. 10, *Rast*; 'Vom Abendrot zum Morgenlicht / Ward mancher Kopf zum Greise' ('Between sunset and dawn / Many a head has turned grey') in no. 14, *Der greise Kopf*; 'Der Winter, kalt und wild' ('The winter, cold and wild') in no. 18, *Der stürmische Morgen*; 'Eis und Nacht und Graus' ('Ice and night and horror') in no. 19, *Täuschung*; 'Wüstenein' (Wilderness) in no. 20, *Der Wegweiser*; 'Gegen Wind und Wetter' ('Against Wind and Weather') in no. 22, *Mut*; 'Barfuß auf dem eise' ('Barefoot on the ice') in no. 24, *Der Leiermann*.

7 Other examples of coquettish play with death are: 'Fühlst in der Still' erst deinen Wurm / [. . .] sich regen' ('In the silence do you feel your worm stirring') in no. 10, *Rast*; 'Treue bis zum Grabe' ('Fidelity to the grave') in no. 15, *Die Krähe*; 'meiner Hoffnung Grab' ('my hope's grave') in no. 15, *Letzte Hoffnung*; 'Eine Straße muss ich gehen, / Die noch keiner ging zurück' ('I must walk a road from which no one has returned') in no. 20, *Der Wegweiser*; the whole of no. 21, *Das Wirtshaus*; 'Ging nur die dritt' erst hinterdrein! / Im Dunkeln wird mir wohler sein' ('If only the third would go after the rest / I will be better off in darkness') in no. 23, *Die Nebensonnen*.

8 The playing of a hurdy-gurdy – and the drone sounds with the appoggiatura from below, representing the rubbing of the wheel against the strings, indicate that it is indeed a hurdy-gurdy and not a barrel organ – requires musical skill and imagination. When Fischer-Dieskau refers in this context to a bagpipe and lyre rather than a hurdy-gurdy I see this is a confusion of terms: '[. . .] the unchanging bagpipe fifths in the left hand [of the piano] (this is the older form of the lyre, and not, for example, a hurdy-gurdy!' (Dietrich Fischer-Dieskau, *Auf den Spuren der Schubert-Lieder. Werden – Wesen – Wirkung* (Wiesbaden, 1971), p. 298.

9 As my friend James Cheung says, 'Don't milk pity from the audience as the protagonist.'

10 Erika von Borries, *Wilhelm Müller. Der Dichter der 'Winterreise'. Eine Biographie* (Munich, 2008).

11 Quoted in ibid., p. 36.

12 Günter Hartung, review of Erika von Borries, *Wilhelm Müller. Der Dichter der 'Winterreise'. Eine Biographie*, in *Mitteilungen des Vereins für Anhaltische Landeskunde*, vol. 17 (2008), pp. 259–74. I am grateful to Dorothee Treiber for this reference.

13 'It probably consisted of a "period of sensuality" mentioned by Müller of sexual dalliances or brothel visits of a kind that would not have been unusual for a twenty-year-old soldier and student, and may be assumed to have come to an end by the early autumn of 1815, after he fell in love with Luise Hensel.' (Ibid., p. 271.)
14 See von Borries, *Wilhelm Müller*, p. 43.
15 Otto Erich Deutsch (ed. and comp.), *Schubert: Die Erinnerungen seiner Freunde* (Leipzig, 1957), pp. 160f.
16 Dedifferentiation is a term that correlates with the malignity cancer cells. When people or social classes are described as cancerous tumours, we might suspect fascism, but for a description of the withdrawal of artistic complexity previously achieved I don't find the term inappropriate. This distortion can thoroughly sweep away artistic achievements by trivialising them for the sake of easier digestibility. But in fact Silcher's treatment is like a slap in the face for Schubert, a frontal attack on the genius of the composer who had, as a student, obediently accepted the advice of his teacher Antonio Salieri to stick to the models of Johann Friedrich Reichardt and Carl Friedrich Zelter, but as a mature composer had simply brushed them aside and invented a new genre: the art song.
17 The traditional *Stollen* and *Gegenstollen* (strophe and antistrophe) of the German *Meistersinger* tradition become the *Vordersatz* and *Nachsatz* (antecedent and consequent) of the simple lied form, which leads to a distorting simplification of the sophisticated structure in Schubert's work.
18 *Umsingen*, as we have seen, is an important characteristic of the folk song: the constant, even substantial change applied to a traditional song that was not originally written down. For me, however, the process of *Umsingen* is fundamentally an elaboration, an indication that a folk song is moving towards the art song and not the other way round.
19 My inestimable friend and adviser Laurenz Lütteken has a less negative vision of Silcher's treatment, because in the *Vormärz*, the period leading up to the 1848 Revolution, an incomparably different aesthetic ambience prevailed, which makes Lütteken, in the context of this idyll, think of the Biedermeier painter Carl Spitzweg (1808–1885) as a 'corrective', not least because by collectivising the message of the lied in the form of a choral piece, Silcher fundamentally moves the goalposts. In fact, I would have to agree with this: but if I compare the two pieces, Schubert's and Silcher's, in the present day, again I can't help sticking with my adamant rejection. The very thought of Silcher, when I'm singing *Der Lindenbaum*, makes me shudder.
20 See Thomas Mann, *Der Zauberberg* (Frankfurt am Main, 1960), pp. 903ff. and 993; *The Magic Mountain*, trans. H.T. Lowe-Porter (New York, 1927).
21 Summer is being sung about and described from the perspective of winter. Here, however, I believe it would be a mistake to see this as a memory of the past. It is in fact about the most culturally reassuring aspect of nature: the annual return of seasonal phenomena.

22 *Portamento* is more or less a sliding but, but unlike *glissando*, a controlled and uneven connection between two notes upwards or downwards. The pitch of the next note is generally reached at the end of the process, before the new note actually begins.
23 As a singer I find it difficult to achieve the melodiousness of this 3/4 rhythm because the extension of the first syllable of 'Bru–nnen' (spring') and of 'träumt" ('dreamt') has to be held so long on a dotted crotchet in the 3/4 *legato*, that the flow of melody is prevented from easily continuing after the count of 'two and'. Because I recognised this, but didn't quite understand it, as a student I wrote '6/8' over this passage as an aid, which is of course not to be understood as meaning that I wanted to place a (completely unthinkable) emphasis on the second count of 'two and' of the 3/4 bar; it was more that I was aiming for a *diminuendo* on the first dotted crotchet. But I find the *portamento* solution even better, the replacement of a dynamic by intonation – something very rare in Schubert.
24 See Bostridge, *Schubert's Winter Journey*, pp. 163–4.
25 In contrast with this gallery of very different stone monuments in *Die Winterreise*, in the earlier *Schöne Müllerin* I find actual and communicative colour as it were in watercolours, while in the Heine lieder of the later *Schwanengesang* I think primarily of woodcuts.
26 See Elmar Budde, *Schuberts Liedzyiklen. Ein musikalischer Werkführer* (Munich, 2003), p. 69.
27 I am referring here to an observation of my friend, the pianist and musicologist Siegfried Mauser.
28 'Sind den in diesem Hause / Die Kammern all besetzt? / Bin matt zum Niedersinken, / Bin tödlich schwer verletzt' ('Are all the rooms here / Occupied? / I am ready to collapse, / I am fatally injured') in *Das Wirtshaus*; 'Ach meine Sonnen seid ihr nicht, / Schaut andren doch ins Angesicht' ('Oh, you are not my sons, / Look others in the eye') in *Die Nebensonnen*.
29 Jean Paul's word *Weltschmerz* (world-weariness) is used as a generalising term for the programmatically melancholic poetry of Wilhelm Müller, Nikolaus Lenau and others of their time.
30 At this point the parallels with Othmar Schoeck's other hugely important orchestral song-cycle, *Lebendig begraben* ('Buried alive'), op. 40, in which generous time is given to this horrific theme, so popular in the nineteenth century, invite additional interpretative approaches: an ironic, macabre, almost cynical self-display would also grant us a new interpretation of *Die Winterreise*, fleeing this vale of tears in favour of Heine, *Tristan und Isolde* or even *Les Fleurs du mal*. See also Derrick Puffett, *The Song Cycles of Othmar Schoeck* (Bern and Stuttgart, 1982), pp. 201ff.
31 Ibid., p. 138.
32 See Chris Walton, *Othmar Schoeck. Eine Biographie* (Zurich, 1994), pp. 190ff.
33 See Puffett, *The Song Cycles of Othmar Schoeck*, p. 144.

Art Nouveau Rose

1 I think a description that Adorno found for *Jugendstil* (*art nouveau*) with regard to Schoenberg is fitting for Mahler's form of formlessness: '*Jugendstil* is based [. . .] on the attempt to break away from the environment of conventional bourgeois forms, while at the same time remaining within the environment of forms outlined by the bourgeois world.' (Theodor W. Adorno, *Kranichsteiner Vorlesungen*, edited by Klaus Reichert and Michael Schwarz (Berlin, 2014), p. 25.)
2 Another kind of game that really should not be audible, being entirely out of my control, is as if forcibly imprinted in me. In the first of Mahler's *Lieder eines fahrenden Gesellen*, at the start of the middle section ('Blümlein blau . . .'), I imagine that the two introductory 6/8 bars are articulated differently, once as a 3/4 bar with three emphases, on the first, third and fifth quavers, and once as a conventional 6/8 bar with two beats, on the first and the fourth quavers. Although it is objectively quite insignificant, I always see it as the expression of the unconditional vitality of this music, which nevertheless I almost always think I can hear.

Meaning or Being

1 Hans Blumenberg, *Nachahmumg der Natur. Zur Vorgeschichte der Idee des schöpferischen Menschen* (Stuttgart, 2020), p. 52.
2 Johann Jakob Bodmer (1698–1783), Swiss historian and critic; Johann Jakob Breitinger (1701–1776), Swiss philologist and author; Friedrich Gottlieb Klopstock (1724–1803), German poet.
3 Friedrich Nietzsche, *Die Geburt der Tragödie. Oder: Griechenthum und Pessimismus* [1871], in Nietzsche, *Die Geburt der Tragödie [. . .] Kritische Studienausgabe*, edited by Giorgio Colli and Mazzino Montinari, vol. 1 (Munich, 1988), pp. 873–90. *The Birth of Tragedy Out of the Spirit of Music*, trans. Shaun Whiteside (London, 1993), p. 13.
4 See the second strophe: 'Seht ihr im Lande der Zwietracht Fackeln lodern? / Hört ihr den Frevel das Recht zum Kampfe fodern? / Drum mit des Herzens Gewalt friedvoller Lieder / Zaubert das wilde Geschrei des Wahnsinns nieder' ('Do you see the torches of strife blazing in the land? / Do you hear the sacrilege demanding the right to fight? / Therefore with the heart's power of peaceful songs / Conjure down the wild cries of madness!'
5 The two poems are also linked very concretely by word-mirroring: 'Über allen Gipfeln ist Ruh' / In allen Wipfeln' ('Peace lies over all / The mountain peaks / In all the treetops') writes Goethe. And 'Wie der Bäume kühne Wipfel / [. . .] Wie der Berge greise Gipfel' (How boldly the treetops / [. . .] How the grey mountain peaks') writes von der Neun.
6 Nicholas of Cusa (1401–1464), German philosopher and theologian, early proponent of Renaissance humanism.

7 If Mahler treated his texts (apart from the Rückert settings) with extreme liberty – he talked of using them as 'quarries' – I would see this as meaning that in effect he anticipated the interpretational gap between the original poem and its musical setting in his poem-editing. This meant that Mahler was to an extent his own poet, as is apparent in his attribution of authorship to himself for his treatment of textual fragments from *Des Knaben Wunderhorn* for the *Lieder eines fahrenden Gesellen*. At the same time, however, Mahler travelled some distance (in a manner untypical of the art song) from the poem to the libretto – his songs are of course nothing less than dramas. See also 'Farewell to the Familiar', pp. 123–46, and 'Art Nouveau Rose', pp. 285–302.

8 *Das Mühlenleben* is one of the three poems by Wilhelm Müller that Schubert did not set for his cycle (apart from the prologue and epilogue). Along with the previous poem, *Am Feierabend*, it makes it particularly clear that in this story, the miller's daughter is not the journeyman's harmless crush but a resolute manager, who runs the mill purposefully and rationally. As such she is universally praised to the skies by all the employees, but is essentially unattainable for all the apprentices and journeymen.

Schubert's Lied Legacy

1 Not only in the Stadttheater in Würzburg (my first engagement) but also in countries where musical and virtuoso tradition is held in high esteem (the violinist Anton Barakhovsky, leader of the Bavarian Radio Symphony Orchestra, told me this is also true of competitions in the Soviet Union), the concert manager's summons would be: 'Musicians and singers to the stage!'

2 The fact that Otto Erich Deutsch gave a number of its own to *Die Taubenpost*, D. 965A, and did not integrate it within the '957' of *Schwanengesang* testifies to the scepticism that has long been applied to the construction of this cycle.

3 The collections of lieder published as opus numbers in Schubert's lifetime don't seem to me to be as relevant in terms of performance practice as is sometimes suggested. I see them, unlike Schumann's lied opus numbers, largely as mere editorial collections; I think the intention was simply to publish lieder in particular volumes and make them accessible in that way. So far, at any rate, I have not really been able to discern any cyclically conceptual meaning in them. According to the autograph, the sequences of the lieder in the two small cycles on poems by Rellstab and Heine, however, seem to have been conceived by Schubert as Haslinger published them.

4 I cannot find a suitable place for the recitative song *Die Wallfahrt* ('The Pilgrimage'), D. 778A, in this group, any more than I can for the previously mentioned Rellstab song *Herbst* ('Autumn'), D. 945, in the first part of *Schwanengesang*.

5 Heinrich Heine wrote to Wilhelm Müller on 7 June 1826: 'Very early on I allowed German folksong to have an influence on me, and later, when I was

studying in Bonn, August Schlegel revealed many metrical secrets to me, but I think in your songs I have for the first time found the pure sound and the true simplicity for which I have always striven' (Das Heinrich Heine-Portal, http://www.hhp.uni-trier. de/Projekte/HHP/briefe/06briefdatenbank/tabelle/ adressaten/ index_html?widthgiven=30&letterid= W20B0177&lineref= 0&mode=1).

6 See 'The Souls of the Crags' pp. 99–122.

7 I cannot understand Fischer-Dieskau's apodictically expressed observation on what irony means in the song *Das Fischermädchen* ('The Fisher Maiden') – he does not provide evidence for his ascription. That could equally be said, of course, of many of my own assertions. See Dietrich Fischer-Dieskau, *Auf den Spuren der Schubert-Lieder* (Wiesbaden, 1971), p. 313.

8 Once again, the message of love is characterised by listing all of animate and inanimate nature in *Frühlingssehnsucht* ('Spring Longing') as the crucial topos that it is for the literature of the nineteenth century's art song: by involving all imaginable messengers – as realised in exemplary fashion in Beethoven's *An die ferne Geliebte*, op. 98, and in Schumann's *Liebesbotschaft*, op. 36 no. 6. See particularly 'Prelude with Low-Flying Fighter Jet', pp. 1–36.

9 A review in the Leipzig *Allgemeine musikalische Zeitung* as early as October 1829 spoke of 'paroxysm' with regard to this song. It consisted of 'defiantly put-down harmonic caricatures', and a 'state of anarchy' would arise if everyone did 'what he felt like doing in a state of intoxication' (quoted from Marie-Agnes Dittrich, 'Die Lieder', in Walther Dürr and Andreas Krause (eds), *Schubert-Handbuch* (Kassel et al., 1997), pp. 142–267; p. 260).

10 I am struck by the concluding ornaments in the second version of the *Greisengesang*, which characterises the end of life, not yet expected from a spiritual point of view in spite of a certain age. And the answer to the end of the epistrophe, the concluding part of the strophe, at the beginning of a reprise written in a very free 'crab' mirror, shows dynamic surprises within this very sonorous song. I find a complete withdrawal of the solidity of sound at 'und nur im Duft der Träume' not only possible but also striking in its depiction of a body failing too soon.

11 This sound quality can be located, with the concentration of the core of sound, in the region just above the upper incisors, and is something particularly sought after and practised in opera. This location of focus is intended to guarantee a sound projection extending far into the auditorium.

12 Unlike other sensory perceptions, we chiefly identify scents through their actual quality and only to a very minor extent in an abstract or intellectual way. That and the fact that we process the perception of scents primarily through memory and association clarifies and explains their high emotional charge.

13 One of my elder son's favourite children's books ends with a solitary dreamer's escape from property developers. He doesn't want to sacrifice his little house to their desire for profit and refuses to budge. So he climbs upwards, picking up the previous step each time and placing it in front of him, in order

to evade his pursuers – something that might also have worked vocally too, as a way of eluding one's own fretful mind.

14 The *passaggio* is the term given to the range across which the different registers of the human voice blend together as seamlessly as possible. In male voices the upper *passaggio*, referred to here, between the mixed and the head voice, is particularly difficult.

Coda with Stifter

1 Adalbert Stifter, *Die Mappe meines Urgroßvaters, Journalfassung* [1841], quoted in Alexander Stillmark, Foreword, Adalbert Stifter, *Die Mappe meines Urgroßvaters, letzte Fassung* (Zurich, 1997), p. 417.
2 Stifter, *Die Mappe meines Urgroßvaters, letzte Fassung*, p. 255.
3 Ibid., p. 273.

ACKNOWLEDGEMENTS

Images

p. 176 © Paul Leclaire (www.leclaire-foto.de)
p. 177 © University Library Heidelberg/Justinus Kerner: Kleksographien. Stuttgart 1890
p. 311 © University Library Erlangen-Nürnberg, MIL 76 u[4], No. 24

Music Examples

1, 2 Ludwig van Beethoven, *An die ferne Geliebte, für Singstimme und Klavier*, op. 98, original keys for high voice, Urtext edn, edited by Helga Lühnung (Munich: Henle (HN 579), 2007)
3 Robert Schumann, *Lieder für eine Singstimme mit Klavierbegleitung*, vol. I, for medium voice, edited by Max Friedlaender from the manuscripts and first editions (Frankfurt am Main: Peters (Nr. 2383b))
4, 5, 7, 14, 15, 16, 17 Robert Schumann, *Lieder für eine Singstimme mit Klavierbegleitung*, vol. III., for medium voice, edited by Max Friedlaender from the manuscripts and first editions (Frankfurt am Main: Peters (Nr. 2385 b))
6 Robert Schumann, *Lieder für eine Singstimme mit Klavierbegleitung*, vol. II, for medium voice, edited by Max Friedlaender from the manuscripts and first editions, (Frankfurt am Main: (Peters (Nr. 2384 b))
8 © The Bodleian Libraries, University of Oxford/MS. M. Deneke Mendelssohn, c. 12, fol. IV
9 Gustav Mahler, *14 Lieder aus des Knaben Wunderhorn*, for low voice and piano (London: Universal Edition (UE 14786 b), 1952)
10 Gustav Mahler, *Das Lied von der Erde*, for high and medium voice and piano, edited by the International Gustav Mahler Society (Vienna: Universal Edition (UE 13937), 1989)
11 Heinz Holliger, *Lunea*. 23 movements by Nikolaus Lenau for baritone and piano (or ensemble) (Mainz: Schott Music (DE 21643), 2016)
12, 13, 18, 19, 20 Heinz Holliger, *Lunea*. Scenes from Lenau in 23 leaves from a life. Libretto by Händl Klaus from texts by Nikolaus Lenau. Piano score. (Mainz: Schott Music (57087), 2017)
21, 22, 23 Othmar Schoeck, *Notturno*, 5 movements for low voice and string orchestra, op. 47 (1931/1933), texts by Nikolaus Lenau and Gottfried Keller, to be performed with string quartet or string orchestra (Vienna: Universal Editions (UE 19042), 1933)

24 Wolfgang Rihm, *Harzreise im Winter* for baritone and piano (Vienna: Universal Edition (UE 36008), 2012)
25, 26, 27 Wolfgang Rihm, *Tasso-Gedanken*, monologues from *Torquato Tasso* by J. W. von Goethe for baritone and piano (Vienna: Universal Edition (UE 38193), 2018)
28, 29, 30, 32, 33, 34 Franz Schubert, *Lieder für eine Singstimme mit Klavierbegleitung*, vol. I, from the first prints revised by Max Friedlander, edition for medium voice (Frankfurt am Main: Peters (No. 20b))
31 Franz Schubert, *Lieder für eine Singstimme mit Klavierbegleitung*, vol. III, from the first prints revised by Max Friedlaender, edition for medium voice (Frankfurt am Main: Peters (No. 790b))

INDEX

References in *italics* indicate images; in **bold**, music examples, and <u>underlined</u>, song texts and translations. For clarity, titles of song-cycles and collections are shown in *semibold italics* when followed by individual songs.

All Quiet on the Western Front (film), 93
Allen, Woody, 325
Altenberg, Peter, 249; *Über die Grenzen*, 249
Amsterdam Concertgebouw Orchestra, 83
Andersen, Hans Christian, 106, 114
Arcadelt, Jakob: *Bianco e dolce cigno*, 327
Asam family, 79
Avatar (film), 61–5, 79

Bach, Johann Sebastian, 174; B minor Mass (BWV 232), 71; Passions, 173
Banse, Juliane, 175, *176*
Barth, Karl, 92
Basle Chamber Orchestra, 260
Bavarian Academy of Fine Arts, Munich, 228
Bayerischer Rundfunk, 16
Beethoven, Ludwig van, 10–13, 167–8, 225; *Adelaide*, op. 46, 225; *An die ferne Geliebte*, op. 98, 6, 9–11, 16, 225: *Auf dem Hügel sitz ich spähend* (1), 11, <u>19–20</u>; *Wo die Berge so blau* (2), 11, <u>20–21</u>; *Leichte Segler in den Höhen* (3), 11–13, **12**, <u>22–3</u>; *Diese Wolken in den Höhen* (4), 11, 14–15, <u>23–4</u>; *Es kehret der Maien, es blühet die Au* (5), 11, <u>24–5</u>; *Nimm sie hin denn, diese Lieder* (6), 11, <u>25–6</u>; Symphony no. 9, op. 125 ('Choral'), 71
Berg, Alban, 13–14, 247, 249; *Altenberg-Lieder*, op. 4, 225: *Über die Grenzen* (3), 249; *Vier Lieder*, op. 2, 246; *Aus 'Dem Schmerz sein Recht'* (1), 249, 250; *Schlafend trägt man mich* (2), 249, 250; *Nun ich der Risen Stärksten überwand* (3), 249; *Warm die Lüfte* (4), 249; *Wozzeck*, op. 7, 13–14, 67, 93
Berlin, 61, 226–7, 249, 266

Bernhard, Thomas, 95; *Dene*, 95; *Einfach kompliziert*, 95; *Minetti*, 95; *Ritter*, 95; *Voss*, 95
Bethge, Hans, 139–40
Biedermeier style, 40, 310, 327, 330
Blomstedt, Herbert, 292
Blumenberg, Hans, 305
Bodmer, Johann Jakob, 305
Börne, Ludwig, 125
Bonaparte, Napoleon, 266
Borchmeyer, Dieter, 112, 239, 246
Borries, Erika von, 265–6, 268
Bostridge, Ian, 52, 274
Brahms, Johannes, 45, 168, 224–5, 281, 306, 346; *Die schöne Magelone*, 163, 223
Braunschweig-Bevern, Duke of, 309
Braunschweig-Lüneburg, Electorate of, 309
Breitinger, Johann Jakob, 305
Britten, Benjamin: *Cantata Misericordium*, 173; *Folksong Arrangements*, 169, 225
Brocken, 228–9, 231
Brod, Max, 297
Bruns, Klaus, 189
Brussels, 265–6
Budde, Elmar, 277
Buddeus, Julius: *Resignation*, 214–15
Burns, Robert: *Hauptmanns Weib*, 48; *Die Hochländer-Witwe*, 47; *Hochländers Abschied*, 47; *Hochländisches Wiegenlied*, 47; *Im Westen*, 48; *Jemand*, 47; *Niemand*, 48; *Weit, weit!*, 48
Byron, George Gordon, Lord: *Hebrew Melodies*, 42, 47, 49

Cameron, James, 61
Casanova, Giacomo, 158
Castellucci, Romeo, 94–5

Chamisso, Adelbert von, 106; *Frauenliebe und Leben*, 40; *Die Kartenlegerin*, 41; *Löwenbraut*, 41; *Die rote Hanne*, 41
Cicero, 94, 326
Claudius, Matthias: *Der Mensch*, 205–6

Da Ponte, Lorenzo, 155
Dante Alighieri: *The Divine Comedy*, 71
Debussy, Claude, 169, 246
Dessau, 266
Don't Look Now (film), 93
Drake, Julius, 44
Dreves, Lebrecht, 108; *Requiem*, 102–3

Eichendorff, Joseph von, 45, 92, 108–9, 206, 260; *Aus dem Leben eines Taugenichts*, 9–10; *Der Einsiedler*, 207–10; *Das Marmorbild*, 167, 331
Eisler, Hanns: *Deutsche Sinfonie*, op. 50, 71
Elmau, 280
Elsheimer, Adam, 79
Empedocles, 235
Endenich, 51
Evin, Franck, 189

Fallersleben, Hoffman von, 92
Fanshawe, Catherine Maria: *Räthsel*, 47
Fauré, Gabriel, 169
Feldkirch, 326
Ferrer, José, 325
Finley, Gerald, 44
Fischer-Dieskau, Dietrich, 258, 328
Frankfurt, 9, 149, 156, 228
Frankfurter Oper, 149

Geibel, Emanuel, 40, 53; *Der Hidalgo*, 40–41; *Der Knabe mit dem Wunderhorn*, 40; *Der Page*, 40
Géricault, Théodore: *The Raft of the Medusa*, 93
German Democratic Republic, 5
Gilhooly, John, 44
Goethe, Johann Wolfgang von, 8–9, 46, 49, 63–79, 131, 227–32, 234–51; *An die Entfernte*, 10, 36; *An Schwager Kronos*, 228; *Erlkönig*, 39; *Faust*, 61–79, 159, 250; *Freisinn*, 47; *Ganymed*, 68, 228; *Grenzen der Menschheit*, 247, 249–50; *Harfenspieler*, 249, 251–3;

Harzreise im Winter, 223, 226–33, 249, 251; *Lied der Suleika*, 47; *Mahomets Gesang*, 228; *Marienbader Elegie*, 250; *Prometheus*, 68, 228, 330; *Prooemion*, 64; *Schäfers Klagelied*, 112; *Seefahrt*, 228; *Talismane*, 47; *Torquato Tasso*, 231–45, 248, 250; *Über allen Gipfeln ist Ruh'*, 163, 312; *West-östlicher Divan*, 8–9, 30–33, 47, 48; *Wilhelm Meisters Lehrjahre*, 247, 252; *Wilhelm Meisters Wanderjahre*, 41–2, 78–9
Goncharov, Ivan: *Oblomov*, 173
Görlitz, 309
Gottsched, Johann Christoph, 259, 310
Grillparzer, Franz, 239
Grün, Anastasius, 109
Gründgens, Gustaf, 68
Gulbenkian Foundation, Lisbon, 292
Gustav Mahler Youth Orchestra, 292

Haitink, Bernard, 83
Handel, Georg Frideric: *Lascia ch'io pianga*, 190
Händl Klaus, 178–9
Hanslick, Eduard, 165–6, 259; *Vom Musikalisch-Schönen*, 165–6
Harnoncourt, Nikolaus, 216, 289
Härtling, Peter: *Niembsch oder der Stillstand: Eine Suite*, 179
Hartung, Günter, 266, 268
Haslinger, Tobias, 326–7, 344
Haydn, Joseph, 167, 174, 225; *The Creation*, 275; *Lob der Faulheit*, 173; *The Seasons*, 275
Hebbel, Friedrich: *Dem Schmerz sein Recht*, 249
Heine, Heinrich, 39, 45–6, 259, 326–32, 344, 346; *Am Meer*, 328, 331; *Der Atlas*, 328, 330; *Du bist wie eine Blume*, 48; *Der Doppelgänger*, 328, 331; *Das Fischermädchen*, 328, 331; *Ihre Bild*, 328, 330–31; *Die Lorelei*, 39; *Die Lotosblume*, 47; *Die Stadt*, 328, 331; *Was will die einsame Thräne?*, 48
Helsinki, 189, 328
Herder, Caroline, 235
Hesse, Hermann: *Demian*, 321
Hoffmann von Fallersleben, August Heinrich: *Der Sandmann*, 331
Hohenems, 326
Hölderlin, Friedrich, 173, 179, 235

Holliger, Heinz, 76, 169, 173–5, 177–90, 195–201, 260; *Lunea* (opera), 173–90, *176*, **182**, **184**, **187**, 195–201, **196–8**; *Lunea* (song-cycle), 173, 175, 181, **183**
Homoki, Andreas, 175, 189
Huber, Gerold, 15–17, 44, 97, 101, 106, 111, 113, 206, 217, 223–8, 235, 246–7, 254, 260, 274, 280, 282, 299, 322, 325–7, 329–32, 359; *Die Seefahrt*, 228, 250

Jean Paul, 46
Jeitteles, Alois: *An die ferne Geliebte*, 6, 9, 19–26
Joyce, James, 152, 157

Kafka, Franz, 296–7; *Before the Law*, 296–7
Kerner, Justinus, 42, 45, 177; *Todebote*, *177*
Kistner (publishers), 111
Klopstock, Friedrich Gottlieb, 305
Knaben Wunderhorn, Das, 85, 88–9, 91, 131–7, 295–6; *Bildchen*, 131–4, 136; *Unbeschreibliche Freude*, 132, 134–5; *Urlicht*, 295–6
Körner, Julius, 50
Krenek, Ernst: *Reisebuch aus den österreichischen Alpen*, op. 62, 223
Kulmann, Elisabeth, 42

La Mettrie, Julien Offray de: *L'Homme machine*, 151
Lappe, Karl: *Der Einsame*, 249, 330
Leitner, Karl Gottfried von, 328
Lenau, Nikolaus, 42, 101, 106, 108–11, 114–16, 173–9, 190–94, 197–200, 260, 281; *An die Entfernte*, 8, 29; *Blick in den Strom*, 190–91; *Faust*, 101, 111–12, 118; *Ein Herbstabend*, 118, 192–7; *Lied eines Schmiedes*, 109–10; *Die Sennin*, 115–16, 120
Leonardo da Vinci: *Madonna of the Rocks*, *63*
Lindau, 16, 326
Lipiner, Siegfried, 131
Liszt, Franz: *Nuages gris*, 190
Loebe, Bernd, 149
Löns, Hermann, 225
Loy, Christof, 149, 156–7
Ludlow, Ivan, *176*
Lyne, William, 44

Mahler, Alma, 291, 301
Mahler, Gustav, 84–98, 168, 224, 246, 287–302, 306, 315; *Kindertotenlieder*, 83, 91–5, 97–8: *In diesem Wetter, in diesem Braus* (5), 97; *Das Knaben Wunderhorn* settings, 85, 88–9, 91, 125: *Rheinlegendchen*, 128; *Urlicht*, 41, 91, 295–7, 295–6; *Wer hat dies Liedlein erdacht?*, 125–7, 127; *Wo die schönen Trompeten blasen*, 129–30, 130–38, **138**, 142; *Das Lied von der Erde*, 71, 125, 139–44: *Der Abschied* (6), 125, 139–41, 142–4; *Lieder eines fahrenden Gesellen*, 83–92: *Wenn mein Schatz Hochzeit macht* (1), 85–6, 90; *Ich hab' ein glühend Messer* (3), 84, 90; *RückertLieder*, 91, 127–8, 131, 287–302: *Blicke mir nicht in die Lieder* (1/2), 127, 287–9, 288–9, 299–300; *Ich atmet' einen linden Duft* (2/1), 287–8, 300–301, 301; *Um Mitternacht* (3/4), 287–8, 297–9, 299; *Liebst du um Schönheit* (4/5), 91, 287–8, 290–92, 290–91, 299, 301–2; *Ich bin der Welt abhanden gekommen* (5/3), 127–8, 287–8, 293, 293–5; Symphony no. 1, 190; Symphony no. 2, 91, 295; Symphony no. 3, 91; Symphony no. 4, 91; Symphony no. 8, 71, 190; *Veni creator spiritus*, 190
Mahler Jubilee Biennial (2010–11), 291
Mann, Thomas: *The Magic Mountain*, 272; *Tonio Kröger*, 239, 321
Mathis, Edith, 44
Mayrhofer, Johann, 315–16; *Beim Winde*, 316; *Sehnsucht*, 315
Mehltretter, Florian, 163
Meier, Andreas, 111
Melanchthon, Philipp, 64
MelosLogos Festival, Weimar, 228
Mendelssohn, Fanny, 42
Mendelssohn, Felix, 42; *Die erste Walpurgisnacht* (MWVD 3), 71; *Sechs Lieder*, op. 71: *An die Entfernte* (3), 8, 29–30; *Was bedeutet die Bewegung?*, 8
Midsummer Night's Sex Comedy, A (film), 325
Minetti, Bernhard, 95
Mombert, Alfred: *Der Glühende*, 249
Mong-Kao-Jen, 139, 142
Monteverdi, Claudio, 315

Moore, Thomas: *Zwei Venetianische Lieder*, 47
Mörike, Eduard, 246, 247–9; *Auf ein altes Bild*, 249, 251; *Auf eine Christblume II*, 249; *Begegnung*, 249, 250; *Lied eines Verliebten*, 249–50; *Schlafendes Jesukind*, 249, 251
Mosen, Julius: *Der Nussbaum*, 47
Moys, 309
Mozart, Wolfgang, 149–59, 167, 174; *Don Giovanni*, 149–59, 167, 227–8; *Masonic Funeral Music*, 175; *Die Zauberflöte*, 106
Müller, Wilhelm, 88, 163, 257, 265–7, 278, 280, 315, 329; *Erstarrung*, 257; *Die schöne Müllerin*, 223, 315–22; *Sieben und siebzig Gedichten*, 280; *Ungeduld*, 7; *Die Winterreise*, 257–9, 265–7, 269–71, 274, 277, 278, 280, 282, 329
Munich, 94, 173, 228, 318, 325

Neun, Wilfried von der, 41, 311; *Gesungen!*, 311; *Himmel und Erde*, 312–13; *Röselein*, 41
Nicholas of Cusa, 313
Nietzsche, Friedrich, 39, 43, 149, 151, 155, 305, 311, 314; 'About Truth and Lies in the Extra-moral Sense', 43

Peters (publishers), 111
Pfarrus, Gustav, 42
Platen, August von, 311; *Ihre Stimme*, 311–12
Plato, 72, 326–7; *Phaido*, 326–7
Plessing, Friedrich, 228–9, 231, 253
Prey, Hermann, 83, 325
Püttlingen, Johann Vesque von, 330

Quadflieg, Will, 68

Reinick, Robert: *Liebesbotschaft*, 3–5, 17
Rellstab, Ludwig, 325–9, 332, 339, 345–8; *Abschied*, 328; *Auf dem Strom*, 327; *Aufenthalt*, 328; *Frühlingssehnsucht*, 328, 332–4; *Herbst*, 327; *In die Ferne*, 328, 341–3; *Kriegers Ahnung*, 328, 340–41; *Liebesbotschaft*, 26–7, 328; *Ständchen*, 328, 336–8
Rhin, Opera du, Strasbourg, 106

Rihm, Wolfgang, 169, 227–48; *Harzreise im Winter* 227–33, 229–30, **233**, 246, 248, 253; *Hölderlin-Fragmente*, 227; *Stilles Stück*, 227; **Tasso-Gedanken**, 228, 231–48, 250–53: Bist du aus einem Traum erwacht (1), 234–7, 234, **237**, 250–52; Ganz ruht mein Gemüt auf diesem Werke nun (2), 236–8, 238–9, 250–52; Gedanken ohne Maß und Ordnung (3), 240–41, 241–2, **242–3**, 251–2; Die Träne hat uns die Natur verlieben (4), 244–5, 245–7, 250–53; *Wölfli-Lieder* 227
Rorschach test, 177
Roth, Joseph, 359
Rückert, Ernst, 92
Rückert, Friedrich, 212, 246–8, 287–301, 328–9; *Aus den östlichen Rosen*, 48; *Blicke mir nicht in die Lieder*, 287–9, 299; *Die Blume der Ergebung*, 210–12; *Dass sie hier gewesen*, 248, 328, 349–51; *Du bist die Ruh*, 248, 352–6; *Greisengesang*, 248; *Ich atmet' einen linden Duft*, 287–8, 300–301; *Ich bin der Welt abhanden gekommen*, 287–8, 293–5; *Kindertotenlieder*, 90–98; *Lachen und Weinen*, 248; *Liebesfrühling*, 54–6; *Liebst du um Schönheit*, 287–8, 290–92, 299, 301; *Lieder der Braut*, 47; *Sei mir gegrüsst*, 248, 253; *Um Mitternacht*, 287–8, 297–9; *Widmung*, 47; *Zum Schluss*, 48
Rückert, Luise, 92, 346

Sade, Marquis de, 151
St John's Gospel, 68
Sams, Eric, 15–16, 50
Sarotie, Tuula, 189
Sawallisch, Wolfgang, 325
Schiller, Friedrich, 69; *Der Geisterseher*, 331
Schlößmann, Frank Philipp, 189
Schober, Franz von, 268
Schoek, Alfred, 281–2
Schoek, Othmar, 83, 118, 192, 280–82; *Elegie*, op. 36, 192, 260, 280–82; *Notturno*, op. 47, 118, 190–92, 190–91, 192–4, 195–6, 199–200, **199–200**
Schoenberg, Arnold: *Das Buch der hängenden Gärten*, 169, 225
Schönmüller, Annette, *176*

Schreiber, Aloys: *Der Blumenbrief*, 8, 28
Schubert, Ferdinand, 326
Schubert, Franz, 14–15, 39, 84, 168,
217, 224–5, 227, 246, 257–79,
280–83, 305–6, 310, 314–22, 325–56;
Abendbilder (D. 650), 247–8; *Abschied*
(D. 475), 275; *Am Fenster* (D. 878),
327–8; *An die Entfernte* (D. 765),
10–11, 36; *An Schwager Kronos*
(D. 369), 228; *Auf dem Strom* (D. 943),
327; *Beim Winde* (D. 669), 316; *Der
Blumenbrief* (D. 622), 8, 28–9; *Dass
sie hier gewesen* (D. 775), 247–8, 328,
346, **347**, 348–51, 349; *Du bist die
Ruh* (D. 776), 247–8, 346, **347**, 348,
352–3, 353–6, **355**; *Der Einsame*
(D. 800), 249, 330; *Ganymed* (D. 544),
228, 306; *Gesängen des Harfners*
(D. 478–80), 306; *Greisengesang*
(D. 778), 247–8, 253–4, 346; *Gretchen
am Spinnrade* (D. 118), 305–6; *Herbst*
(D. 945), 327; *Himmelsfunken* (D. 651),
247–8; *Im Freien* (D. 880), 327–8;
Lachen und Weinen (D. 777), 226,
247–8, 346; *Mahomets Gesang* (D. 721),
228; *Petrarch Sonnets* (D. 628–30),
306; *Prometheus* (D. 674), 228, 306;
Schäfers Klagelied (D. 121), 112; *Der
Schiffer* (D. 694), 275–6; **Die schöne
Müllerin** (D. 795), 7–8, 14–15, 84–5,
87–8, 101, 163, 223, 257, 315–22,
325: *Das Wandern* (1), 306, 316–19,
316–18, 321–2; *Wohin?* (2), 325; *Am
Feierabend* (5), 320; *Ungeduld* (7), 7,
8; *Tränenregen* (10), 321; *Eifersucht
und Stolz* (15), 14; *Schwanengesang*
(D. 957), 6, 9, 225, 247, 259, 306,
325–48: *Liebesbotschaft* (1), 6, 15–17,
26–7, 306, 328, 338–9, 344–5; *Kriegers
Ahnung* (2), 328, 338–9, 340–41,
341, 344–5; *Frühlingssehnsucht* (3),
328, 332–4, 334–6, 338–9, 344–5;
Ständchen (4), 328, 336, 336–8,
338–9, 345; *Aufenthalt* (5), 328, 338,
341, 344–5; *In die Ferne* (6), 328, 338,
341–3, 343–5; *Abschied* (7), 328, 338,
341, 343–5; *Der Atlas* (8), 328–30;
Ihr Bild (9), 328–30; *Das Fischermädchen* (10), 328–31; *Die Stadt* (11),
328–30, 332; *Am Meer* (12), 328–30;
Der Doppelgänger (13), 328–30; *Die
Taubenpost* (14) (D. 965a), 9, 15,
33–5, 326–8, 344, 348; *Sehnsucht*
(D. 516), 315–16, 328; *Sei mir gegrüsst*
(D. 741), 247–8, 253, 253, 346, **347**,
348; *Suleika I* (D. 720), 8–9, 30–32;
Suleika II (D. 717), 9, 32–3; Symphony
no. 9 in C ('The Great') (D. 944), 338;
Der Wanderer an den Mond (D. 879),
328; *Wandererfantasie* (D. 760), 338;
Der Winterabend (D. 938), 275;
Winterreise (D. 911), 86–8, 180, 223,
227, 257–79, 280–83, 329, 343, 346:
Gute Nacht (1), 180, 262, 268, 276–7;
Die Wetterfahne (2), 260–62; *Gefrorne
Tränen* (3), 261–2, 276; *Erstarrung* (4),
262, 273, 276; *Der Lindenbaum* (5),
87, 262, 268–9, 269–71, 271–4, **275**;
Wasserflut (6), 52, 262, 274, 276; *Aus
dem Flusse* (7), 262; *Rückblick* (8), 262;
Irrlicht (9), 261, 263, 268; *Rast* (10),
263, 276; *Frühlingstraum* (11), 263,
268, 276; *Einsamkeit* (12), 263, 268;
Die Post (13), 263, 276; *Der greise Kopf*
(14), 263, 266, 278; *Die Krähe* (15),
263, 278; *Letzte Hoffnung* (16), 263,
265, 268, 278; *Im Dorfe* (17), 259,
263, 267–8, 278, 282; *Der stürmische
Morgen* (18), 263, 268; *Täuschung* (19),
263, 268; *Der Wegweiser* (20), 263,
278, 282; *Das Wirthaus* (21), 263,
267, 278; *Mut* (22), 263, 278; *Die
Nebensonnen* (23), 257–8, 263, 278;
Der Leiermann (24), 86–7, 180, 259,
261–2, 264, 276–7
Schubertiade (Lindau), 16; (Vorarlberg),
325
Schumann, Clara, 41, 46, 48, 51, 55,
111
Schumann, Robert, 13, 17, 39–57, 61–79,
101–121, 168, 174, 179, 183–6,
206–20, 224–5, 246, 305–115, 325,
330, 346; **Dichterliebe**, op. 48, 43,
45, 83, 223, 227, 325–6: *Ich grolle
nicht* (7), 325; **Drei Gedichte von
Emanuel Geibel**, op. 30: *Der Knabe
mit dem Wunderhorn* (1), 40; *Der
Page* (2), 40; *Der Hidalgo* (3), 40–41;
*Drei Gedichte aus den Waldliedern von
Gustav Pfarrius*, op. 119, 42; **Drei
Gesänge**, op. 31, 41: *Löwenbraut* (1),
41; *Die Kartenlegerin* (2), 41; *Die rote*

Hanne (3), 41; ***Drei Gesänge***, op. 83, 44, 206–13: Resignation (1), 214–15, 216–20; Die Blume der Ergebung (2), 210–12, 212–14, 220; Der Einsiedler (3), 206–10, 207–8, 220; ***Drei Gesänge aus Lord Byron's Hebräischen Gesängen*** (Byron-Lieder), op. 95: Die Tochter Jephtas (1), 42; An den Mond (2), 42; Dem Helden (3), 42; ***Frauenliebe und Leben***, op. 42; ***Fünf Lieder***, op. 40 (Andersen-Lieder), 39, 44, 106–8, 111–14, 330: Märzveilchen (1), 106–7, **107**, 111–12; Muttertraum (2), 107; Der Soldat (3), 107; Der Spielmann (4), 107; Verratene Liebe (5), 107; Gedichte der Königin Maria Stuart, op. 135, 42; Geistervariationen, WoO 24, 51; Genoveva, op. 81, 57, 71; Lieder und Gesänge I, op. 27, 40; Lieder und Gesänge II, op. 51, 42; ***Lieder und Gesänge III***, op. 77, 41, 43: Geisternähe (3), 41; ***Lieder und Gesänge IV***, op. 96, 41, 43, 307–14, 322: Nachtlied (1), 312; Schneeglöcken (2), **185**, 185, 307–9, 307–11, *311*, 314; Ihre Stimme (3), 311–12; Gesungen! (4), 311; Himmel und Erde (5), 312–13, 312–13; ***Lieder, Gesänge und Requiem aus 'Wilhelm Meister'*** (Wilhelm-Meister-Lieder), op. 98a/b, 41–2, 44: Mignon (1), 45; ***Liederalbum für die Jugend***, op. 79, 44–5, 307: Schneeglöckchen (27), 307; Lied Lynkeus des Türmers (28), 45; Mignon (29), 45; ***Liederkreis***, op. 24, 39: Ich wandelte unter den Bäumen (3), 39–40; Schöne Wiege meiner Leiden (5), 40; Berg' und Burgen schau'n herunter (7), 40; ***Liederkreis***, op. 39, 45, 206; ***Minnespiel***, op. 101, 54–5: Mein schöner Stern, ich bitte dich (4), 54–5; ***Myrthen***, op. 25, 40, 44, 46–52; Widmung (1), 47, 48; Freisinn (2), 47, 48; Der Nussbaum (3), 46–8; Jemand (4), 46–8; ***Lieder aus dem Schenkenbuch im Divan***: Sitz'ich allein (5), 47, 48; Setze mir nicht, du Grobian (6), 47; Die Lotosblume (7), 47, 49; Talismane (8), 47, 49; Lied der Suleika (9), 47, 49; Die Hochländer-Witwe (10), 47, 49; Lieder der Braut: Mutter, Mutter (11), 47, 49; Lass mich ihm am Busen hangen (12), 47; Hochländers Abschied (13), 47, 49; Hochländers Wiegenlied (14), 47, 49; Aus den hebräischen Gesängen (15), 47, 49–50, **50**, 51; Räthsel (16), 46–7, 51; Zwei Venetianische Lieder, 47, 51: Leis' rudern hier (17), 48; Wenn durch die Piazzetta (18), 48; Hauptmanns Weib (19), 48, 51; Weit, weit! (20), 48, 51; Was will die einsame Thräne? (21), 48, 51; Niemand (22), 48, 51; Im Westen (23), 48, 51; Du bist wie eine Blume (24), 48, 51; Aus den östlichen Rosen (25), 48, 51; Zum Schluss (26), 48, 51; Das Paradies und die Peri, op. 50, 57, 216; Requiem für Mignon, op. 98b, 57; Romanzen und Balladen I, op. 45, 42; Romanzen und Balladen II, op. 49, 39; Romanzen und Balladen III, op. 53, 42, 44; Romanzen und Balladen IV, op. 64, 42; Der Rose Pilgerfahrt, op. 112, 57; ***Sechs Gedichte von N. Lenau und Requiem***, op. 90 (Lenau-Lieder), 39, 44, 101–9, 113–15, 185–7, 190, 192, 330: Lied eines Schmiedes (1), 109–10, 111, 114–15; Meine Rose (2), 114, **186**, 186–8; Kommen und Scheiden (3), 114; Die Sennin (4), 75, 114–21, 115–16, **118**, *118*; Einsamkeit (5), 114; Der schwere Abend (6), 103, 114, **185**, 185; Requiem (7), 101–5, 101–3, **104**, **105**, 114–15, 213; ***Sechs Gedichte aus dem Liederbuch eines Malers***, op. 36, 3, 6, 39: Liebesbotschaft (6), 3–6, 15, 17; ***Sechs Gesänge***, op. 89: Röselein (6), 41; ***Sechs Gesänge***, op. 107, 41; ***Sieben Lieder von Elisabeth Kulmann***, op. 104, 42; ***Spanische Liebeslieder***, op. 138, 53–4, 56–7: Flutenreicher Ebro (5), 54; Hoch, hoch sind die Berge (8), 54; Dunkler Lichtglanz (10), 54; ***Spanische Liederspiel***, op. 74, 54, 56–7: Erste Begegnung (1), 54; Intermezzo (2), 54; Liebesgram (3), 54; Melancholie (6), 54; Geständnis (7), 54; Botschaft (8), 54; Szenen aus Goethes Faust (WoO 3), 17, 57, 61, 63, 66–79, 115; ***Vier Husarenlieder von Nikolaus Lenau***, op. 117, 42, 183–5: Da liegt der Feinde gestreckte Schar (4), **184**, 184–5; ***Zwolf Gedichte aus F. Rückerts Liebesfrühling***, op. 37

(*Rückert-Lieder*), 44, 55–6: *Der Himmel hat eine Träne geweint* (1), 55; *Er ist gekommen* (2), 55; *Liebst du um Schönheit* (4), 55; *Ich hab' in mich gesogen* (5), 55; *Liebste, was kann denn uns scheiden?* (6), 56; *Schön ist das Fest des Lenzes* (7), 55–6; *Rose, Meer und Sonne* (9), 56; *O Sonn! O Meer, o Rose!* (10), 56; *Warum willst du andre fragen* (11), 55–6; *So wahr die Sonne scheinet* (12), 56; *Zwolf Gedichte von Justinus Kerner* (*Kerner-Lieder*), op. 35, 42–5, 325
Schumann Brothers (publishers), 50
Schurz, Anton, 175
Second Berlin Lieder School, 52, 168
Seidl, Johann Gabriel, 327–8; *Am Fenster*, 327; *Im Freien*, 327; *Sehnsucht*, 328; *Die Taubenpost*, 34–5, 327
Seven Years War, 309
Shakespeare, William, 315; *Hamlet*, 247; *King Lear*, 93
Shostakovich, Dmitri; Piano Trio no. 2, op. 67, 225; Symphony no. 13 in B flat minor, op. 113 (*Babi Yar*), 71
Siemens Music Prize, 227
Silbert, Johann Peter, 248–9; *Abendbilder*, 247–8, 250; *Himmelsfunken*, 247–8, 250
Silcher, Friedrich, 269, 273; *Der Lindenbaum* (arrangement for men's choir), 269, 273
Spaul, Josef von, 268
Stockholm, 328
Stokes, Richard, 111–12
Sprau, Kilian, 108
Stifter, Adalbert, 359–60; *Die Mappe meines Urgroßvaters*, 359–60; *Der Nachsommer*, 359
Strasbourg, 106
Straubing, 5, 136, 144, 227, 325
Strauss, Richard, 42, 346
Stravinsky, Igor, 83
Stuart, Mary, 42
Sun, Sarah Maria, 175, *176*

Tieck, Ludwig: *Die schöne Magelone*, 223
Twain, Mark, 226

Urania (almanac), 280
USA, 144

Vaughan Williams, Ralph: *Songs of Travel*, 169
Vogl, Johann Michael, 339

Wagner, Richard, 13, 79, 216, 306–7; *Tannhäuser*, 94
Walser, Robert, 179
Walton, Chris, 281
Wang-Wei, 140, 142
Weimar, 9, 228, 231
Wiener Festwochen (2014), 94
Wieck, Clara, *see* Schumann, Clara
Wieck, Friedrich, 46, 48
Wigmore Hall, London, 44
Willemer, Marianne von, 9, 49; *Lied der Suleika*, 47; *West-östlicher Divan*, 9, 30–33
Wittgenstein, Ludwig, 166
Wolf, Hugo, 168, 246–9, 306, 315, 346; *Auf ein altes Bild*, 249–50; *Auf eine Christblume II*, 249–50; *Begegnung*, 249–50; *Grenzen der Menschheit*, 246–7, 249–50; *Harfenspieler*, 246, 248; *Wer sich der Einsamkeit ergibt'* (1), 248, 251–2; *An die Türen will ich schleichen* (2), 248; *Wer nie sein Brot mit Tränen aß* (3), 248; *Lied eines Verliebten*, 249–50; *Schlafendes Jesukind*, 249–50
Wunderlich, Fritz, 225
Würzburg, 228
Würzburg Mozart Festival, 227

Yeats, William Butler: *The Lake Isle of Innisfree*, 287

Zelenka, Jan Dismas, 174
Ziesak, Ruth, 106
Zurich, 173, 175